AIA Guide to the Architecture of Washington, D.C.

AIA

THIRD EDITION

GUIDE TO THE ARCHITECTURE OF WASHINGTON, D.C.

by Christopher Weeks

for the Washington Chapter of the American Institute of Architects

with an Introduction by Francis D. Lethbridge, FAIA

Alan Karchmer, Photo Editor and Principal Photographer

THE JOHNS HOPKINS UNIVERSITY PRESS
BALTIMORE AND LONDON

The Johns Hopkins University Press
2715 North Charles Street
Baltimore, Maryland 21218-4319
The Johns Hopkins Press Ltd., London

AIA Washington DC
1777 Church Street, N.W.
Washington, D.C. 20036
202-667-1798

LIBRARY OF CONGRESS CATALOGING-IN-PUBLICATION DATA

Weeks, Christopher, 1950–
    The AIA guide to the architecture of Washington, D.C. / by Christopher Weeks with
an introduction by Francis D. Lethbridge for the Washington Chapter of the American
Institute of Architects. — 3rd ed.
        p.   cm.
    Rev. ed. of: A Guide to the architecture of Washington, D.C. / written and edited by
Warren J. Cox.
    Includes index.
    ISBN 0-8018-4712-5 (hc : acid-free paper). — ISBN 0-8018-4713-3 (pbk. : acid-free
paper)
    1. Architecture—Washington (D.C.)—Guidebooks.   2. Washington (D.C.)—
Buildings, structures, etc.—Guidebooks.   3. Washington (D.C.)—Guidebooks.
I. American Institute of Architects. Washington Chapter.
II. Guide to the architecture of Washington, D.C.   III. Title.
NA735.W3W44 1994
720'.9753—dc20   93-34867

A catalog record for this book is available from the British Library.

Contents

Preface and Acknowledgments

In the early 1960s some of Washington's leading Young Turk architects—Warren J. Cox, Hugh Newell Jacobsen, Francis D. Lethbridge,
and David R. Rosenthal—decided to do a take on Andy Hardy. But instead
of putting on a show, they put out a book, *A Guide to the Architecture of
Washington, D.C.* Written and published for the Washington Metropolitan
Chapter of the American Institute of Architects, it appeared in 1965 and
quickly sold out; a second, somewhat revised edition hit the gift shops in
1974 and it, too, quickly sold out. This time the four impresarios, busy
with other things, decided to pass on a third edition.

As a consequence, the national capital was suddenly without an AIA
guide. This state of affairs continued for more than a decade, until the late
1980s, when Arnold Prima, chapter president, decided that the hiatus had
gone on long enough and looked into publishing an updated version of the
out-of-print book. Chapter member William Hooper agreed to serve as
point man for this project, a moment of weakness that he has undoubtedly
regretted over and over and over again.

Prima, Hooper, and company looked at the 1965 and 1974 editions of
the *Guide* and agreed to make a number of fundamental changes. First,
they narrowed the focus of the new book. The boundaries of the District
should provide the book's boundaries, they felt, so, with the single exception of the Arlington National Cemetery complex, the more-remote sites
included in the earlier editions (sites ranging from Columbia, Maryland,
to Mount Vernon) were red-penciled out. While important, they simply
do not belong in a guide to the District of Columbia.

That hurdle cleared, Prima and Hooper turned their attention to buildings (and gardens) within what is left of George Washington and Thomas
Jefferson's original ten mile square (the portion south of the Potomac was
given back to Virginia 150 years ago). Happily for all, Charles Atherton,
Donald Canty, and Benjamin Forgey—who, as the saying goes, have forgotten more about Washington architecture than any other trio has ever
known—agreed to act as a review committee. Applying the single standard
of architectural prominence, these gentlemen reappraised every entry in
the first two editions and eliminated sites that had been demolished,
altered beyond recognition, or had in some other way failed to measure up

to their exacting criteria. (One or two buildings experienced a slight editorial reshuffling; for example, a discussion of Hartman-Cox's exquisite St. Alban's Tennis Club, it was felt, more properly belonged in a general overview of the National Cathedral grounds than in a separate entry of its own.)

A far more daunting task then loomed, namely, to examine the whole body of District architecture past and present and to select buildings to add to the core group. Those familiar with the tremendous amount of high-quality construction that has taken place in Washington in the past twenty-five years, as well as the richness and depth of the District's corpus of historic structures, can appreciate the magnitude of this undertaking. Innumerable cups of coffee later, the review committee agreed on approximately one hundred new buildings and sites. Most of them represent recent work. They range from Maya Ying Lin's somber Vietnam Memorial to Arthur Cotton Moore's rambunctious Washington Harbour. A few important and unaccountably overlooked older buildings were included as well, such as the Adas Israel Synagogue and the Hay-Adams Hotel. To keep the text as up-to-the-minute as possible, Atherton and Forgey met again in the summer of 1992; joined this time by Deborah Dietsch, they suggested another twenty just-completed (or nearly completed) projects to be included.

Finally, it quickly became clear that a massive rewrite was in order. Many of the entries retained from the 1965 and 1974 editions lacked any descriptions whatever, and certain other texts required revisions to reflect new information or changes in thinking within the profession. Then there were those ten dozen new entries. In addition, Prima and Hooper felt that most of the earlier editions' photographs warranted replacement. To find someone to tackle the text and a publisher willing to handle the venture, the chapter went far afield, to the wilds of Baltimore; the primary photographer they found closer to home, in Washington resident Alan Karchmer. The result of all this reworking is not a simple update; it might be viewed as the equivalent of an architectural adaptive reuse project, for the outcome is a new book, albeit one created within the carefully preserved framework of the old.

Part of that framework, of course, is the very organization of the entries. After much discussion, everyone involved liked the Cox-Jacobsen-Lethbridge-Rosenthal concept of dividing the city into walkable neighborhood tours. Careful readers will see that a few neighborhoods have been renamed: the label "Downtown," for example, while satisfactory in 1964, simply makes no sense a generation later. Thus, one finds the entries "Pennsylvania Avenue and Downtown" and "Judiciary Square." While it is assumed that most people who use this book will do so as pedestrians, the author, who himself visited every site on foot, must regretfully urge walkers to exercise care and common sense when plotting their routes: not every Washington neighborhood provides the setting for a quiet, safe stroll.

Concerning the rewrite itself, the author wrote for an ideal reader, someone who combines the best features of an intelligent tourist and an interested local professional. While the *Guide* will find a home in many area libraries as a reference work, it should be intelligible to the general public. Perhaps, if it isn't hoping for too much, it will stimulate a wider appreciation of the District's early architecture and a concerned interest in what gets built (or torn down) in the future.

It also must be noted that every care has been taken to ensure accuracy: the editors of the 1975 edition corrected many mistakes of the first volume; Atherton, Canty, and Forgey did their best to give proper credit and dates to the new entries; Gerard Martin Moeller, Jr., executive director of the District AIA chapter, devoted hours to checking facts, names, dates, and phone numbers; and the author talked to scores of practicing Washington architects about their projects and spent hundreds of hours poring over primary and secondary source material in the Library of Congress (particularly the Historic American Buildings Survey), the Historical Society of Washington, D.C. (formerly the Columbia Historical Society), the National Archives, and the Fiske Kimball Library at the University of Virginia School of Architecture. Even so, a work of this scope will inevitably spark differences of opinion: a seemingly simple matter like dating a building, for instance, can become a field filled with land mines of conflicting judgments. Some reputable sources date buildings to the completed working drawings, others to the day ground was broken, and still others use a datestone for its intended purpose; sometimes work on a single structure spans decades. Just what date should one assign to the National Cathedral or the Washington Monument? The upshot is that the author, the Chapter, and the Press encourage readers to submit any comments and corrections that they feel are warranted.

Notwithstanding all that—and not forgetting two daylight muggings—work on this book has proven both more fun and more interesting than anyone could have predicted. It would not have been so without the help and hard work of a large and varied cast. It is a pleasure to be able to thank them publicly. Those making definable contributions include Warren J. Cox, Hugh Newell Jacobsen, Francis D. Lethbridge, and David R. Rosenthal, by graciously allowing use of their earlier work. Judith Robinson and Joey Lampl of Robinson & Associates reviewed several drafts of the manuscript and suggested several welcome changes to it. Deep, deep thanks go to Marty Moeller of the AIA and Robert J. Brugger of the Johns Hopkins University Press for keeping track of the project's myriad threads and to Anne Whitmore, editor *extraordinaire* at the Press, for smoothly tying up loose ends, for regularizing my spelling and punctuation, and for tactfully making scores of prose improvements. Humble bows also go to Professors Mario di Valmarana and William B. O'Neal of the University of Virginia School of Architecture and to John Dorsey of the Baltimore *Sun* for tirelessly acting as sounding boards over the years, for patiently reeling me in from my more exotic flights of fancy, and for offering countless specific suggestions that all substantially improved the text.

Further thanks are happily given to Ambassador Sir Robin Renwick and Mr. Peter Turner of the British Embassy for generously permitting me to use material on Lutyens's Massachusetts Avenue commission; to Bill Allen for sharing his limitless knowledge of the Capitol; to Betsy May-Salazar, much appreciated staff member of the District AIA chapter, for ensuring that this project ran smoothly; to Elizabeth Chanler Chatwin for her thoughts about her grandfather, Irwin Boyle Laughlin of Meridian House; to Eleanor Davies Chesebrough Tydings Ditzen for her generously offered "deep background" reflections on 20th-century Washington; and to Alan Karchmer for his splendid photography. An equally diverse cast assisted in less definable ways and thanks are hereby given, in somewhat random order, to Al and Bettye Chambers, Susan Tobin, Betty Baker Supplee di Valmarana, John Eggen, Claire V. Cox, Mr. and Mrs. George Constable, Mrs. Brodnax Cameron, David W. Roszel, S. Kyle Glenn, Gerald Gagnon, Ron Andrews, David Fogle, Tom Gump, Ellen Coxe Price, Osborne Mackie, and Eldon Scott. While every architectural office contacted proved helpful and cooperative, a few firms and their representatives should be singled out: David Bennett (HOH Associates), Mark C. Huck (architrave p.c.), Patricia Moore (Arthur Cotton Moore/Associates P.C.), Susan Samad-Zadeh (AEPA, p.c.), Thomas Green (David M. Schwarz/Architectural Services, PC), Warren Cox (Hartman-Cox Architects), Allison Matthews (Shalom Baranes Associates), Carolyn Davis (Keyes Condon Florance Architects), Karen Cooper (Cooper, Robertson + Partners), and David Yerkes.

Finally, Bill Hooper, although mentioned above, must be thanked again for his inestimable help in conceiving the book and seeing it through some truly trying times.

C.W.

The Washington Chapter of the American Institute of Architects gratefully acknowledges the generous financial support of Hartman-Cox Architects; Arnold J. Prima, Jr., FAIA; and the Washington Architectural Forum.

The following individuals contributed significant time and expertise to the preparation of this book: Judith Helm Robinson/Robinson & Associates; Charles H. Atherton, FAIA; Benjamin Forgey; Donald Canty, Hon. AIA; Deborah K. Dietsch; and Janet B. Rankin, AIA.

The following persons constituted the Washington Chapter/AIA Guidebook Committee for this revised edition: William D. Hooper, Jr., AIA, chair; Raj Barr-Kumar, FAIA, RIBA; Jerrily R. Kress, AIA; Arnold J. Prima, Jr., FAIA; Joseph H. Sacco, AIA; Sharon F. Washburn, AIA; and G. Martin Moeller, Jr., Associate AIA, Executive Director.

AIA

The Architecture of Washington, D.C.

FRANCIS D. LETHBRIDGE, FAIA

The selection of a site for the federal capital was finally settled in New York City one evening in the summer of 1790, when Thomas Jefferson and Alexander Hamilton dined together and concluded what might be described as a political deal. Bitter political enemies though they were, Jefferson and Hamilton that year each wanted something that only their combined influence in Congress could bring about. And so it came to pass that sufficient Southern votes supported the Funding Bill; Pennsylvanians, wooed by the prospect of removal of the federal capital to Philadelphia for the next ten years, cast their votes for the Residence Bill; and, to the accompaniment of cries of rage from New York and New England, the federal government assumed the debts of the states and made plans to set up its home on the shores of the Potomac River.[1]

The planning of the city of Washington is a familiar tale, yet one that bears repeating, for the quality, durability, and persistent effect of that plan upon the city must always be a central theme in the story of its architecture. We must first, however, go somewhat farther back in time, for long before the construction of the federal city began, there was a flourishing colonial society on the shores of the Potomac near the place where the tidewater country ends. The fall line—that abrupt rise from the eastern coastal plain that marks the end of navigable water—may be traced as an uneven line from New England southward and westward. The cities of Trenton and Richmond, for example, lie at the falls of the Delaware and the James, and if the capital had never been established on the Potomac, the ports of Georgetown and Alexandria would doubtless have prospered and grown into thriving cities by virtue of their location at this crossroads of travel by land and river.

The Chesapeake Bay had been explored by the Spanish before the end of the sixteenth century, but not until 1608, when Captain John Smith sailed up the Potomac River, quite possibly as far as the Little Falls, north of the present site of Georgetown, was very much known of the area that became the capital of the New World. Smith's *General Historie of Virginia, New England and the Summer Isles,* published in England in 1627, was accompanied by a remarkable map that was the basis for all cartography of the Chesapeake region for nearly a hundred years. His description of the river is still a vivid one:

> The fourth river is called Patawomeke, 6 or 7 myles in breadth. It is navigable 140 myles, and fed as the rest with many sweet rivers and springs, which fall from the bordering hills. These hills many of them are planted, and yeeld no lesse plentie and varietie of fruit, then the river exceedeth with abundance of fish. It is inhabited on both sides. . . . The river above this place maketh his passage downe a low pleasant valley overshaddowed in many places with high rocky mountaines; from whence distill innumerable sweet and pleasant springs.

In the next twenty-five years the Potomac became a scene of increasing activity on the part of traders, who began to tap a rich supply of furs, not from the adjacent country alone, but from the lands beyond the Alleghenies, from which they were carried by the Indians to the headwaters of the river. These adventurers were necessarily a hardy and resourceful lot, who plied their trade, in small shallops, from the lower reaches of Chesapeake Bay; and some of them, such as Henry Spelman and Henry Fleete, knew the Algonquin language well from having lived with the Indians as hostages or captives.

In March 1634 Leonard Calvert arrived upon this Potomac scene in two ships, the *Ark* and the *Dove,* with a cargo of Protestant and Roman Catholic settlers, the Catholics seeking their fortunes but also haven from English religious persecution. Near the mouth of the river they founded St. Mary's City, which served as the capital of Maryland until a Protestant revolt late in the century. The St. Mary's City Commission has been engaged in an ambitious reconstruction program on the site of the old capital, and a visit there repays the trip. But there are, in fact, very few remaining examples of seventeenth-century construction on either the Maryland or the Virginia shores of the river. You must travel farther south, to the banks of the James River, to the sites of the Thomas Rolfe house (1651), the Allen house, or "Bacon's Castle" (1655), and St. Luke's Church (c. 1650), to see the only recognizable survivals of Jacobean architecture in the tidewater country. It is ironic that the most famous example of the period, Governor Berkeley's mansion "Greenspring" (1642), which Thomas Tileston Waterman terms "probably the greatest Virginia house of the Century," was destroyed in 1806 to make way for Benjamin Henry Latrobe's house for William Ludwell Lee, which in its turn was demolished during the Civil War.[2]

Despite recurring troubles with the dwindling Indian tribes until the beginning of the eighteenth century, settlement along the Potomac continued steadily. Large land grants were taken up in both Virginia and Maryland, and estates of many thousands of acres were not unusual.

Compared to the lands of Robert Carter of Nomini Hall, who owned 63,093 acres, and William Fitzhugh of Bedford, who had acquired over 45,000 acres, the 8,000-acre holdings of George Washington at Mount Vernon and George Mason's combined holdings of about 15,000 acres along the river seem modest in size. Cheap land, abundant labor, easy transportation from private landings to ships, and a ready market for tobacco in England made possible the development of the great plantations of the tidewater country.

At least for the planters who prospered, the country offered a gracious life, which flourished in the early and mid-eighteenth century and resulted in some handsome houses. Within a relatively few miles of Washington you can see many noble examples of these country mansions,[3] and a short trip to Williamsburg, Virginia, will help you to imagine what life was like in a provincial capital of that period.

The prosperity of the plantations and the settlements of tracts beyond the borders of the river and its navigable tributaries stimulated the founding of the ports of Alexandria (1748) and Georgetown (1751).

Another earlier port, Garrison's Landing, known later as Bladensburg (1742), on the Eastern Branch, or Anacostia River, sank into commercial obscurity at the end of the eighteenth century when the river silted up beyond that point. Two of these Potomac ports were the scene of an important event in colonial history not long after they had been established. In the year 1755 General Braddock embarked with his army from Alexandria, landed near the foot of Rock Creek, and marched up the path of what is now Wisconsin Avenue, on the ill-fated expedition against the French and Indians that ended in disaster near Fort Duquesne. One of the few provincial officers to return unscathed from the campaign was a young Virginian who had been spared to play a greater role in history.

Georgetown and Alexandria still retain some of the atmosphere and much of the scale and texture of colonial river port towns. From the accounts of travelers it would seem that by the latter part of the century they were thriving, pleasant places. Thomas Twining, after a rough all-day wagon journey from Baltimore in 1795, described Georgetown as "a small but neat town. . . . the road from Virginia and the Southern States, crossing the Potomac here, already gives an air of prosperity to this little town, and assures its future importance, whatever may be the fate of the projected metropolis."[4] The fate of the future "metropolis" was, in fact, frequently in doubt during the succeeding seventy-five years.

At George Washington's request, the act of 1790 specifying the location of a federal district of "ten miles square" to be located at any point *above* the Eastern Branch, was modified to include the town of Alexandria, several miles below that point. (Alexandria was ceded back to Virginia in

L'Enfant's 1791 plan for Washington (published in The Universal Asylum and Columbian Magazine *of March 1792) put Capitol Hill in the center of things.*

1846.) Congress enacted this change on March 3, 1791, and by the ninth of that month Maj. Pierre L'Enfant had arrived in Georgetown to commence the planning of the capital city. Andrew Ellicott and Benjamin Banneker had already been employed to survey and map the federal territory, and they proceeded without delay to carry out as much of this work as they could before Washington's arrival at the site.

On the evening of March 29 a crucial meeting took place after dinner at the home of Gen. Uriah Forrest,[5] at which the president, the newly appointed commissioners, and the principal landowners of the federal district were present. The next day Washington recorded in his diary:

> The parties to whom I addressed myself yesterday evening, having taken the matter into consideration, saw the propriety of my observations; and whilst they were contending for the shadow they might lose the substance; and therefore mutually agreed and entered into articles to surrender for public purposes, one half the land they severally possessed within the bounds which were designated as necessary for the city to stand.
>
> This business being thus happily finished and some directions given to the Commissioners, the Surveyor and Engineer with respect to the

mode of laying out the district—Surveying the grounds for the City and forming them into lots—I left Georgetown, dined in Alexandria and reached Mount Vernon in the evening.[6]

It was only fitting that the commissioners agreed in September that the federal district be called "The Territory of Columbia" and the federal city "The City of Washington"!

L'Enfant had less than a year to prepare the plan of the capital city before he was dismissed for his failure—or his temperamental inability—to acknowledge the authority of the commissioners over his work. To the end, he maintained that he was responsible to the president alone, and when Washington himself reluctantly denied that this was so, L'Enfant's dismissal was inevitable. He had sufficient time, nevertheless, to set the mold into which the city would be formed, and with the sole exception of Washington himself, no one's influence upon its conception and development was greater.

The architecture of the area since 1791 may be conveniently divided into four major phases. The first, which extended to the middle of the nineteenth century, is generally characterized by work in the Late Georgian and Classic Revival styles. Some designs in the Gothic Revival style also appeared in this period, but they were limited principally to small examples of ecclesiastical architecture. The second phase, in a variety of

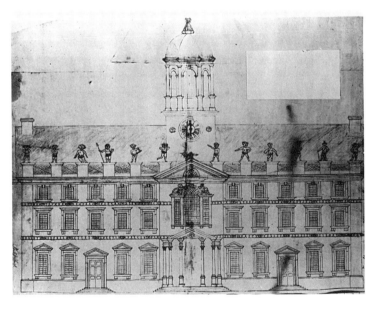

Phillip Hart proposed this design for the new Capitol. Nothing more was ever heard of Mr. Hart—or his humanoid finials.

styles that might be grouped under the term Romantic Revival, dominated from about 1850 to the end of the century. The third period, Classic Eclecticism, was to a large degree an outgrowth of the Columbian Exposition of 1893 and the McMillan Plan for Washington of 1901. The fourth and last phase can be said to extend from about the beginning of the Second World War to the present day.

From the first, the federal capital attracted the talents of many of the most gifted designers of the period. They included architect-builders or "undertakers," such as William Lovering; self-taught gentleman-architects like Dr. William Thornton; and trained professional architect-engineers, of whom Benjamin Henry Latrobe was the most notable example. Some, like James Hoban, architect of the White House, and Charles Bulfinch, who succeeded Latrobe as architect of the Capitol in 1818, do not fit neatly into any of these categories.

In an era that was not distinguished by temperance of speech and writing in the political arena, architects frequently indulged in bitter personal invective. Architects have been inclined to disagree with one another since the beginning of time and will probably continue to do so until the end, but they have seldom expressed themselves so forcefully in writing as in the case of:

(a) Thornton versus Latrobe:
This Dutchman in taste, this monument builder,
This planner of grand steps and walls,
This falling-arch maker, this blunder-roof gilder,
Himself still an architect calls.

(b) Latrobe versus Hoban:
. . . the style he [Jefferson] proposes is exactly consistent with Hoban's pile—a litter of pigs worthy of the great sow it surrounds, and of the wild Irish boar, the father of her.

(c) Hadfield versus Thornton, et al.:
This premium [for the best design of the Capitol] was offered at a period when scarcely a professional architect was to be found in any of the United States; which is plainly to be seen in the pile of trash presented as designs for [the Capitol] building.[7]

Paradoxically, the men who hurled such violent criticism at one another lived in an age of harmonious urban architecture, for, despite personal animosities and professional jealousies, they were all working within the limits of generally accepted standards of taste, and perhaps just as importantly, within fairly narrow limits of available construction materials and techniques.[8]

Although work on the first major public buildings, the White House and the Capitol, had begun in 1793—seven years before the government

Published in London, this engraving marks the day the British took Washington in the War of 1812: "we burnt and destroyed their Dock Yard . . . , Senate House, President's Palace, . . . and the Great Bridge." The tabloid press never changes.

moved to Washington—they were virtually built anew after British troops sacked and burned Washington in 1814. The rout of the hastily assembled militia at the Battle of Bladensburg (known thereafter as "The Bladensburg Races") caused President Madison, Madame Madison, and the rest of official Washington to beat a hasty retreat to the suburbs. The president returned to take up temporary residence in Col. John Tayloe's town house, the Octagon; the Treaty of Ghent, which ended the War of 1812, was signed in the round room on the second floor.

In the early 1830s the commercial leaders of Washington City thought its future lay in the success of the Chesapeake and Ohio Canal, which was supposed to connect the Potomac with the headwaters of the Ohio River. After 1850 the canal did tie Washington to Cumberland, Maryland, and it continued in operation until 1923. But it was never a profitable investment, because the more successful Baltimore and Ohio Railroad, following much the same route and with its eastern terminus at Baltimore, had been begun at exactly the same time (a remarkable act of optimism, since steam locomotives had not yet been tried on such a scale). The canal today provides a valuable recreational area—an attractive stretch for hiking, cycling, and canoeing. (Barge trips are conducted by the National Park Service during the summer months from the lock at the foot of 30th Street in Georgetown.)

Early-20th-century District schoolchildren evidently liked both straw boaters and C & O Canal boatmen. The waterway didn't prove equally popular among merchants, who preferred the speed and reliability of the B & O Railroad, and the canal was closed to commercial traffic in 1923.

When Robert Mills served as architect of public buildings in 1841, he supplemented his modest income by producing the *Guide to the National Executive Offices and the Capitol of the United States,* a slim paperbound volume of only fifty pages that is of interest today chiefly because within those covers he was able to include plans of the Capitol and of all the executive buildings, to list the names and room numbers of all federal employees, and to have room left over to print the menu for the congressional dining room or "Refectory for Members of Congress."[9]

Mills (who had been a pupil of Latrobe), Ammi Young, and Thomas U. Walter were probably the last federal architects of the period to design work in the Classic Revival style. In 1849 Robert Dale Owen, son of Robert Owen, leader of the utopian colony of New Harmony, published *Hints on Public Architecture.* A former representative from Indiana, the younger Owen served as chairman of the building committee of the Smithsonian Institution, and his book supplied an elaborate presentation of, and argument for, the honest functional qualities of James Renwick's design, "exemplifying the style of the twelfth century," as contrasted with the false qualities of the Greek and Roman manners of other public buildings in Washington. The book and the design appear to have been strongly influenced by the writings of A. Welby Pugin and Andrew Jackson Downing. Some of the text gives one the impression that, though time may pass and styles may change, architectural jargon remains usable for any occasion: ". . . to reach an Architecture suited to our own country and our own time

*The just-opened Smithsonian; although this engraving, published c. 1854, exagger-
ates the depth of the "Castle," it accurately illustrates how the picturesque beauty of
the building is enhanced by the lively interplay of light and shade.*

. . . an actual example, at the Seat of Government, the architect of which
seems to me to have struck into the right road, to have made a step in
advance, and to have given us, in his design, not a little of what may be fitting and appropriate in any manner . . . that shall deserve to be named as a
National Style of Architecture for America."[10]

Not many architects chose to follow Renwick's new "national style"
(Renwick himself, when he designed the old Corcoran Gallery some years
later, adopted the style of the French Renaissance), but most architects
thereafter seemed determined to submit their own candidates for that
honor.

Before his death in a Hudson riverboat explosion in 1852, Downing
had laid out the grounds of the Smithsonian and the White House in the
romantic, meandering style of the period. His popular books on landscape
design and rural architecture publicized residential designs by A. J. Davis,
Richard Upjohn, and Downing's own partner, Calvert Vaux, who planned
houses for some of the fashionable and wealthy citizens of Georgetown.
Vaux's houses show, in an interesting way, the transition of residential
design from the late Classic Revival through the relatively chaste Italianate
or Tuscan Villa style to the heavily ornamented, mansard-roofed houses of
the latter part of the nineteenth century.

The Civil War turned the city of Washington into an armed camp. The
location of the capital, selected so carefully to be near the line between the

North and South, became a position at the edge of the battlefront. A ring of defensive forts appeared on the hills surrounding the city, and although in 1864 a Confederate army led by Jubal Early reached the outskirts of the federal district at Fort Stevens, the city's defenses were never penetrated.[11]

Apart from the completion of the new Capitol wings and dome, work on which continued despite the war, little construction of a permanent nature went on in the city until the end of hostilities. A significant aftermath, however, was the increased influence and activity of the U.S. Army Corps of Engineers—not restricted to works of engineering alone, but extending to the design or supervision of construction of major public buildings such as the Pension Building and the old State, War, and Navy Building. Most prominent in the corps at that time was Gen. Montgomery Meigs, the talented officer who had earlier challenged Thomas U. Walter's authority as architect of the Capitol. Meigs designed the astonishing post–Civil War Pension Building but left what may be his most enduring monument in the Washington aqueduct system, extending to the city from above the Little Falls of the Potomac. Two of the bridges along its route are especially notable—the Cabin John Aqueduct Bridge, which for many years was the longest stone arch in the world (220 feet), and the Rock Creek Aqueduct Bridge, where the road was carried on the arched tubular metal pipes of the water supply system.

Construction of the old State, War, and Navy Building after the Civil

Merchant Robert Dodge built this "suburban villa" in Georgetown to the design of Calvert Vaux and A. J. Downing. Robert and his brother Francis watched over the family warehouse near the C & O Canal from the glass-enclosed tower.

The Franklin School featured prominently in Joseph West Moore's Picturesque Washington *(1886); architect Adolf Cluss designed the octagonal corner turrets as ventilators to show that function and ornament need not be mutually exclusive.*

War was considered by many to signify the permanence of Washington, D.C., as the site of the national capital. If cost of construction and permanence of materials were any measure of that intent, it must have served admirably to make the intention clear. Alfred B. Mullett was not an architect whose work rested lightly upon the earth (the Post Office Building in St. Louis is another good example of his work). Like MacArthur's Philadelphia City Hall, his buildings expressed as much civic confidence as architectural diligence.

The Smithsonian's Arts and Industries Building, designed by Cluss and Shulze, is an interesting survival from the exhibition architecture of the 1876 Philadelphia Centennial Exposition. The Oriental flavor of its form and polychrome decorations was echoed in some of the city's market buildings, schools, railroad stations, and residences of the 1880s, of which relatively few remain. The influence of H. H. Richardson and the Romanesque Revival made an impression on Washington architecture from about 1880 to 1900, and although Richardson's Hay and Adams houses were destroyed to build the hotel that bears their names, the Tuckerman House, built the year of his death, 1886, on an adjoining site, was carried out by Hornblower and Marshall in a direct continuity of style and exterior detailing. The Presbyterian Church of the Covenant, designed by J. C. Cady, architect of the Museum of Natural History in New York, and the old Post Office on Pennsylvania Avenue, are other important examples of the period.[12]

The Washington firm of Smithmeyer and Pelz was prominent on the architectural scene toward the end of the nineteenth century, with buildings to its credit as widely different as Georgetown's Healy Hall, a Victorian neo-Gothic college building, and the Library of Congress, a competition-winning design in the Renaissance style. Some of the more startling designs of this versatile firm were never built; they included a Gothic multi-towered bridge across the Potomac, a new White House spanning 16th Street at Meridian Hill, and Franklin Smith's proposal for the "Halls of the Ancients," a sort of permanent world's fair of architecture that would have extended from the west side of the Ellipse to the river.

The lack of any effective controls over its rapid and haphazard growth was gradually destroying any evidence of the capital as a uniquely planned city, but in the year 1901 the American Institute of Architects played a central role in the initiation of the McMillan Plan, which modified, enlarged, and reestablished L'Enfant's plan of Washington. Glenn Brown, an architect whose deep interest in the history of the Capitol later produced a monumental two-volume account of its development, had been appointed secretary of the institute in 1899, and it was largely through his efforts that the program for the AIA convention of 1900 was prepared. The meeting convened in Washington on the centennial of the establishment of the federal city, and the papers delivered at that meeting inspired Senator James McMillan, chairman of the Senate District Committee, to appoint a commission to study the planning of the city. He asked the institute to suggest who would be most qualified to serve, and the names of Daniel H. Burnham and Frederick Law Olmsted, Jr., emerged by common consent. The Chicago Columbian Exposition of 1893 was still fresh in the minds of all, and Burnham, having headed the group of architects and artists who planned the exhibition, was a logical choice, as was Olmsted, son and successor of the famous landscape architect who had designed the grounds and terraces of the Capitol. Burnham and Olmsted, in turn, asked for the appointment of architect Charles Follen McKim and sculptor Augustus Saint Gaudens, both of whom had worked intimately with Burnham during the Columbian Exposition. The report of this group, the Park Commission, was published in 1902 and was a remarkable document. These talented men—bound together by friendship, respect, and common purpose—made the most of the opportunity to describe and delineate a vision of what the city might become.

Some of the Park Commission's recommendations were never carried out—among them ideas that could be profitably restudied today—but many of them were, and the effect upon Washington's architectural style was just as pronounced as the effects upon its plan. The formality of L'Enfant's plan was restored, and the argument that an architecture derived from classical antecedents was the only suitable style for such a plan was persuasively presented in visual terms. Whatever weight or merit this argument may have had, some of the finest buildings in Washington date from the early decades of this century quite simply because the best architects in the country designed them.

It was a time of great optimism, clients wanted and would pay for the best, and art was respectable enough to sit at the table when the money was being served. Not only were prominent architects of the period, such as Burnham, the firm of McKim, Mead and White, Henry Bacon, Paul Cret,

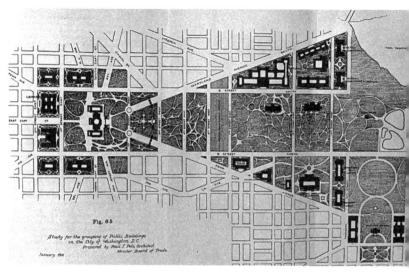

Fig. 85

Study for the grouping of Public Buildings
in the City of Washington, D.C.
Prepared by Paul J. Pelz, Architect
January 1901   Member Board of Trade

By the turn of the 20th century, people had had enough of a chaotic, unkempt Mall.
Architect Paul Pelz, who had helped design the Library of Congress, thought that
this relandscaping and new construction might improve things. He was on the right
track. He proposed buildings for the sites that eventually housed the Supreme Court
and the House and Senate Office Buildings (all on Capitol Hill) and he envisioned,
farther down Pennsylvania Avenue, a prototype of the Federal Triangle. On the
other hand, he kept the Mall's unclassical serpentine paths and left what he labeled
"PENN RAILROAD DEPOT" in place on the Mall between 6th and 7th Streets.

and Cass Gilbert, given important commissions in the capital, but their
buildings were embellished by the work of sculptors such as Saint Gaudens, Daniel Chester French, and Lorado Taft.

The spirit pervading the best work of that period seems gradually to
have been lost. Whether it was dried up by the Depression, squeezed out
by the weight of bureaucracy, or simply enfeebled by lack of conviction
and talent would be hard to say. Whatever the cause, work in the style of
Academic Classicism, with few exceptions, seemed to become progressively larger, more sterile, and less graceful in conception and execution.

It is difficult to view architecture in Washington since 1940 in any
clear historical perspective. Dating a new phase of architectural development from a period at the beginning of World War II is in itself a somewhat arbitrary decision, but the Saarinen competition-winning design for
the Smithsonian Gallery of Art in 1939 (which was never constructed)
and William Lescaze's Longfellow Building in 1940 probably mark as distinct a point of change as any that might be named. Since that time,
certain other isolated examples, such as the Dulles Airport Terminal

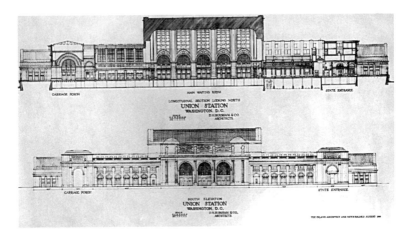

Daniel Burnham, a member of the Beaux-Arts–minded McMillan Commission, did get the train station off the Mall: here is his 1908 proposal for Union Station.

building, loom up as important and serious works of architecture, but a leveling influence of sorts has been at work. The majority of contemporary commercial office buildings and governmental office buildings tended to become larger and more standardized to the point where they were virtually indistinguishable in form. This was perhaps inevitable, since the functions of these structures were very nearly the same. The great variety of industrially produced materials and building components that became available after the Second World War, along with the economies of modern curtain wall construction, created a new element in the cityscape that was both monotonous and distracting: monotonous because many of the newer buildings were wrapped, like packages, in an overall pattern of windows and spandrels; distracting because there seemed no limit to the number of unsuitable patterns that one could place in juxtaposition to one another.

Washington is a horizontal city. The maximum building heights Congress established in 1910 to prevent our principal federal monuments from being overshadowed by commercial construction are in general still considered to be a desirable limitation. But these height limits, coupled with building programs calling for hundreds of thousands of square feet of construction, have created architectural and planning problems within the city that remain unresolved.

Southwest Washington remains interesting to architects and planners, not only as one of the first large-scale applications of the powers of urban renewal, but also as an architectural sampler of the mid-twentieth century. Rarely may one view such a variety of architectural solutions to essentially the same problem, constructed in such a relatively concentrated area, over such a short period of time. Some examples of planned communities near Washington—ranging from Greenbelt, Maryland, the most famous of the government-sponsored resettlement housing projects of the 1930s, and Hollin Hills in Virginia, a pioneer example of postwar contemporary development planning, to Reston, conceived as a New Town, in nearby Fairfax County—also are of particular interest.

The 1960s and 1970s brought significant changes in the expectations, attitudes, and demands of the city's people, both black and white. The riots of 1968, Resurrection City, and the outpouring of young demonstrators against the Vietnam War offered dramatic evidence of change, but there were less dramatic shifts just as important to the architectural and topographical future of the city. Concern for the preservation of older buildings and places within the city grew, contributing to its cultural vitality and variety. Disenchantment with the wholesale demolition that accompanied (and the overbearing scale that characterized) so much of the federal city planning and reconstruction mounted in these years. Resistance to the construction of more freeways within the city, organized opposition by communities within the city to overly permissive zoning, and, on a smaller scale, the struggle to save the old Post Office on Pennsylvania Avenue all reflected changing beliefs of what constitutes progress. These movements questioned the sanity of any planning that fails to sustain and encourage the humane qualities of the city—those qualities making life within it bearable.

Reconstruction of Pennsylvania Avenue supplied a good case in point. Early plans, unveiled in 1964, swept away all existing buildings on the north side of the avenue from the Treasury Building to the Capitol and retained only the tower of the Post Office on the south side as a relic of the nineteenth century. Ultimately, however, those plans gave way, as had earlier proposals to "Federalize" Lafayette Square, to less drastic reconstruction. The Pennsylvania Avenue Plan, after being restudied and modified, saved some fine older buildings instead of demolishing them and brought more mixed commercial and residential uses into the area. It was well that planners reconsidered, for the FBI Building (as the first block to conform to the earlier plan, but without the arcaded street façade recommended by the commission) hardly warmed one's enthusiasm for an avenue filled with a succession of such structures. To the credit of Nathaniel Owings and others who were active in the planning process, they remained receptive to changing needs and conditions in their efforts to move this important project ahead.

From the Rayburn Building, to the Kennedy Center, to the FBI Building and Washington Convention Center, the planning and architectural problems of such immense, relatively low buildings within the city were nearly insurmountable. The area south of Independence Avenue, as it parallels the Mall, has been filled with federal office buildings just as monumental and just as lifeless as those spawned by the Federal Triangle project of the 1920s but lacking that undertaking's unity of concept and style. The Mall has become the site of a newer group of buildings for the Smithsonian Institution, which share only the general discipline of their location. Fortunately, the scale of the great central lawn, with its flanking panels of trees, is so vast that aberrations of form are visually submerged with scarcely a ripple.

If the work of any architect during the 1970s is to be singled out for its contribution to the city, one must note I. M. Pei's Christian Science Church at 16th and I Streets and office buildings at L'Enfant Plaza. Both stand well above the level of quality of similar buildings of the period in their maturity of concept and execution. Pei's East Wing of the National Gallery, completed in 1978, stands as one of the capital's most original and exciting structures—complex but complete in its logic and form.

In 1967 President Johnson requested the development of a new "racially and economically balanced community" on one of the largest single undeveloped sites still remaining within the District of Columbia. Fort Lincoln New Town, to be built on the grounds of the former National Training School for Boys, was conceived as an urban community, a prototype for other federally sponsored new towns-within-towns, and a laboratory for innovative social, ecological, and educational planning. The project never received the support that had originally been envisioned; it remains, under the aegis of private developers, an architectural (as well as social) disappointment.

Mushrooming construction in Rosslyn, just across the river from the old port of Georgetown, and in Crystal City—an office and residential complex close to the National Airport—has transformed parts of the nearby Virginia skyline (someone called it Houston-on-the-Potomac) with a forest of high-rise office buildings unrestricted by the height limits of the city of Washington. The Georgetown waterfront, long depressed by anachronistic industrial zoning and by the blighting influence of an unattractive elevated freeway, now constantly stirs to the sound of new construction, and an effort is being made to reconcile opportunities for residential and commercial development on what is potentially one of the most advantageous sites in the city with the need to preserve the valuable historic buildings and enclaves that enrich the area.

And last, one must mention the Metro, the Washington Metropolitan Transit Authority. Washington's Metro was one of the most extensive, and expensive, public works projects in history, spending more than three billion dollars on construction. The architectural design of the system was under the direction of Harry Weese and Associates, with DeLeuw Cather and Company acting as general engineering consultants. The subway, with rail extensions reaching far out into Maryland and Virginia, unquestionably has had a profound influence upon the present and future development of the city and its suburbs.

NOTES

1. See Kenneth R. Bowling and Helen E. Veit, eds., *The Diary of William Maclay and Other Notes on the Senate Debates*, vol. 9 of the *Documentary History of the First Federal Congress of the United States of America, March* 4, 1789–March 3, 1791 (Baltimore, 1988), pp. 307–8. Maclay, a senator from Pennsylvania, had no illusions. His journal entry for June 30, 1790 reports: "I am fully convinced Pennsylvania could do no better. The Matter could not be longer delayed. It is in fact the Interest of the President of the United States, that pushes the Potowmack, he by means of Jefferson Madison Carroll & others Urges the Business, and if We had not closed with these Terms a bargain would have been made, for the Temporary Residence in New York."

2. Thomas Tileston Waterman, *The Mansions of Virginia, 1706–1776* (Chapel Hill, 1946).

3. Gunston Hall, Virginia (1753); Mount Vernon, Virginia (1757–1787); Montpelier, Laurel, Maryland (1770). See also Mills Lane, *Architecture of the Old South: Virginia* (New York, 1987) and *Architecture of the Old South: Maryland* (New York, 1991) for other examples.

4. Thomas Twining, *Travels in America* 100 Years Ago (New York: Harper & Bros., 1893), pp. 98–99.

5. The building that was Forrest's home, 2550 M Street, though mutilated by commercial alteration, remains standing.

6. Donald Jackson and Dorothy Toohig, eds., *The Diaries of George Washington* (Charlottesville: University Press of Virginia, 1979), vol. 6.

7. Talbot Hamlin, *Benjamin Henry Latrobe* (New York: Oxford University Press, 1955), pp. 285, 294; George Hadfield, *The Washington Guide* (Washington, D.C.: S. A. Elliott, 1826), p. 22.

8. See, for example, Thornton's "Tudor Place," and the Octagon; Latrobe's Decatur House and St. John's Church, Lafayette Square; The White House—central façade by Hoban and Latrobe; and Hadfield's Arlington House and Old City Hall.

9. Some of the fixed prices were: venison steak, 37 1/2 cents; beefsteak, 25 cents; pork steak, 25 cents; mutton chop, 25 cents; veal cutlet, 25 cents; one dozen raw oysters, 12 1/2 cents; ham and eggs 37 1/2 cents; one plate of common turtle soup, 25 cents; one plate of green turtle soup, 50 cents; wine and water, and malt liquor, per tumbler, 6 1/4 cents.

10. Robert Dale Owen, *Hints on Public Architecture* (New York: G. P. Putnam, 1849), pp. 104, 109.

11. See Barnard, *Defenses of Washington* (Washington, D.C., 1871). The remains of this chain of earthwork defenses are now under the jurisdiction of the Park Service. Fort Stevens, at the head of Georgia Avenue, N.W., is probably the most interesting, historically if not topographically.

12. Of these three buildings, only the old Franklin Post Office still remains, the Tuckerman House and Church of the Covenant having been demolished in the late 1960s to make way for new speculative office buildings.

The Architecture of Washington, D.C., 1970s to 1990s

CHRISTOPHER WEEKS

As the District of Columbia concludes its second century the city's architects, consciously or not, have marked the bicentennial with a coda: after Chloethiel Woodard Smith, Charles Goodman, David Yerkes, and Winthrop and Waldron Faulkner nurtured Washington's modern movement to its full flowering, architectural thinking in the capital has returned—with a vengeance—to themes begun in the 1790s. But, like most things in Washington, this "return" is not as neat and tidy as it may first seem, because both decades, the 1790s and the 1990s, can be characterized by inherently contradictory themes. Architecture in 1990s Washington seems driven by an uneasy fusion of up-to-the-minute technological advances sheathed in historical, even archaeological, forms. Flashing back two hundred years one will find the exact same tension in the District's air, only in the 1790s the tension was the result of grafting ancient architectural forms onto revolutionary politics.

One could certainly argue that, of all the Founders, Washington and Jefferson did more than any other two people to bring this radical new nation into existence, one with his battlefield wiles, one with his potent pen. It could also be argued that these two played similarly pivotal roles in establishing the new city on the Potomac. Yet what did the two revolutionaries plan for the capital city? Working with the moody Pierre Charles L'Enfant, they created a plan for the new nation's capital that was thoroughly steeped in the traditions of absolutist Europe (many scholars suggest that the plan simply superimposed the axes of Versailles onto the banks of the Potomac). In addition to giving the city this retrospective framework, both men agreed that the proposed broad avenues should be lined with buildings based on the ancient temples of Rome and Greece and on the 16th-century villas of Palladio.

Washington and Jefferson fully understood the value of symbols and recognized the need to create an instant history to legitimize the new nation to the generally hostile Europeans. "Architecture is my delight," Jefferson himself wrote, "but it is an enthusiasm of which I am not ashamed, as its object is to improve the taste of my countrymen, to increase their reputation, to reconcile them to the rest of the world, and to procure them its praise." In 1791 Jefferson asked his secretary to get him "a complete set of Piranesi's drawings of the Pantheon. . . . I wish," he explained, "to render them useful in the public buildings now to be begun at Georgetown."[1]

Benjamin Henry Latrobe, more of a professional architect and less of a philosopher than his sponsor, Jefferson, mused on his own difficulties in reconciling "my principles of good taste," which he said were "rigid . . . [and] Grecian" with the knowledge that "Roman and Greek buildings . . . are inapplicable to the objects and uses of our public buildings."[2] Latrobe was unable to see, as Washington and Jefferson did, that this 18th-century historicism had practical purposes. The Italian critic Manfredo Tafuri has written volumes on "the pragmatism of American eclecticism" and argues that Jefferson valued this or that monument of ancient architecture as a "ready-made object to be transported by means of a minimum of functional modifications, since its interest lies entirely in the values it embodies . . . which are beyond discussion."[3] Thus, from the beginning the District's architecture was born out of an uneasy truce between the contemporary forces of change and the pull of the past.

Few of the District's modern architects are worried about legitimizing America in the eyes of Europe, but nearly all seem driven by the same professional dichotomy that plagued Latrobe: after a decade or so of hard-

Thomas Jefferson himself anonymously entered the White House design competition. He based his elevation (shown here) on Palladio's Villa Rotonda near Vicenza. His design did not win, but he retained his belief that adherence to neoclassicism would "improve the taste of my countrymen" and "increase their reputation" among citizens of more established nations.

edged modernism, when new construction was often imposed onto a site, architects now seem primarily concerned with having their new buildings fit into the existing urban scene. As Haynes Johnson of the *Post* has suggested, 1990s Washington architects work "with an eye to modesty and charm." David Schwarz hopes his buildings are thought "appropriate"; David Childs wants his to be "handsome"; Warren Cox, perhaps the most verbally gifted of the generation, has been quoted as saying "once you start looking at and working on these good Washington buildings [of the past] . . . you realize there's a richness, interest in detail, and caring *about how things work together* that makes the average elderly graduate of the GSD look like he's doing spec houses. I'm tired of drywall . . . and Formica."[4] The dichotomy of the 1990s is not one of combining a reverence of past forms with fiery, innovative politics; it is one of combining a reverence of past forms with unprecedented technological advancement and change.

This combination has produced a body of work that sometimes borders on the eccentric—most strikingly Arthur Cotton Moore's Washington Harbour. Easily the most talked-about building of the 1980s, Washington Harbour, according to Moore, represents his attempt "to reflect . . . Victorian Georgetown" and the "columnar quality" of the neoclassical monuments with contemporary materials and technology.[5] Washington Harbour strikes some observers as extreme, but its philosophical basis seems clear enough. Moore worked on an abstract level; when designers give literal form to the fusion of past and present, the results can only be called surreal. Such certainly is true of the State Department's diplomatic reception rooms, where curator Clement Conger and architects Allan Greenberg and John Blatteau took the seventh floor of a banal 1960s office building and inserted a series of sumptuous 18th- and 19-century rooms, suites, and furniture. Heads are still being scratched at the results, noted *Abitare* magazine, which deemed the endeavor "curious, to say the least."[6]

Washington Harbour and the reception rooms are extreme cases, but the fusion theme appears all over town. Sometimes it takes the form of façadism, whereby shells of older buildings are preserved while interiors are altered or gutted. More often than not, new floorspace—sometimes new floors—appear through more or less harmonious infill. Warnecke's Lafayette Square is the grand-daddy of these conversions; Skidmore, Owings and Merrill's Evening *Star* Building and Shalom Baranes's Southern Building are two of the more successful grandchildren. Less frequently, reverence for the past has produced whole new buildings (or distinct additions) built all-of-a-piece but built following earlier dogmas. When done well, the result is not copywork but reinterpretation—much as one might regard Sargent's portraits. These new/old buildings vary widely, and range from the near-literal, such as Keyes Condon Florance's

Hartman-Cox's 1982 addition to the Folger Library: a bit of French Enlightenment, a smattering of high-tech, and a superabundance of talent combined to produce a room as perfect as it is humanly possible for a room to be.

Republic Place, to the somewhat abstract, such as Hartman-Cox's exquisite addition to the Folger Shakespeare Library.

It should be pointed out that landscape architecture seems to have become more appreciated during the 1980s and '90s than it was a generation or so ago, at least in Washington. This change involves an understanding not only of nature and of growing things (which might be said to have been regenerated by Lady Bird Johnson's plea that we "plant a tree, bush, or shrub") but also of the theories and implications of garden design as an art form equal to bricks and mortar building design. Sometimes literal monuments control landscape, as in EDAW's Column Garden at the National Arboretum; sometimes abstractions do, as in Venturi, Rauch, and Scott Brown's Freedom Plaza.

Contemporary architects in Washington must feel that they hear as many voices as Joan of Arc did, for, in addition to the ongoing professional debates, architects in the District must perforce work with a dizzying array of review committees. The sheer numbers of these groups—and their codified, statutory power—makes them enormously influential players in the late-20th-century design process. Bureaucrats and officials empowered by the Pennsylvania Avenue Development Corporation, the Fine Arts Commission, and the forces unleashed by the National Historic Preservation Act of 1966 dictate, on a large, sweeping scale, how the city looks, while seemingly dozens of neighborhood volunteer groups monitor proposed construction (and demolition) at the grassroots level. There is precedent for all this, of course: ninety years ago the McMillan Plan gave bureaucrats influence over design; two hundred years ago George Washington created a citizens committee to pass judgment on designs for the proposed Capitol and President's House. It seems at least arguable, though, that none of these earlier amateur bodies had the power their modern volunteer counterparts enjoy. Some professionals feel this intervention is bad and some feel it is good, but no one can deny that it gives contemporary architecture a lively, public airing.

Yet what other design process could operate in the capital of citizenry democracy? This leads to another two-hundred-year-old constant in Washington's architectural history, namely, the presence of well-intentioned, well-researched, deeply held, contradictory opinions. Every one of the District's "masterpieces," those seemingly foreordained creations—the Capitol, the White House, the Washington Monument, the Mall, the National Cathedral, the Lincoln Memorial, and Arlington Bridge—every one of them is a result of years (sometimes of generations) of push and pull and compromise, of architects sometimes yielding to half-baked congressional opinion and sometimes finding somewhat devious ways to circumvent it. Or take the L'Enfant Plan and the McMillan Plan: each bears a single name, but in truth they reflect the thinking of Washington and Jefferson filtered through a prickly Frenchman's aesthetic and modified by congressional committees all working in what John Dos Passos has called the "miasma of contention" that envelops every project along "the muddy flats of the Potomac."[7]

Again, what else is new? What else is possible—or desirable—in our pluralistic society? Everyone older than age twelve seems to hold an opinion about every building project in the city, and no citizen seems the least bit shy about expressing such opinions in a letter to the editor of the *Washington Post*. In addition, members of the American Institute of Architects fill the pages of professional journals with reviews of each other's works and with rebuttal letters.

Artistic tension can produce spectacular results. While it is obviously too early to render a final verdict on the recent works of, say, David Schwarz or Amy Weinstein, it seems equally obvious that such men and women are just as serious about the art of building—and about the implications they respond to and create—as their counterparts of two centuries ago. Will critics in 2193 feel comfortable mentioning Warren Cox, David Childs, and Hugh Newell Jacobsen in the same breath as Latrobe and Bulfinch and Mills? No one can say, of course. But that one is able to pose the question says a good deal about the calibre of contemporary building in the nation's capital.

NOTES

1. The basic work on this much-discussed subject remains Fiske Kimball's *Thomas Jefferson, Architect* (Boston: privately printed, 1916). See also Dumas Malone, *Jefferson and the Rights of Man* (Boston: Little, Brown, 1951), pp. 371–87, as well as William Howard Adams, ed., *The Eye of Jefferson* (Washington, D.C.: National Gallery of Art, 1976), pp. 234–37.

2. See, among others, Malone, *Jefferson*, pp. 373–74.

3. Quoted in Fulvio Irace, "Il Classicismo Pragmatico: Una Costante Americana," *Abitare* (July–August 1988): 203.

4. Wolf Von Eckardt, "Filling in the Gaps," *Washington Post,* August 30, 1980; "With Respect to Cret, Folger Library Additions and Alterations," *Progressive Architecture* (July 1983): 65–73; Benjamin Forgey, "The Penn is Mightier," *Washington Post,* June 14, 1986; Andrea Oppenheimer Dean, "Contextualism Continues Strong in the Capital," *Progressive Architecture* (November 1986); Paul Goldberger, "A Pat on the Back for Some Modest Buildings," *New York Times,* June 18, 1989; Margaret Gaskie, "Neo-eclecticism on the Potomac," *Architectural Record* (July 1984).

5. Quote related to author by Patricia Moore.

6. Irace, "Il Classicismo Pragmatico," p. 167.

7. John Dos Passos, *Prospects of a Golden Age* (Englewood Cliffs, N.J.: Prentice-Hall, 1959), p. 265.

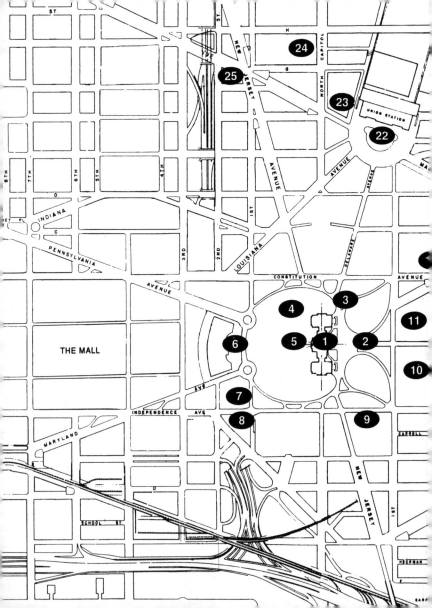

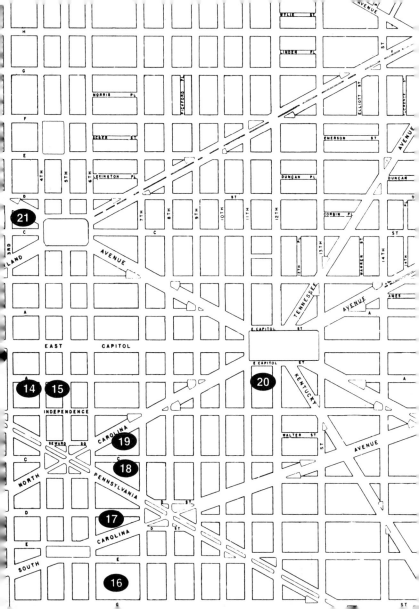

Lined with arching elms and radiating from the Capitol Plaza, L'Enfant's gracious avenues reach into every quadrant of the city to ensure that the spirit of the great dome is felt throughout the District. It is certainly felt everywhere in this charming neighborhood, from marbled governmental palaces to low-scale residential side streets.

This c. 1920 aerial view shows that (even without the yet to be built Supreme Court building) the Capitol, Union Station, Senate and House offices, and Library of Congress made Jenkins Hill appropriately monumental in scale and style.

Congress first convened in "the Capital City" in 1800; when the legislators arrived, Capitol Hill boasted eight boarding houses, a general store, an oyster house, and a washerwoman. Things remained a bit primitive until after the Civil War, although a few prescient visitors saw the potential beauty of it all. For instance, as early as the 1830s Frances Trollope openly admired the city, in counterpoint to the snickers and sneers that generally characterized Europeans' opinions of the new town. (Some 1804 British doggerel reads, "This embryo Capital, where fancy sees / Squares in morasses, obelisks in trees / Which second-sight seers, even now adorn / With shrines unbuilt to heroes unborn!") Mrs. Trollope, less well known than her novelist son, Anthony, proved herself an equally keen observer of social scenes in her 1832 *Domestic Manners of the Americans*. "I was delighted with the whole aspect of Washington," she wrote. "Light, cheerful, and airy, it reminded me of one of our fashionable watering holes. . . . I confess I see nothing in the least degree ridiculous about it; the original design, which was as beautiful as it was extensive, has been in no way departed from, and all that has been done has been done well." And yet a correspondent for the *Sacramento Daily News* complained as late as 1871 that Washington's "streets are seas or canals of liquid mud, varying in depth from one to three feet and possessing as geographical features conglomerations of garbage, refuse, and trash."

Enter local politico Alexander "Boss" Shepherd, who served—reigned, really—as governor of the District from 1871 until 1874. Shepherd drained swamps and canals, laid sewer and water lines, built 128 miles of sidewalks, installed over 3,000 gas lights, and improved 300 miles of city streets—when he left office Washington boasted more paved streets than any other city in the country! He also encouraged new construction in Capitol Hill (and in the Dupont Circle area) and he himself built more than 1,000 speculative houses. His complicated financial network eventually collapsed, however, and he had to flee to Mexico.

Jefferson, Washington, and L'Enfant all assumed that the new city would grow to the southeast, towards the then-navigable Anacostia River; Washington even engaged in a bit of land speculation, buying a few lots in the "town" of Carrollsburg, located at the junction of the Anacostia and the Potomac. To everyone's surprise, however, building activity shifted to the northwest, rendering the Capitol Hill neighborhood a quiet backwater. But no longer: a favored enclave of that unique Washington type, the bohemian bureaucrat, Capitol Hill booms as one of the "hottest" of Washington neighborhoods, the darling of city realtors.

---

1   The Capitol

1793–1802	William Thornton	1803–1817	Benjamin Henry Latrobe
1819–1829	Charles Bulfinch	1836–1851	Robert Mills
1851–1865	Thomas U. Walter	1865–1902	Edward Clark
1902–1923	Ellicott Woods	1923–1954	David Lynn
1954–1970	J. George Stewart	1971–present	George M. White

9:00 A.M. TO 4:30 P.M. DAILY   PHONE: 225-6827

In 1791, after examining the new Federal District in search of a site suitable for the Capitol, Pierre Charles L'Enfant reported that he "could discover no one [situation] so advantageously to greet the congressional building as that on the west end of Jenkins Heights." Near the center of the city-to-be, and some 88 feet above the Potomac, Jenkins Hill, he believed, stood like "a pedestal waiting for a monument." The "monument's" rough-and-tumble career—two centuries of stop-and-go construction, seven generations of changes and modifications of rethinkings and "master plans"—shocks the orderly-minded but is precisely what one would expect, and perhaps hope for, in this symbol of participatory democracy; indeed, in a very real way, the architectural history of the Capitol simply gives three-dimensional form to the philosophical history of the Republic.

In 1792, the site having been selected, Congress, at the urging of Secretary of State Jefferson, arranged to hold competitions for the design of the Capitol and the President's House and ran a series of newspaper ads to announce "a premium of a lot in the city of Washington . . . and $500 shall be given by the Commissioners of the Federal Buildings to the person who before the 15th of July, 1792, shall produce to them the most approved plan for a Capitol to be erected in this city."

Sixteen proposals crossed the desk of George Washington. Some were bizarre; most were amatuerish; none was good enough for the new nation's most important building. Three months after the official deadline, William Thornton, a physician from the Virgin Islands, submitted his design and Washington immediately endorsed it: "The grandeur, the simplicity, and the beauty," he wrote to the other judges of Thornton's sketch, "will, I doubt not, give it a preference in your eyes as it has in mine." They concurred and selected Thornton's design in 1793. Architectural design was rather free and easy back then; Thornton once described his own method thus: "I got some books and worked a few days, then gave the plan in the ancient Ionic order which carried the day." Partly because of such statements, everyone worried about the amateur Thornton's ability to oversee construction, so builder Stephen Hallet, first runner-up in the contest, was hired to supervise things.

In one of the few peaceful moments in the building's history, on September 18, 1793, George Washington, following Masonic ritual, laid the cornerstone using a silver trowel and a marble-headed gavel. Then trouble broke out and egotism surfaced: Hallet inserted so many of his own ideas that he had to be fired. James Hoban, winner of the competition for the President's House, was put in charge, with Hallet as his assistant. (It took a direct appeal from Washington and the mediating efforts of Jefferson to reach that compromise.) Funds were limited. As Irish journalist Isaac Weld noted in 1799, "numbers of people . . . particularly in Philadelphia" tried to sabotage work on the Capitol by withholding funds. In this penny-pinching, intrigue-filled atmosphere, Jefferson and Washington had laborers concentrate their efforts on the north wing alone, which was finished in 1800. Congress met in Washington for the first time that November. Looking at the present building from the Library of Congress, one can still see the small dome (to the right) that crowned that earliest structure.

The small dome to the left, atop the present House wing, dates to a section completed in 1807 under the auspices of Benjamin Henry Latrobe, a *professional* architect, whom Jefferson admired and appointed surveyor of public buildings in 1803. Jefferson, vitally interested in architecture, took a more than passive role in the Capitol's construction. Under Latrobe's guidance, with Jefferson peering over his shoulder (and Thornton, *éminence grise*), both the south and north wings lurched to what everyone thought was completion. When Jefferson retired from the presidency he hopefully expressed to Latrobe his wish that this building might stand as "the first temple dedicated to the sovereignty of the people embellishing with Athenian taste the course of a nation looking far beyond the range of Athenian destinies."

William R. Birch's 1800 sketch of the Capitol's north (Senate) wing shows an idealized White House floating in the misty distance, like Bali Hai. Birch accurately showed that Jenkins Hill, site of the Capitol, really was a hill.

When Congress fired Latrobe in 1817, the Capitol's House and Senate wings were up with only a wooden walkway to connect then, as this c. 1819 watercolor shows.

But it was one problem after another. Two years after Jefferson wrote those optimistic words, war intervened, when British admiral Sir George Cockburn torched "this harbor of Yankee democracy" on August 24, 1814, leaving what Latrobe called "a most magnificent ruin." After the war, Congress moved temporarily to the "Brick Capitol," on the site of the present Supreme Court, and Latrobe began reconstructing the earlier building, all the while supervised by Thornton.

Latrobe and Thornton constantly feuded—a classic case of professional versus amateur. Although both Jefferson and Madison forced Latrobe to follow Thornton's original design on the exterior work, they gave him a looser rein on the rooms within—and he consequently achieved greater success there. Jefferson perhaps best summed up Latrobe's contribution when he wrote the architect, "I declared on many and all occasions that I considered you as the only person in the United States who could have executed the [project]."

Among Latrobe's many gifts to the Capitol, perhaps his corn-cob and tobacco-leafed capitals most deserve their own paragraph. Latrobe (and Jefferson) sought to create a truly American replacement for the acanthus-leafed capitals of Greece and Rome. Latrobe was well pleased with his invention and wrote his Virginia friend that they had "more applause from members of Congress" because of these capitals "than all the Works of Magnitude that surround them." Mrs. Trollope was just as impressed—

One of Latrobe's deservedly acclaimed corn-cob columns: in addition to replacing the traditional acanthus-leaf design with indigenous maize, he made the shaft a bundle of corn stalks.

and for all the right reasons—and she commented in 1832 that "the beautiful capitals . . . composed of the ears and leaves of Indian corn" were "the only instance I saw in which America has ventured to attempt national originality; the success is perfect. A sense of fitness always enhances the effect of beauty."

However successful, Latrobe eventually fell victim to political and professional intrigue and was forced to resign in 1817. (The somewhat prickly architect's outspokenness didn't help him: in 1813, for example, he likened President Madison to "a little shrivelled spider.") Latrobe's departure left a most curious structure on Jenkins Hill, the completed Senate and House wings and the wooden walkway that connected them creating a U-shaped profile. Before he was fired, however, he had sketched out an overall scheme for the entire building and thus, as historian William Pierson has written, "was able to impose something of his own artistic and practical vision upon the building, and . . . elevate it from the depths of mediocrity to levels of quality, both in appearance and convenience."

President Monroe then brought the brilliant New England architect Charles Bulfinch to Washington to complete the structure. According to a Bulfinch biographer, Harold Kirker, "not the least of Bulfinch's talents . . . was the extraordinary political tact that" marked a sharp break from the "almost thirty years of party strife . . . which had brought the construction of the Capitol to a standstill." (Even the amiable Bulfinch met with complaints, but he stoically wrote, "Architects expect criticism and must learn to bear it patiently.") His major task was to fill in that gaping U; this he did in 1827, by completing and doming the link between the two wings. Both Latrobe and Thornton had, miraculously, agreed that the dome should be low and gentle, but a few congressmen and some cabinet officers told Bulfinch they wanted, in the architect's words, a "bold . . . picturesque . . . lofty dome." (One cabinet member even demanded "a gothic form," but Bulfinch gently dismissed this idea as "too inconsistent.") If Congress wanted a taller dome, Bulfinch was the right man for the job, and he gave the Capitol a 55-foot-high dome, modeling it closely on the dome he had

Bulfinch, invited to Washington by James Monroe, added the center section and dome to Latrobe's wings. His dome might not seem high enough to modern eyes, but it is a good deal taller than that envisioned by Latrobe or Jefferson, both of whom wanted something more akin to the Pantheon or to Monticello. This 1849 engraving celebrates what everyone assumed was the finished building.

designed for the Massachusetts State House in the 1790s and creating a much more vertical silhouette than Latrobe and Jefferson had envisioned. So, in the matter of the dome, it was politicians 1, architects 0.

Bulfinch also finished the old House Chamber, which was used until 1857, when it was vacated for larger quarters. The old chamber began to deteriorate and was even used as a market stall until Congress passed a bill in the early 1860s to "throw the hucksters out." By about 1864 it had evolved into the Statuary Hall. (Congress decided that each state could place a statue of one or two favorite sons or daughters there. It is said that the Missouri delegation chose to honor Sen. Thomas Hart Benton instead of Mark Twain because they and their peers took umbrage at Twain's witticism, "Suppose you were an idiot. And suppose you were a member of Congress. But I repeat myself.") Bulfinch, concerned about the appearance of the Capitol grounds, added steps, terraces, gatehouses (see D-8), and fences. Frances Trollope saw what was essentially a Bulfinch Capitol when she visited Washington. It rendered her speechless— "the beauty and majesty of the American capitol might defy an abler pen than mine"— so she simply told her English readers that both "the magnificent western façade" and the "elegant eastern façade" struck her as "exceedingly handsome . . . [and] most splendid."

Walter's 1859 cross-section of the Capitol's newly designed dome.

As the government and the nation grew, the Thornton-Latrobe-Bulfinch building began to bulge, so in 1850 Congress authorized enlargements and launched another competition. This time architect Thomas U. Walter was the winner. He proposed building new quarters for the House and Senate and replacing the already-tall old center dome with a still-larger one. Overseen by engineer Montgomery C. Meigs, work began more or less immediately and all seemed rosy. But then Meigs and Walter began to quarrel, and the architect had to ask Congress to dismiss his "disobedient and rebellious assistant." Workmen, however, plugged away, oblivious to upper-level wrangling, and managed to complete the House extension in time for that body to convene there on December 16, 1857. The Senate moved into its completed quarters on January 4, 1859.

Both wings have proven great successes, but Walter's tour-de-force was, of course, that great dome. All those 1850s extensions had more than doubled the building's length (from 351 feet to 746 feet), thus reducing Bulfinch's "too large" dome to visual insignificance. So in 1855 Walter designed a huge new replacement, a truly magnificent creation consisting of two trussed cast-iron shells, one superimposed on the other. (The iron reportedly expands three to four inches on hot summer days.) All of the trim, cornices, and columns are cast iron painted to resemble marble.

Inside, the dome forms the Capitol Rotunda, 180 feet high and one of the nation's great spaces. The very top of the ceiling is filled with Constantin Brumidi's fresco, "The Apotheosis of Washington," in which various classical gods and goddesses hobnob with the Founding Fathers. Brumidi, born in Rome in 1805, worked at the Vatican before emigrating to the United States in 1852 and beginning work on the Capitol in 1855. He is said to have stated, "My one ambition is that I may live long enough to make beautiful the Capitol of the one country on earth in which there is liberty," but his ambition was thwarted by his death in 1880, when his

It was the American centennial, and the Illustrated London News *chose to adopt an ironic tone in this "typical" scene in the Capitol corridors. No doubt the magazine's readers were amused, but isn't this co-equal, mixed bag of humanity precisely the point?*

frescos were but partially completed. (He was succeeded by Filippo Costaggini, who, according to legend, tried to secure his imprint on the building by cramming nine panels into a space Brumidi had designed to hold seven. Congress objected and fired the upstart painter.) Closer to eye-level, the Rotunda's walls are embellished with eight historical paintings by John Trumbull, "the Artist of the Revolution." Trumbull was a serious (if crotchety) artist and, to ensure accuracy, took the trouble to travel to London and Paris as well as throughout the United States to paint his subjects from life. His paintings, such as "The Signing of the Declaration of Independence," have achieved a near-religious stature that surpasses their very real value as works of art and historical reportage.

One might think that the Civil War would have slowed construction of the Capitol, since troops bivouacked in the building's halls and some rooms even became bakeries; but Lincoln continued the building during the war because he believed that "if people see the Capitol going on . . . it is a sign we intend the Union shall go on." This wonderful use of architectural symbolism came to a climax on December 2, 1863—coinciding most fittingly with the Emancipation Proclamation—when Thomas Crawford's 19-foot statue, "Freedom," was lifted into place at the peak of the great cream-colored, cast-iron dome. (She took her perch after a circuitous five-year voyage that began in Rome and included gales and storms and a stop-over in Bermuda.)

Technological change produced a series of renovations and functional improvements throughout the 19th century: steam heat arrived in 1865, then elevators (1874), fireproofing (1881), and drainage (1882).

The 20th century has not been quiet for the Capitol, either. In 1959–60, under the direction of J. George Stewart, then holder of the office of Architect of the Capitol, the East Front was extended outwards 32 1/2 feet. This single stroke added 102 rooms and provided a visually deeper base for the dome. The stonework was changed from local Aquia Creek sandstone to Georgia marble in the process, and the old sandstone columns now grace the National Arboretum (see Q-9). Although wildly controversial at the time, such an extension had actually been proposed by Thomas U. Walter a century earlier. Another expansion scheme surfaced in the 1970s, but this time public outcry was so great that Congress scrapped the plans and voted to restore, not enlarge, the West Front. Accordingly, the stone walls were reinforced with steel rods and roughly one-third of the façade's crumbling sandstone was replaced. This work was completed in 1988.

What a bumpy ride! Henry James well described the results of all this bickering as "a vast and many-voiced creation." To James, the Capitol stood as the "compendium of all the national ideals, a museum, crammed to the full, even to overflowing, of all the national terms and standards, weights and measures and emblems of greatness and glory, and indeed as a built record of half the collective vibrations of a people; their conscious spirit, their public faith, their bewildered taste, their ceaseless curiosity, their arduous and interrupted education . . . association really reigns there, and in the richest, and even again and again in the drollest forms; it is thick and vivid and almost gross, it assaults the wandering mind." Yet it all works. Despite the diversity of personnel involved and the diversity of their talents, the parts miraculously come together in a harmonious, seemingly foreordained whole.

---

2 Lampstands

East Capitol Street
1877 Frederick Law Olmsted

In 1874 Congress commissioned Frederick Law Olmsted, certainly the greatest landscape architect of the times, to design a coherent, rational landscaping scheme for the Capitol grounds. Olmsted obliged by drawing up plans that were bold in their comprehensiveness—he had thoughts about everything, from broad, open lawns and shady walkways to details such as cast-iron planters—and a surprising amount of Olmsted's original street furniture, such as these lampstands, endures in situ on the Capitol's leafy grounds.

3 Waiting Station

Near the East Front of the
Capitol

c. 1875 Frederick Law
Olmsted

These hipped-roof stations
(there are two) show how surely
and completely Olmsted guided
the design of the late-19th-century Capitol grounds towards a unified artistic creation. These stations were once known as "Herdics" after the Herdic Phaeton Company, whose line of horse-drawn, plushly upholstered trolleys they served.

4 Spring Grotto

Near the West Front of the
Capitol

1874–1875 Frederick Law
Olmsted

Olmsted called this sheltered
spring his "cool retreat during
hot summer" and built it as part
of his general landscaping of the Capitol grounds. The hexagonal grotto, with its brick and terra-cotta walls and red tile roof, still serves its intended purpose, although it now flows with city water, since the original spring soured and had to be diverted. A stone tower, also designed by Olmsted, stands guard nearby and manages to be both decorative and functional: its upward thrust neatly balances the declivity of the grotto and a vent within it allows fresh, cooled air to be wafted into the Capitol through a series of underground tunnels.

The purity of congressional air evidently weighed heavily on Olmsted's mind. He suggested that "if . . . there was a body of trees along the base of Capitol Hill . . . it would in all probability be an efficient means of protecting the Capitol from malarial poison originating on the banks of the Potomac and in the low grounds between the river and the hill." Thus, in May 1875 he drew up a proposal for planting a "belt of woods" south of the Capitol grounds, more or less from the current Rayburn House Office Building to L'Enfant Plaza.

5 The Capitol—West Terrace

1874–1875 Frederick Law Olmsted

Olmsted, having rethought Latrobe's plan of stressing the Capitol's East Front, designed this elaborate system of terraces and walkways, completed in 1890, to draw attention to the west façade and simultaneously to ease the transition from it to the then-informal Mall. The view from the west side had been commended by no less than Emerson, who in 1843 wrote, "If Washington should ever grow into a great city, the outlook from the Capitol will be unsurpassed in the world. Now at sunset I seem to look westward far into the heart of the Continent from this commanding position." The view from the west steps and terraces still inspires such visions, and it allows one to see how well L'Enfant's broad avenues and open spaces lead the eye, the motorist, and the pedestrian to this most important building. Here is one bit of proof that baroque concepts of city planning remain valid in the late 20th century. The views *towards* the seat of government are wonderful too, for, as Olmsted noted, "the full proportions and beauty of a great building like the Capitol can only be comprehended from a distance at which its various parts will fall into a satisfactory perspective."

6 Grant Memorial

1st Street and East Mall

1922 pedestal: Edward Pearce Casey; statuary: Henry M. Schrady, sculptor (completed after his death by Edmond R. Amateis)
1976 reflecting pool: Skidmore, Owings & Merrill

About 252 feet long, this is the most expansive statuary grouping in the city and includes the second largest equestrian monument in the world (only the bronze Victor Emmanuel in Rome is larger). Here, at the center of it all, sits General Grant, wearily hunched astride his horse, Cincinnatus. Subservient figures represent the artillery and cavalry units Grant commanded with such doggedness during the Civil War.

The six-acre Reflecting Pool in front of the memorial resolved two different issues that arose when Interstate 395 was tunneled under the Mall. First, because the underground roadway covers a huge area, it requires a similarly huge "roof," and second, nothing substantial could be planted on the "roof," since roots and tunnels don't mix. The pool provided a happy solution and Skidmore, Owings & Merrill discovered that, by fiddling with the angles and edges, the shallow pool's vast watery surface could be laid out to capture, in reflection, the entirety of the Capitol dome.

Other notable—and somewhat earlier—commemorative sculptures nearby include the Garfield Memorial at 1st Street and Maryland Avenue, S.E. (1887, J. Q. Adams Ward), which depicts the recently assassinated president as a statesman, student, and warrior, and the Peace Monument at 1st Street and Pennsylvania Avenue, N.W. (1877, Franklin Simmons, sculptor, and Edward Clark, architect), in which Neptune, Mars, Victory, and Peace surround and console America, who is leaning on History while weeping for her dead heroes.

7 United States Botanic Garden

1st Street, Maryland Avenue, and Independence Avenue

1931 Bennett, Parsons & Frost

9:00 A.M. TO 5:00 P.M. DAILY
PHONE: 225-8333

Its multiarched rusticated façade, which suggests a 17th-century French *orangerie*, ensures that the dignified Mall side of the gardens makes a suitable mate to its important and formal neighbors. Just go around the corner, though, and view the rear façade, where the large glazed archways and glass-domed rotunda glisten, the exuberant—and functional—responses to the problem of how to grow full-sized trees indoors. Pay particular attention to the greenhouse's ribcage: it is made of aluminum and when built was the largest such construction in the world.

The federal government has maintained some sort of garden in Washington since 1842, when explorers brought exotic botanical souvenirs from the South Seas to the shores of the Potomac. Those plants were watered and kept warm in the old Patent Office Building and at various other sites in the city until achieving their permanent root-runs here.

8 Bartholdi Fountain

1st Street and Independence Avenue, S.W.

1876 Frédéric Auguste Bartholdi, sculptor

A bravura performance in bronze, glass, and water, this fountain, impressive enough today, was once even more spectacular. When Bartholdi (1834–1904, his best-known work is the Statue of Liberty) originally sculpted it for the 1876 Philadelphia Centennial Exhibition, the fountain represented the power that could be unleashed when disparate elements worked together: water spouted and swirled and flaming gas jets hissed. When the exhibition closed, the federal government bought the fountain and moved it to Washington. Electric lights have replaced the gas-fired flames, but the composition still produces a joyously dramatic effect. The park around the fountain picks up the theme, and the grounds blaze with color, thanks to thousands of annuals (and a few perennials) planted in a "bedding out" manner appropriate to the period.

9 Cannon House Office Building

New Jersey and Independence Avenues, S.E.

1908 Carrère & Hastings

The commission to erect offices for the Senate and the House—the first structures in the city (excepting only the Capitol) built specifically for congressional use—was divided between two architects who made up one firm. Hastings received responsibility for the House Office Building (illustrated here); Carrère for the (perhaps more successful) Senate Office Building. The pleasing result was a set of nonidentical neoclassical twins that, with their giant columns and gleaming white surfaces, visually merge to form a unified and proper background for the Capitol.

---

10 Library of Congress

1st Street and Independence Avenue, S.E.

1886–1892 Smithmeyer & Pelz
1892 Edward Pearce Casey
1993 restoration: Arthur Cotton Moore/Associates PC

8:30 A.M. TO 9:00 P.M. MONDAY, WEDNESDAY, THURSDAY; 8:30 A.M. TO 5:00 P.M. TUESDAY, FRIDAY, SATURDAY   PHONE: 707-5458

Thomas Jefferson argued that "there is no subject to which a Member of Congress may not have occasion to refer," so, to be prepared, Congress in 1800 voted $5,000 to buy books and create a library for its use. Those original tomes were destroyed when the British burned the Capitol in 1814. To replace them, Jefferson sold his great private library to the government at cost. He had purchased many of his 6,487 volumes while serving as Minister to France, writing that he had spent long, happy hours among the Parisian bookstalls, "turning over every book with my own hands, putting by everything which related to America, and indeed, whatever was rare and valuable in every science." From this core, the Library of Congress has grown into the largest and best-equipped library in the world, containing roughly 90 million items housed on 540 miles of shelves.

The library's design is based on the Paris Opera House. Its off-putting granite exterior has been the subject of some severe complaints. The critic Russell Sturgis, for instance, grumbled about the main façade and "that false idea of grandeur which consists mainly in hoisting a building up from a reasonable level of the ground, mainly in order to secure for it a monstrous flight of steps which must be surmounted before the main door can be reached." But the dazzling interiors win over even the most curmudgeonly skeptics. They should be credited to Casey, who came onto the scene with a team of 22 sculptors and 26 painters. The central stair hall, superbly heroic, consists of a profusion of statues set amidst colorful, swirling seas of marble, stained glass, and bronze. The octagonal main

The reading room of the Library of Congress shortly after Henry James penned his admiration for it. The statue in the foreground depicts a heroic, determined-looking, pre-revisionist Columbus.

reading room, all marble and wood beneath a 160-foot-high domed ceiling, forms the virtuosic finale; it rendered even Henry James (almost) speechless. The novelist had giggled a bit at the exterior (the "wondrous Library of Congress . . . fresh and almost frivolous"), so when he walked into the reading room he was skeptical; but when he left, he was a convert: "The great domed and tiered, galleried and statued central hall, the last word of current constructional science and artistic resource . . . crowns itself with grace." Here, the opening of a book becomes a noble rite.

---

11 Supreme Court Building

1st and East Capitol Streets, N.E.

1935 Cass Gilbert, Jr.; John R. Rockart, associate architect; James Earle Fraser, Herman A. MacNeil, and Robert Aitken, sculptors

9:00 A.M. TO 4:30 P.M.
WEEKDAYS   PHONE: 479-3030

Together, this structure, the National Archives, and the Lincoln Memorial form the last major body of academic neoclassicism in Washington that works. Well on the wane by the 1930s, that school did, however, prove itself perfectly appropriate here. A century earlier, Alexis de Tocqueville wrote that "a more imposing judicial power was never constituted by any people," and this building's massive scale and deep grandeur, all rendered in gleaming Vermont marble, certainly suggest that power. Although now unanimously praised as a smashing success, when new the building had its detractors: Dean Acheson complained, "the massive building . . . seems to shrink the members of the Court," and Justice Harlan Fiske Stone fussed that Gilbert's edifice was "wholly inappropriate for a quiet group of old boys such as the Supreme Court." (Perhaps as a nod to these critics, Gilbert kept the flanking wings relatively austere; or perhaps he kept them clean-lined to harmonize with the neighboring Folger Library.) The panels on the great bronze entrance doors (great indeed—each door weighs 13,000 pounds) depict the history of the legal system from ancient times into the 20th century; the doors were fashioned by John Donnely, Jr.

12 Sewall-Belmont House (National Woman's Party Headquarters)

144 Constitution Avenue, N.E.

1800 Robert Sewall, owner-builder

1814 burned

1820 rebuilt

PHONE: 546-3989

It *looks* quiet enough, but this restrained brick building actually marks the tumultuous capstone of the career of Alva Smith, among the most flamboyant characters in an era that specialized in flamboyant characters. In the early 20th century, Smith, an Alabama-born belle who married two of the world's richest men (William K. Vanderbilt and Oliver H. P. Belmont) and who forced her daughter, Consuelo, to marry the brutish ninth Duke of Marlborough, decided to abandon the world of society and throw herself into politics. She spearheaded the women's suffrage movement by organizing conventions, writing speeches and articles, lobbying congressmen up for reelection, and picketing the White House. Based in New York, she also wrote a suffragette opera and leased a floor in a Fifth Avenue building for her group's headquarters.

Woman's suffrage achieved with the 19th Amendment, she then cast her lot with the more militant National Woman's Party. That group, too, was located in New York, but Smith decided that they belonged in Washington, so in 1929 she bought this brick house and made it party headquarters. Alice Paul, who wrote the original Equal Rights Amendment (in 1923!) lived here for a while, and much of the house is a museum of her work. Meanwhile, Alva Smith Vanderbilt Belmont rolled inexorably on, organizing rallies and boycotts, leading hunger strikes, and comforting her weary troops with the immortal words, "Just pray to God: *She* will help you."

13 Folger Shakespeare Library

201 East Capitol Street, S.E.

1932 Paul P. Cret; Alexander B. Trowbridge, consulting architect
1975–1982 addition: Hartman-Cox Architects

10:00 A.M. TO 4:00 P.M.
MONDAY THROUGH SATURDAY PHONE: 544-7077

Nineteen thirties art deco classicism without and 16th-century Tudor within, the library houses one of the world's greatest collections of material on Shakespeare, his works, and his period.

Agents for Henry Clay Folger, chairman of the board of Standard Oil, approached Cret as early as 1928 about designing a building "of a modern flavor but retaining the classic spirit . . . to be a little more explicit, classic architecture from which the ordinary details such as columns, pilasters, etc., have been removed but in which the classic spirit has been retained by a nice use of sculptured ornament in relief." But not too much ornament—in 1933 Cret himself advised his fellow architects of "the value of restraint, the value of designing volumes instead of merely decorating surfaces, and the value of empty surfaces as elements of composition."

A few critics have fussed about the sharp difference between the library's interior and exterior. Cret delivered his rebuttal in a paper read at Amherst College: "To those who have wondered why the architecture of the façades is at such variance with the somewhat archaeological character of the rooms. . . . The reason is quite simple. Mr. and Mrs. Folger desired surroundings . . . reminiscent of England. . . . On the other hand, the architect . . . could readily see that the site selected, facing a wide, straight avenue in one of the most classical of cities . . . would be inappropriate for an Elizabethan building."

The library proved an immediate success, and its somewhat restrained elevations successfully keep the structure in sympathy with the surroundings while eschewing the cheap tricks of historicism. When the AIA awarded the French-trained Cret its Gold Medal in 1938, his citation read in part, "He has brought . . . the sound sense, the clear logic, the discriminating taste that belong to the classic tradition of an older civilization. Thus armed, he has met and mastered with outstanding skill those problems that are inherent . . . in a new world."

Those self-same qualities shine through 50 years later in Hartman-

Cox's new reading room. Drawing inspiration from Boullée's *Bibliothèque Nationale*, Hartman-Cox gave the Folger's new room a vaulted ceiling with skylights that bathe the interior with a soft glow. Everything here works in concert: function, form, scale, and light—and the space comes as close to being perfect as it is possible to be in this imperfect world.

14 Saint Mark's Episcopal Church

3rd and A Streets, S.E.

1888–1894 T. Buckler Ghequier
1965 Kent Cooper & Associates, interior alterations

Here Romanesque revival details dwell somewhat uneasily within a Gothic revival shell. The church certainly meets the standard of structural "honesty," for its elements are completely exposed inside and out: layered brick, timber roofing, and cast-iron columns. Stained glass in the front sections of the clerestory came from the studio of Louis Comfort Tiffany.

St. Mark's began as a mission church of Christ Church on G Street; it became a parish in 1869, and for a glorious spell between 1896 and 1902 it served as the Episcopal cathedral for the Diocese of Washington. Nonetheless, there have been some rough moments, and its survival is a tribute to one of the most alive-and-well and community-minded congregations in the city.

15 120 4th Street, S.E.

c. 1867 architect unknown
1958–1968 C. Dudley Brown, restoration

Brownstone steps, intricately cast iron, and a vigorous, bracketed wood cornice give the Italianate exterior of this town house special distinction. Within, one finds the marble mantles, ornate plaster-work, and high ceilings one expects in such a grand creation of this period. The painter Filippo Costaggini lived here from 1880 until 1888 while working on the friezes and frescos in the

Capitol Rotunda, a project which his teacher, Constantin Brumidi, had begun in the 1850s.

16 Christ Episcopal Church

620 G Street, S.E.

1805 Benjamin Henry Latrobe
1824, 1849 extensions: architects unknown
1877 William H. Hoffman
1953–1954 Horace W. Peaslee

This charming little building was not only frequently attended by presidents Madison, Monroe, John Quincy Adams, and Jefferson (as much as he frequented any church), it was also one of the first and finest Gothic revival buildings in this country. But it has been much altered: it grew extensions in 1824 and 1849 (the latter including the narthex and bell tower), and the extensions themselves were extended in 1877 and 1891. Finally, in this century, Peaslee restored the highly important building to Latrobe's rational and coherent intentions.

17 Friendship House Settlement (The Maples)

630 South Carolina Avenue, S.E.

1795 William Lovering, architect-builder
1936 restoration: Horace W. Peaslee

"This fine house in the woods between Capitol Hill and the Navy Yard," as George Washington is said to have described it, has now had a city grow up around it. Still, in spite of changed surroundings, in spite of the addition of wings, in spite of a succession of occupants (including a hospital), and in spite of its present state of decay, the sturdy brick structure has retained most of its character. Lovering, one of early Washington's best-known master craftsmen, built the place for William Mayne Duncanson, a rich planter who made and lost a fortune in District real estate; later owners included Francis Scott Key.

18 The Penn Theater Project

650 Pennsylvania Avenue,
S.E.
1935 John Eberson
1985–1986 David M.
Schwarz/Architectural
Services, PC

David Schwarz has often said that he prefers the designation "contextual-ist" to "post-modernist." Whatever label one applies to him, this three-part project surely ranks among the city's greater architectural successes of the 1980s. It consists of a playfully appropriate addition to an art deco movie house on Pennsylvania Avenue, a red brick, vaguely Victorian apartment complex on C Street, and a modernist-Mediterranean courtyard in between.

Amusingly, each of the new component parts outdoes its model. The details of the C Street apartments (broken massing, gabled skyline, and limestone trim) resemble elements of 1890s Capitol Hill town houses—only more so. The stark white grid of the plaza walls has been likened to a three-dimensional di Chirico painting—only *more so*. But the greatest applause goes to the office building built into and around the old theater: overriding objections from the city's Art Deco Society, Schwarz selected terra cotta, blue-glazed tiles, and limestone stripping for the Pennsylvania Avenue structure, and the result easily out-decos the deco theater. All that's missing is a madcap heiress walking a leopard.

19 Eastern Market

7th and C Streets, S.E.
1873 Adolph Cluss
1908 addition to north:
architect unknown

Washington once boasted several of these expansive empori-
ums—*the* places for the freshest meat, fish, fruit, eggs, cream, and bread—but the Eastern Market is the only functioning survivor. The venerable Capitol Hill Market, established in 1813, stood at East Capitol and E Streets until area residents complained to Congress that the building had become "a common nuisance and a great annoyance to all persons" and in

1838 Congress responded by authorizing removal of that "unsightly use-less old building." Fortunately, attitudes have changed, and 20th-century residents of Capitol Hill value the Eastern Market and have made it the unofficial center for their neighborhood.

A cast-iron shed, originally intended to shelter vendors, spans the 7th Street exterior, while arched and bull's-eye windows provide light for the stalls inside. It is all supported by impressive, exposed iron roof trusses, visible from within. Eastern Market makes a refreshing change from the standardized and depersonalized supermarkets of today. It is also a depressing reminder that although people *may* have lived in less-sanitary conditions a century ago than most of us would tolerate, they certainly ate better.

The German-born and Brussels-trained Cluss (1825–1905), a brilliant although essentially esoteric architect and engineer, became one of the city's most prolific mid-19th-century builders. From 1862 to 1876 his office designed or supervised construction of nearly every public building erected by the D.C. government and he managed to secure many private commissions as well. Politically, Cluss was a thorough Victorian progressive—in fact, he numbered Karl Marx among his cronies and translated Marx's writings into English for the New York *Tribune*. A firm believer in "modern" technology, he despised what he thought of as "anachronistic" bits of construction, such as the Washington Monument, which he dismissed as "a huge, unsightly pile of masonry."

20 Philadelphia Row

132–154 11th Street, S.E.
c. 1860 George Gessford

According to oral tradition (supported by the name historically attached to this group of buildings), Gessford built these side hall–plan row houses to assuage the homesickness of his Quaker City–born wife. The row certainly evokes sections of the town along the Schuylkill. Note the calm yet steady rhythm of the uniform façades, punctuated only by regularly placed doors (snug within their arched openings) and windows (generally flanked by paneled shutters), always marked by white stone sills and lintels. Marble steps and foundations provide another nice touch. The row may be Victorian in date and detail, but its overwhelming spirit is federal. *Philadelphia* federal. In the 1960s the row was nearly demolished to make room for a highway, but citizen outcry carried the day. Sadly, that was not the outcome in 1887 when a similar—and genuinely federal—group of town houses called Carroll Row had to be removed to make way for the new Library of Congress building.

21   317 Massachusetts Avenue, N.E.
1986 Weinstein Associates Architects

How tempting to cry, "At last!" At last architects have begun to take notice of the quintessential Capitol Hill building, the two-bay brick town house: hundreds— thousands—of these structures march along the streets of this neighborhood, their pedimented and projecting squared towers creating an unforgettable urban rhythm. These houses meant home to generations of Washingtonians, and it's nice to see that the buildings' potential for modern office use has at last been recognized. Amy Weinstein and her associates have certainly captured the essence of the form in this new building's Massachusetts Avenue façade. They seem to have had a particularly good time designing the lobby: reached from an arched opening and an interior stairway, the space features wildly carved newel posts, patterned floor tiles, and tubular brass lighting, which all compete for attention in an authentically late-Victorian manner. Weinstein recently completed a couple of other noteworthy Capitol Hill projects, including 303 7th Street and 666 Pennsylvania Avenue.

22   Union Station and Plaza
Massachusetts and Louisiana Avenues, N.E.

1908 Daniel H. Burnham; Lorado Taft, sculptor; Frederick Law Olmsted, Jr., landscape architect
1908 Columbus Memorial Fountain: Lorado Taft, sculptor
1988 restoration: Harry Weese & Associates; Benjamin Thompson & Associates

This building was the first product of the McMillan Commission's grand plan for the city—not totally surprising, since its architect was a quite-vocal member of the commission. Imbued with the principles of the new City Beautiful movement, Burnham and other commission members hoped that a neoclassical train station might simultaneously impose order on the capital's out-of-control urban landscape and help tame the ruthless railroad industry. To those ends, they recommended a new station for Washington, to be built near the Capitol at the confluence of L'Enfant's grand avenues.

Having settled on this location, Burnham (often credited with the lines "Make no little plans; they have no power to stir men's blood. . . . Let your watchword be order and your beacon beauty.") then proved himself as good as his word, for he went right to the top, to President A. J. Cassatt of the Pennsylvania Railroad, and persuaded that industrialist to relay the line's tracks to this site from the old station on the Mall. Cassatt agreed, thus in one stroke making the grand new station possible and freeing the Mall of a sooty eyesore. (Cassatt was a man of no little plans himself, overseeing simultaneously the completion of two of the nation's greatest rail depots—Union Station in Washington and Penn Station in New York.)

Sheathed in glistening white Vermont marble, Union Station's style—vigorous and Roman with arches aplenty and massive Ionic columns—set the tone for most of the city's early-20th-century official buildings. The main waiting room and the concourse, two of Washington's most gloriously monumental interior spaces, create just what McMillan and company had in mind—a triumphant gateway to the capital of an increasingly imperial nation. The waiting room—measuring 219 feet by 120 feet—lies beneath a gilded, coffered ceiling, while the Grand Concourse—760 feet long, 130 feet high, and based on the Baths of Diocletian in Rome—remains among the largest public spaces ever created in the United States. The neoclassical exterior sculpture is appropriately eye-catching and features allegorical figures such as Prometheus (fire), Thales (electricity), and Archimedes (mechanics).

After a shameful period of neglect and misuse, the station underwent a $150 million restoration and was reopened in 1988. Today, the nine movie theaters, the tee-shirt shops, and the fast-food joints make Union Station a busy place, frequented by more than train travelers. With much of its grandeur restored, it once again superbly fills the role of ceremonial gateway to the nation's capital. And its spruced-up state has encouraged much laudable new work nearby: the old post office is being restored, and just to the east on Columbia Plaza, Edward Larrabee Barnes's new Federal Judiciary Building presents interesting stripped-down interpretations of the station's Beaux-Arts devices.

In all, the station, its welcoming forecourt, plaza with fountain, and radiating rows of trees leading to the Capitol and Mall make up one of the country's most thorough Beaux-Arts/City Beautiful experiences. Nowhere else in the Washington does one sense so well what the McMillan Plan was all about or what Henry James admired about the District when he called it "a city of palaces and monuments and gardens, symmetries and circles and far radiations, with the big Potomac for water-power and water-effect and the recurrent Maryland spring, so prompt and so full-handed, for a perpetual benediction."

23 National Postal Museum (City Post Office)

Massachusetts Avenue and North Capitol Street, N.E.

1914 Graham and Burnham
1992 renovation: Shalom Baranes Associates; museum interior:Florance Eichbaum Esocoff King

Adhering to the 1902 McMillan Plan for the city, the architects here took pains to make the post office, with its central Ionic colonnade and slightly projecting entrance pavilions, harmonize with but defer to the Ionic Union Station across the street. Graham and Burnham also continued the Ionic order inside in the main service room, whose noble lines, once hidden by a less-than-pleasing 1959 remodeling, have now been restored.

24 Government Printing Office

North Capitol Street between G and H Streets, N.W.

1861 architect unknown

What may be the world's largest printing establishment buzzes away within this massive block. A few architectural devices do much to lessen the bulkiness of the red brick box—note the three-story arched "loggia" half way up the façades, the two-story rusticated "basement," and the whimsical crest of terra cotta shells and cast iron. The huge GPO has recently gained some equally impressive office building neighbors; two of the best may be Shalom Baranes's 751 North Capitol Street and Hartman-Cox's 800 North Capitol Street.

25 Edward Bennett Williams Law Library at the Georgetown University Law Center

Massachusetts and New Jersey Avenues, N.W.

1991 Hartman-Cox Archditects

Proof positive that cost-conscious academic buildings need not look cheap, the gleaming buff façades and baroque plan of Hartman-Cox's new library create, in the words of *Architectural Record,* "a gentle monument to civility." Intended as an adjunct to the law center (1971, Edward Durrell Stone), the new library has already replaced the somewhat boxy older structure as dominant player on the streetscape. It certainly evinces the architects' well-known skill at cross-referencing: the library's basement podium suggests similar features common among the city's c. 1800 buildings; its heroic massing evokes Hartman-Cox's own nearby Market Square; and hallways and rooms radiate from the cylindrical three-story entrance lobby, much as L'Enfant's streets radiate from traffic circles. Yet Hartman-Cox knew that the university valued economy in construction just as much as elegance in design. To cite but one example of their ingenious thrift: they used inexpensive, precast concrete, innovatively molded in such a way that its neoclassical forms lose nothing when compared to similar motifs rendered nearby in marble.

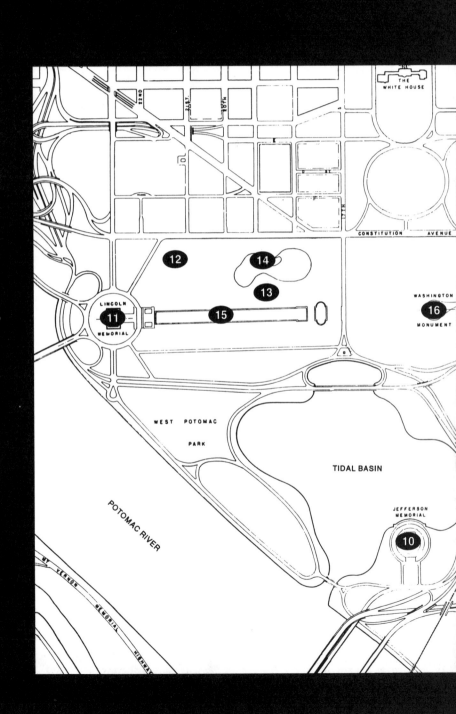

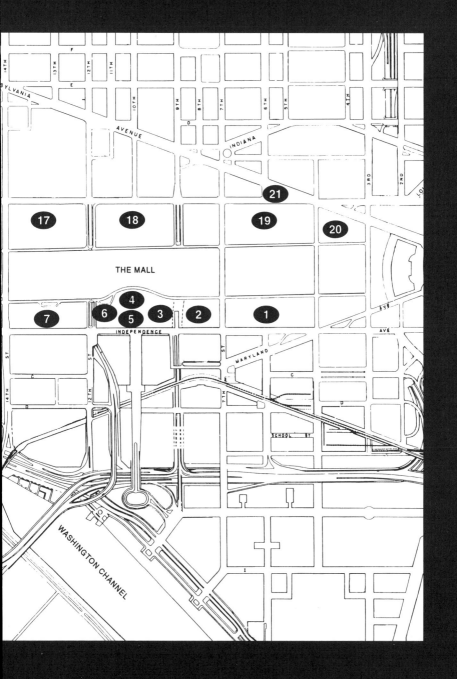

The Mall is the oldest—and most tinkered with—of the federal parks. In 1791 L'Enfant envisioned it as a grand, two-mile axial sweep from the Capitol to Washington's Monument; but for most of the Mall's history the space fell far, far short of these ambitious hopes and the great national park was—in a word—squalid.

During much of the 19th century, Pennsylvania Railroad trains chugged in and out of a station located in the center of the Mall; the trains generated smoke and cinders; the station was surrounded by a jumbled mass of shacks, assorted vegetable patches, and miscellaneous mounds of rubbish. Open sewers, euphemistically called canals, criss-crossed the Mall, while off towards the Potomac stank the largest marsh in the city. Any leftover space got landscaped in a "romantic" manner that interspersed winding paths and carriage drives with what A. J. Downing conceived as a "public museum of living trees and shrubs." The ruddy sandstone turrets of the Smithsonian "Castle," built, as the railroad station was, right on the Mall, contributed the right touch of Gothic horror. Finally, for a considerable interval, the partially completed shaft of the Washington Monument loomed at the terminus of the Mall's western axis, as if to mock the unkempt chaos of it all.

Then, in 1902, the McMillan Commission, headed by Senator James

Baltimore's famed Sachse Company in 1852 published this engraving, partly accurate and partly wishful thinking. The Mall is depicted as an open grassy swath, clear of rubbish, and bordered by a swift-flowing Tiber Canal, none of which was the case. Sachse's misleading representation of the Washington Monument shows Robert Mills's original concept, complete with base perisphere, not the quarter-completed simplified stub then standing. James Renwick's new Smithsonian "Castle," built right on the Mall, is, however, accurately portrayed.

McMillan of Michigan, launched the opening attack to change the Mall from a national embarrassment to a national treasure. The commission found, dusted off, and implemented L'Enfant's plans, at least as far as the give-and-take of politics made practicable. Downing's serpentine paths were straightened out, the railroad agreed to relocate to the northeast (and received the new Union Station for being so public-spirited), the swamps and canals were drained and filled in, and the Lincoln and Jefferson memorials rose in neoclassical splendor in the reclaimed marshlands. Dazed, perhaps, by these successes, the commission found it easy to compromise with the recalcitrant Smithsonian and, after a good deal of haggling, allowed the institution to remain holed up in its castle on the Mall. Now, lined with many of the nation's most important art galleries and museums, the three-mile-long Mall comes closer than ever in its 200-year history to meeting L'Enfant's hopes to "unite the useful with the commodious and agreeable."

---

1 National Air and Space Museum

Jefferson Drive between 4th and 7th Streets, S.W.

1976 Hellmuth, Obata & Kassabaum, PC; Gyo Obata, architect in charge
1988 restaurant: Hellmuth, Obata & Kassabaum, PC

10:00 A.M. TO 5:30 P.M. DAILY
PHONE: 357-2700

In a superlative balancing act, Hellmuth, Obata and Kassabaum placed their monumental glass and granite blocks in a manner that complements the dignified, neoclassical massing of the National Gallery across the Mall while providing a suitable shelter for this up-to-the-minute museum. That latter accomplishment was no small task, for the museum's 23 galleries sprawl through 200,000 square feet of exhibition space and contain material as varied as 50 missiles, the Wright brothers' *Kitty Hawk,* the Apollo 11 space capsule, Lindbergh's *Spirit of St. Louis,* the Einstein Planetarium, a re-created World War I battlefield, and a TV set featuring a continuously running video of "The French Chef" in which Julia Child fruitily announces, "Today we're going to make air." It all works, and the building is reportedly the most popular museum in the world.

Mrs. Child, incidentally, would probably feel right at home whipping up a batch of air in the museum's restaurant: placed in an extension to the east, the inviting space continues the exposed framing and dramatic angles that work so well in the main building.

2 Joseph H. Hirshhorn Museum and Sculpture Garden

Independence Avenue at 7th Street, S.W.

1974 Skidmore, Owings & Merrill; Gordon Bunshaft, architect in charge
1981 redesign of sculpture garden: Lester Collins

10:00 A.M. TO 5:30 P.M. DAILY   PHONE: 357-2700

Yet another part of the Smithsonian. When this structure was in the talking stage, S. Dillon Ripley, secretary of the Smithsonian from 1964 to 1984, told the planning committee that if the final building "were not controversial in almost every way, it would hardly qualify as a place to house contemporary art." The committee listened. While the building's shape—a four-story cylinder, 231 feet in diameter—has caused various wags to liken it to a steamship's funnel, a concrete doughnut, or a military bunker, it does make a comfortable home for one of the nation's great collections of contemporary art. Actually, the pieces flow beyond the building's shell; some dot the courtyard at the cylinder's center while many more accent the nicely landscaped sunken garden, as if to divert viewers' attention from the garden's encroachment upon the Mall.

3 Arts and Industries Building

900 Jefferson Drive, S.W.

1879–1881 Cluss & Schulze, with Montgomery C. Meigs; Casper Buberl, sculptor
1897–1903 modifications: Hornblower & Marshall

1976 restoration: Hugh Newell Jacobsen; Smithsonian Institution Office of Facilities Planning and Engineering Services

10 A.M. TO 5:30 P.M. DAILY   PHONE: 357-2700

This 2 1/2-acre fairy tale castle in polychrome brick, built a generation after the "Castle," might be viewed as the junior member of the Smithsonian Institution's feudal twins. Something of a legend among architects and contractors, the Arts and Industries Building is not only the least expensive major structure ever put up by the federal government (it cost less than $3 per square foot) but is also among the most speedily and efficiently constructed. Work began in 1879 after Congress voted to approve "a fireproof building for the use of the National Museum, 300-foot square" and was finished in time to house President Garfield's 1881 Inaugural Ball.

The great trussed sheds, meandering iron balconies, and complex roofing system of 36 separate coverings have a character at once industrial and nostalgic, which seems perfectly appropriate to the collections. Cluss, the quintessential late-Victorian progressive, had a limitless faith in the possibilities of technology (see A-19), and this building clearly reflects that optimism. The creation is reminiscent of the fanciful structures that housed world's fairs and international exhibitions in the Victorian era, and appropriately so, since many of the treasures here were assembled for just such an occasion, the 1876 Philadelphia Centennial. (They wound up in Washington only after the company formed to curate them went broke.) A notable Casper Buberl sculpture, "Columbia Protecting Science and Industry," at the main entrance lets you know you've come to the right place.

---

4   The Smithsonian Building
    ("The Castle")

Jefferson Drive between 9th and 12th
Streets, S.W.

1855 James Renwick

10:00 A.M. TO 5:30 P.M. DAILY
PHONE: 357-2700

When James Smithson, a bastard son of
the eccentric first Duke of Northumber-
land, died in 1829, his executors were surprised to discover that he had willed his
entire fortune of £104,000 "to the United States of America, to found in
Washington, an establishment for the increase and diffusion of knowledge
among men." The bequest shouldn't have been surprising, for Smithson
was one of the leading chemists and mineralogists of his time (the element
smithsonite is named for him) and something of a political radical, and he
had dismissed the British monarchy as a "contemptible encumbrance" and

publicly predicted that the future lay with the new democracy across the Atlantic.

After a good deal of debate and anti-British posturing, Congress accepted Smithson's largesse in 1846 and hired Renwick to design what would prove the first of the institution's many buildings. Working in accordance with Andrew Jackson Downing's plans to relandscape the Mall in a "naturalistic" manner, the architect produced one of the greatest examples of Gothic revival design in America. And despite Renwick's modest observation that "the business of an American architect is to build something that will stand and be fairly presentable for about thirty years," his "Castle," sculpted of local Seneca sandstone, has excited visitors and critics alike for a *hundred* and thirty years.

Incidentally, whoever decided to lay out the Smithsonian rose garden as a horticultural connector between the Castle and the Arts and Industries Building had a good thought. That's more than can be said for whoever did the actual planting, since the rose beds are filled with hybrid tea roses: certainly someone could and should correct this solecism and plant some rugosas.

---

5 Quadrangle Museums Project, Smithsonian Institution

1987 Shepley, Bulfinch, Richardson & Abbott; Jean-Paul Carlhian, architect in charge; Junzo Yoshimura, design concept; Lester Collins, landscape architect

10:00 A.M. TO 5:30 P.M. DAILY   PHONE: 357-2700

Ever expanding, the Smithsonian keeps a'building. The very names of these latest additions, the Sackler Gallery for Asian Art, the National Museum of African Art, the S. Dillon Ripley Center, and the Enid A.

Haupt Garden, suggest the breadth and depth of the institution's interests.

Shepley and company faced a rather daunting task here, for they had to create something that would harmonize with the new galleries' wildly divergent neighbors, particularly with the cool neoclassical Freer to the west and the rambunctious, florid "Castle" and Arts and Industries Building to the north and east. They met the challenge in a disarmingly simple way: they built in gray granite (a nod to the Freer) yet enlivened the façades with hundreds of inset diamond patterns. Collins's four-acre Haupt Garden, created on the rooftop of an underground parking garage (the garage roof is covered with eight feet of top soil), underscores this effort, since the garden's stated purpose is to "feature design elements complementing the architecture of the surrounding buildings." Thus, one finds a granite and water "theme garden," which suggests the Freer, the monuments, and the Reflecting Pool, as well as specimen trees and shrubbery, a brilliantly colored, diamond-shaped 19th-century parterre (adapted from a similar design at the 1876 Philadelphia Centennial Exposition), and a collection of antique garden furniture, all in stylistic deference to the red brick fantasies nearby.

---

6 Freer Gallery of Art

12th Street and Jefferson
Drive, S.W.

1923 Charles A. Platt
1993 restoration: Shepley,
Bulfinch, Richardson &
Abbott; Cole & Denny/BVH

10:00 A.M. TO 5:30 P.M. DAILY
PHONE: 357-2700

Charles Lang Freer made a fortune manufacturing railroad cars, but his real interest always lay in art: indeed, one Detroit industrialist famously complained that Freer "would rather discuss the tariffs on early Italian art than the price of pig iron." Freer's collecting focused on the work of contemporary Americans, particularly James A. McNeill Whistler, and on the painting and sculpture of ancient Asia. Once he had assembled his collection, Freer hired Platt, one of the giants of American neoclassicism, to design this simple, symmetrical building. He then deeded the whole package to the nation, the most valuable gift ever presented to the government by an individual.

7 Department of Agriculture

14th Street and Independence Avenue, S.W.

1905 Rankin, Kellogg & Crane

Members of the McMillan Commission issued their report in 1902, and this vast pile was the first project built on the south side of the Mall in accordance with their neoclassical dicta. Controversy raged as to the best location for the building—it took the direct intervention of President Theodore Roosevelt to stop them from building smack in the middle of the Mall—but the cornerstone was eventually laid here in 1905, on a site the Smithsonian had used for greenhouses. Funding problems regularly halted construction, and by the time the structure was completed in 1930, its massive, classically-inspired walls were facing the neoclassical Federal Triangle across the Mall.

If one looks hard enough at Agriculture's behemoth façades, one encounters a few flashes of wit and humanity: note particularly the tympanums of the two lower wings, in which innocent yet well-muscled children hold escutcheons labeled, variously, "Forests," "Cereals," "Flowers," and "Fruits," as these products bountifully tumble about the putti.

8 Auditors Main Building (Bureau of Engraving and Printing)

14th Street and Independence Avenue, S.W.

1880 James G. Hill
1989 renovation: Notter Finegold + Alexander Inc./Mariani, Architects

With its red brick walls and romantic profile, this dark pile, along with Meigs's Pension Building and Cluss's Arts and Industries Building, offers a break—albeit a brief one—from the District's "official" pale-hued neoclassicism.

9 U.S. Holocaust Memorial Museum

Raoul Wallenberg Place (between 14th and 15th Streets, S.W.)

1993 Pei Cobb Freed & Partners; Notter Finegold + Alexander Inc., associated architects

10:00 A.M. TO 5:30 P.M. DAILY   PHONE: 488-0400

This passionately brutal structure stands as the American government's three-dimensional memorial to the millions of Jews, homosexuals, prisoners of war, and others murdered in the Nazi death camps in the 1930s and '40s. Although two of the façades harmonize with the memorial's neighbors, including the old Bureau of Engraving, the overall impression is one of discordant shock. And that's as it should be. James Ingo Freed has explained that he felt he had to design an architectural slap-in-the-face to grab visitors and shake them out of the complacency Washington's visually safe and reassuring brick and marble temples encourage. "You cannot deal with the Holocaust as a reasonable thing," he explained; this "wholly un-American subject" can only be treated in "an emotional dimension."

10 Jefferson Memorial

The Tidal Basin

1943 John Russell Pope, architect; Rudolph Evans, sculptor

8:00 A.M. TO MIDNIGHT DAILY

L'Enfant's plan doesn't show a site for a Jefferson Memorial, but then the plan was drawn up a decade before Jefferson's first inauguration. For that matter, the memorial's site didn't even exist in the 18th century, since the Potomac River flowed over this spot. But in the 1930s, the Squire of Hyde Park felt it was high time to honor the Sage of Monticello, and architects and planners selected this watery location for the memorial.

Workmen got busy scooping out and moving tons of river bottom to create dry land for the memorial, and John Russell Pope, *the* unofficial neoclassicist for the unofficially neoclassical city, devised this *retardataire* neo-Pantheon, which FDR dedicated on Jefferson's 200th birthday in April 1943. But by then the heyday of the classical revival had passed and, put simply, Pope's structure just doesn't work. Jefferson himself, of course, enjoyed great success with the Pantheon form in his University of Virginia library 125 years earlier. Yet Pope's polite creation seems tired and passé, lacking the twin fires of inspiration and revolution that so characterized the man.

11 Lincoln Memorial

West Potomac Park (west end of the Mall)

1911–1922 Henry Bacon; Daniel Chester French, sculptor; Jules Guerin, muralist

8:00 A.M. TO MIDNIGHT DAILY

Standing on a reclaimed swamp, the white and columned Lincoln Memorial plays a key role in Washington's monumental composition, as a counterbalance to the Capitol. That characteristic aside, the memorial's nobility truly defies analysis. To stand in front of French's statue and read Lincoln's words inscribed on the walls is akin to hearing a Bach mass sung in a cathedral.

A movement to erect some sort of monument to our sixteenth president began almost immediately after his assassination. Congress, however, waited until 1911 to do anything, and by then there were nearly as many notions for the monument's design as there had been for the Washington Monument. Some people favored an obelisk to echo Washington's and to respect the Egyptian taboo against erecting solitary obelisks; others wanted a pyramid; the new but already powerful automobile lobby pushed for a 70-mile parkway to link Washington and Gettysburg. Even site selection caused problems. Illinois congressman Joseph Cannon balked at this marsh ("I'll never let a memorial to Abraham Lincoln be erected in that god-damned swamp," he bellowed) and pressed for a spot on the high ground across the Potomac. Then someone pointed out that perhaps Virginia might not be *quite* right so the congressman backed down and this moist location prevailed.

Workmen quickly filled in the marsh, and architect Henry Bacon sketched a design loosely based on the Parthenon. But Bacon made Lincoln's memorial differ from its prototype in several respects; for example, he replaced the classic pedimented roof with a squared and recessed attic and moved the entrance from the short end to the long façade. A firm believer in the power of symbolism, Bacon gave the memorial 36 columns, the number of states in the Union when Lincoln was elected president, and 48 festoons, the number when the memorial was completed.

12 Vietnam Veterans Memorial

The Mall, near 21st Street, N.W.

1982 Maya Ying Lin, designer; Cooper-Lecky Architects, PC, architects of record

Quietly and deeply moving, this black marble slash in the Mall is inscribed with the names of the Americans killed or missing as a result of the undeclared war in Southeast Asia. Architect Lin said she envisioned the memorial as a symbol of regeneration: "Take a knife and cut open the earth," she explained, "and with time the grass will heal it." And to walk through the memorial, to move from sunlight down into the abyss and then out again, is to sense how eloquently Lin has given architectural expression to that hope.

13 Constitution Gardens

The Mall, near 19th Street, N.W.

1976 Skidmore, Owings & Merrill

Designed to "establish the historic [Mall] buildings in a comprehensive landscape" and completed to mark the Bicentennial of the United States, these gardens meander over 52 acres between the Washington Monument and the Lincoln Memorial. Ironically, the elements used—a six-acre lake, meadows, clumps of trees, hillocks, and serpentine paths—are precisely what A. J. Downing and Calvert Vaux had romantically planned for the entire Mall 120 years earlier and precisely what the classically oriented promulgators of the McMillan Plan swept away. Circles of taste.

For much of the 19th century the Department of Agriculture used a tract nearby as a garden and nursery to propagate roses, begonias, and flowering shrubs. During World War I that site (and more) got filled with dozens of "temporary" structures to house government offices and workers. The buildings lingered on and on (causing wits to remark that nothing is so permanent in Washington as a temporary building), until the "tempos" were finally removed in the 1960s to make way for these gardens.

14 Signers Memorial

Constitution Gardens, West Potomac Park

1981 EDAW Inc.; Kurt Pronske, civil engineer

Built on a little island in a lake in Constitution Gardens, this low-key creation is Washington's only monument to the signers of the Declaration of Independence. Each signer is represented by a block of red marble, and each block is incised with an enlarged replica of that man's signature. EDAW arranged the blocks in a semicircle to suggest the composition of figures in John Trumbull's famous painting of the signing.

15   Reflecting Pool
The Mall

c. 1920   Henry Bacon, Charles F. McKim, and others

The 1902 McMillan Plan called for a cruciform pool between the Washington and Lincoln memorials, but the First World War came and brought with it the "temporary" Navy and Munitions Buildings along Constitution Avenue. These "tempos" encroached upon the area set aside for the pool's north arm, so the cruciform was changed to the current 2,000-foot-long rectangular basin with a small transverse axis at the eastern end. When the scenographic ensemble of monuments and water was near completion, Bacon, who had also designed the Lincoln Memorial, and several of his cronies staged a moonlight flotilla on the Reflecting Pool in flower-bedecked boats.

16   The Washington Monument
The Mall

1848–1884   Robert Mills and others

8:00 A.M. TO MIDNIGHT DAILY

At 555 feet 5 1/8 inches, this is the tallest masonry structure in the world. Is it stating the obvious to suggest that it's also the noblest?

   Its origins and surprisingly tumultuous history go back to 1783 when the Continental Congress voted to build a statue of General Washington on horseback "at the place where the residence of Congress shall be established." The District of Columbia was created and President Washington and Pierre L'Enfant agreed on a site for the statue. But then Washington died, and in 1800 Congress jettisoned the original plan in favor of a mausoleum "to be of American granite and marble in pyramidal form." In 1804 President Jefferson drove a marker into the proposed site, but the ground proved to be a sodden marsh (one wonders why this wasn't noticed before) and the stone sunk from sight.

Whether because of embarrassment or inertia, little was heard of either idea for a generation. In 1832, the centenary of Washington's birth sparked renewed interest in creating some sort of monument to him. The Washington National Monument Society was formed in 1833, and in 1836 its members launched a national competition for a suitable design, which architect Robert Mills won. Mills, who had some familiarity with monuments to Washington since he had designed the nation's oldest, in Baltimore, in 1815, devised a scheme calling for a circular "Greek" peristyle temple around the base and an obelisk slightly taller (600 feet) and blunter than the present shaft. Lack of funds caused more delay, but ground was finally broken—on a higher, drier site 350 feet northeast of Jefferson's swallowed spike—on July 4, 1848.

The construction period sputtered along in a near-farcical series of delays and complications: the books and records of the monument society were stolen, a virulent strain of anti-Catholicism broke out when Pope Pius IX donated a stone to the project (the enraged local Know-Nothings rioted and smashed the papal gift), and the Civil War halted progress altogether. Then, during the 1870s, a spate of revisionism nearly wrecked the whole effort: one well-meaning soul wanted the monument redesigned as a 12th-century northern Italian campanile; someone else suggested one of "the better Hindu pagodas." Each proposal was given due (or excessive) consideration, but, after heated discussion, each was tossed aside, and the simple shaft continued its fitful rise. The aluminum capstone was set and the monument was dedicated on December 6, 1884.

This is how the Washington Monument looked for much of the 19th century.

One of the many late-1870s proposals to redesign the Washington Monument. This one has everything: a Renwick-ish Second Empire dome (crowned by a version of the Capitol's Liberty statue) and what seems to be an early version of the Pension Building's historical frieze.

Sharing top honors only with the Capitol building itself, the Washington Monument's dignified profile—the eloquent distillation of the aspirations of millions—and its chaotic and seemingly aimless construction history have made it the perfect symbol of the city and a true icon for the nation.

17 National Museum of American History

Constitution Avenue and 14th Street, N.W.

1964 Steinman, Cain & White

10:00 A.M. TO 5:30 P.M.
PHONE: 357-2700

Columnist Russell Baker summed it up best when he wrote that "most of the commentary" on this building "has emphasized [its] . . . architectural failure." But, he added, "what should also be said is that the exhibits inside are an unqualified success." (Baker went on to suggest that "the failure here has not been with Father and Grandfather and their forebears, whose worldly goods are on display, but with ourselves. Our own generation is unable to build a shelter worthy of housing what the old people left us.") While no one claims that the museum is beautiful, it does display a dizzying number of varied artifacts—from Judy Garland's ruby slippers to mementos of the Nisei prison camps of World War II—in an efficient and imaginative manner. Roger Kennedy, who headed operations here from 1979 until 1992, stated that his goal was to celebrate "people who are often ignored but who have something very important to say." Under his spirited direction the museum did just that.

18 National Museum of Natural History

Constitution Avenue between 9th and 12th Streets, N.W.

1911 Hornblower & Marshall
1965 wings: Mills, Petticord & Mills

10:00 A.M. TO 5:30 P.M. DAILY
PHONE: 357-2700

The Department of Agriculture was the first building on the south side of the Mall erected in accordance with the McMillan Commission's neoclassical tenets, and this, with its marble walls and low dome, was the first on the north. Operated by the Smithsonian, the museum contains a spirited hodge-podge that might be taken as a microcosm of the parent institution: highlights include the "striding" bull elephant which greets visitors in the building's rotunda, an enormous array of shells and sponges, a plastic model of a 92-foot blue whale, an Easter Island stone head, the Hope Diamond, and what must be the world's largest ant farm.

19 National Gallery of Art (West Building)

Constitution Avenue at 6th Street, N.W.

1941 John Russell Pope
1983–1985 reorganization and renovation: Keyes Condon Florance Architects

10:00 A.M. TO 5:00 P.M.
MONDAY THROUGH SATURDAY, 11:00 A.M. TO 6:00 P.M. SUNDAY
PHONE: 737-4215

Many feel that this building is more distinguished for the scale of its halls and rotunda and the quality of its materials and workmanship than for its overall design. (*New York Times* art critic John Canady summed up this school of thought when he dismissed the gallery as a "synthetic palace," a structure of "chilly perfection.") Nevertheless, the building's neoclassical lines make it a stylistically sympathetic neighbor to the massive Federal Triangle, and its hushed rooms showcase their magnificent collections most effectively.

Founded in 1937, the National Gallery owes its existence to Andrew Mellon, who gave it both his own collection of Old Master paintings and a sizeable endowment. Magnates who subsequently made notable bequests include Joseph Widener, Lessing J. Rosenwald, Col. and Mrs. Edgar Garbisch, and Chester Dale. The 1980s reorganization, which was prompted by the addition of the new East Wing, vastly improved how the gallery works, both for museum staff and for the visiting public.

20 National Gallery of Art (East Wing)

Constitution Avenue and 4th Street, N.W.

1978 I.M. Pei & Partners; Dan Kiley, landscape architect

10:00 A.M. TO 5:00 P.M. MONDAY THROUGH SATURDAY, 11:00 A.M. TO 6:00 P.M. SUNDAY PHONE: 737-4215

A sculptural work of art in itself, this abstract essay in the acute and the oblique makes superb use of a potentially awkward trapezoidal site. Yet upon reflection it all seems so obvious: Pei simply split the trapezoid into two overlapping triangles; the larger, isosceles triangle contains gallery space, while the smaller, right triangle contains offices. Gallery officials discovered that the quarry that had supplied marble for the West Building had been closed long before Pei designed the new wing, but they managed to get it reopened so that the stone of the two structures would match; otherwise Pei's and Pope's projects have little in common.

21 Andrew Mellon Memorial Fountain

6th Street at Constitution and
Pennsylvania Avenues, N.W.

1952 Eggers & Higgins

How does one memorialize a
man who was at once billionaire
industrialist, banker, Secretary
of the Treasury to presidents Harding, Coolidge, and Hoover, Ambassador
to the Court of St. James, and art collector extraordinaire? This is one
solution, and it seems a highly suitable one, for the fountain's gentle tiers
echo the nearby dome of Mellon's pet project, the National Gallery.

Judiciary Square

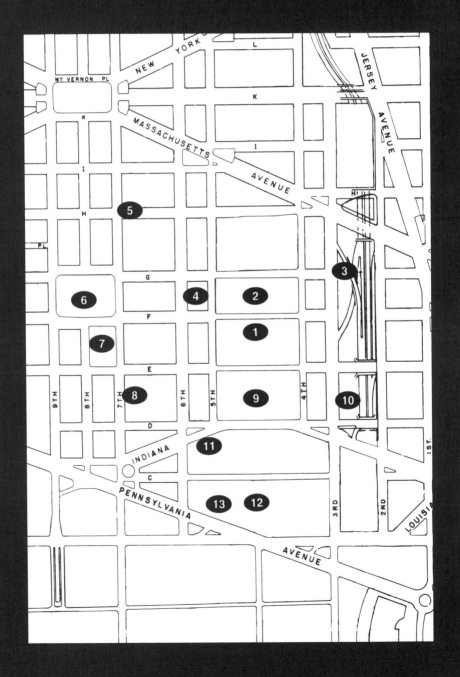

L'Enfant and Washington envisioned this roughly 20-acre neighborhood as the hub of the District's civic life, the site of the post office, the city hall, the court buildings, the jail, the hospital, and so on. All went according to plan, and the area soon boasted some of the nation's earliest and finest Greek revival civic structures, including Robert Mills's post office and patent office and George Hadfield's city hall. Henry Adams, trenchant observer of 19th-century Washington, marveled at the effect and wrote that the "white marble columns and fronts of the Post Office and Patent Office . . . [look] like white Greek temples in the abandoned gravel-pits of a deserted Syrian City."

The best-laid plans generally gang a-gley in Washington: a gaggle of hotels, residences, and shops quickly insinuated themselves among the grand governmental buildings. The innkeepers and homeowners were not drawn here by the beauty of the monumental structures but by a powerful stream that began at a spring near 5th and L Streets and raced southwards to join the Tiber Creek near the Mall. Sometimes, according to the *Washington Star,* the water in the canal was "deep enough for canoeing," but more often it was simply a fast-moving sewer.

The stream has since been covered over, sewer pipes now service the buildings, many once-abandoned structures in the neighborhood have recently found new uses, and thanks to such 20th-century construction projects as the Superior Court building, Judiciary Square again successfully fills its role as the center of law and government for the District of Columbia.

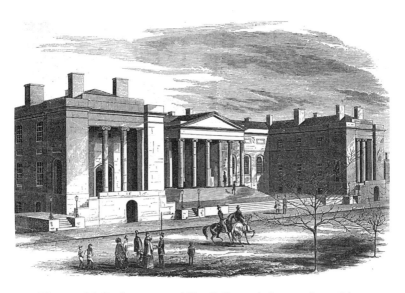

The powerful, Greek, monumental City Hall around 1853, now home of the District's superior court (C-9).

1 Judiciary Square Metro Station

4th and E Streets, N.W.

1975 Harry Weese & Associates; entry signage: Vignelli Associates

"A solid gold Cadillac for transporting the masses"—that's what *Fortune* magazine called Washington's Metro system. And the stations, which are basically vast, coffered vaults, do have a solid—even lavish—feel to them belying their inexpensive materials. Moreover, at each stop one experiences a constant interplay of light and dark that would have enchanted Piranesi.

This station is a worthy representative of the breed, although all regular Metro passengers doubtless have their own favorites. Car-burdened commuters value the large parking lots adjacent to the many above-ground stops, e.g., New Carrollton and Silver Spring; freer spirits, particularly those with a flair for the dramatic, tend to favor the stations at Dupont Circle and Woodley Park, where riding the escalator up to the sunshine makes one hum the Prisoners' Chorus from *Fidelio*.

2 National Building Museum (Pension Building)

4th and F Streets, N.W.

1882–1887 Montgomery C. Meigs; Casper Buberl, frieze sculptor

1989 restoration: Keyes Condon Florance Architects; Giorgio Cavaglieri, associated architect

10:00 A.M. TO 4:00 P.M. MONDAY THROUGH SATURDAY; NOON TO 4:00 P.M. SUNDAY   PHONE: 272-2448

Now universally esteemed as one of the District's undisputed (if quirkish) masterpieces, when new, this 400-foot by 200-foot pile was just as universally derided as "Meigs's Old Red Barn." (William Tecumseh Sherman, according to District lore, took one look at the building and sighed, "The worst of it is, it is fireproof.") Montgomery C. Meigs, quartermaster general during the Civil War, had seen and admired Michelangelo's Palazzo

The Pension Building has hosted innumerable national celebrations, including nine inaugural balls. This photograph, taken in 1901, shows the wonderful structure welcoming the advent of both Teddy Roosevelt and electric lights.

Farnese on a trip to Rome in 1867; and when asked to design a building for the staff administering Civil War veterans' pensions, the general decided to build his own bigger and better version of the palace.

But this is no facile copy, and in several respects Meigs—one trembles to write this—actually improved on Michelangelo, for the general was able to incorporate technological advantages unknown in the 16th century, including the fireproofing that so distressed Sherman. He also simplified the original palace's somewhat complex floor plan by affixing a narrow sheathing of offices to the exterior walls and leaving the interior hollow. He thus formed what may be the most astonishing room in Washington, a vast open space 316 feet long, 116 feet wide, and 159 feet high, ringed by four stories of arcaded passages, and crowned by a cast-iron roof supported by colossal 75-foot-high Corinthian columns.

General Meigs also had a fondness for sculptural historical friezes. Thwarted in an earlier attempt to place a three-dimensional frieze inside the Capitol dome (the dome's present grisaille frieze is painted), he got to play out his fantasies here in a 3-foot-tall, 1,200-foot-long terra-cotta frieze on the belt course. The frieze, which depicts various aspects of life in the Union army and navy during the Civil War, is now as dear to area hearts as the building itself, although it too has suffered bouts of critical disfavor. For example, in 1927 in his *Art and Artists of the Capitol*, Charles Fairman sniffed, "Whether the Pension Office frieze is really worth while or not we shall not attempt to determine." The best Fairman could say about it was, "if a person starts with an object in view and never loses sight of such formulated plans they usually materialize."

Once nearly demolished, the Pension Building, restored, sparkling, and splendid, now makes the ideal home for the National Building Museum, an organization dedicated to promoting the American building arts.

3   Adas Israel Synagogue (Jewish Historical Society)

701 3rd Street, N.W.

1873–1876 architect unknown; Max Kleinman, draftsman
1969 moved to present site

PHONE: 362-4433

This, the oldest synagogue in Washington, was dedicated in the nation's centennial year, 1876. It came into being when 35 families grew dissatisfied with the increasingly liberal Washington Hebrew Congregation (founded in 1852) and left to form Adas Israel, so that they could worship along more traditional lines. Their new building, red brick and highly restrained in design, was perfectly appropriate to the congregation's conservative bent. Exterior decoration is restricted to a wooden sunburst over the main door and a charming cast iron fence with Star of David and menorah motifs. Inside, note the ark for the Torah and the cupola; note also the women's gallery, an important feature, for it was such practices as allowing men and women to sit together during services that prompted members to leave their original place of worship.

    This building originally stood at 600 5th Street. Adas Israel left it in 1908 for new quarters and the building began a somewhat checkered history. By the 1960s demolition loomed, but then the District government, which had taken title to the building, negotiated a deal with the Jewish Historical Society of Greater Washington whereby the government agreed to give the building to the society if the society agreed to move it and operate it as a museum. The move took place in 1969, and the Lillian and Albert Small Jewish Museum opened in the old synagogue in 1975.

4   Operations Control Center Building, Washington Metropolitan Area Transit Authority

5th Street between F and G Streets, N.W.

1974 Keyes, Lethbridge & Condon, Architects

The interplay of light and void seen here contrasts with the dark and solid mass of the nearby Pension Building. At the same time, the widely spaced columns suggest the classicism of the Federal Triangle and Old City Hall.

5 Chinatown Gateway

7th and H Streets, N.W.

1986 Alfred H. Liu; Beijing Ancient Architectural Construction Corporation, construction and ornamentation

Given as a gesture of friendship in a Beijing-Washington sister-city exchange program, the 47-foot-high, 61-foot-wide archway is a carefully crafted and carefully authentic expression of an arch that might have come from the Qing Dynasty (1649–1911). It is also a fine example of how modern technology and ancient motifs can, in the right hands, work together. Liu combined venerable *dou gong* carved wood systems, which do not allow the use of nails or other metal connectors, to balance seven roofs weighing 63 tons with a steel and reinforced concrete base to create the largest single-span Chinese archway in the world. The surface decoration, according to the architect, is "full of color reflecting the kaleidoscopic combinations of hues, shades, primaries, and pastels that imitate the diversity of life itself."

6 National Portrait Gallery and Museum of American Art (Old Patent Office)

8th and F Streets, N.W.

1836 A. J. Davis, Ithiel Town, and William P. Elliot; additions: Robert Mills, Edward Clark, Thomas U. Walter, and others

1969 Faulkner, Stenhouse, Fryer; Faulkner and Underwood; Victor Proetz; restoration: Bayard Underwood

10:00 A.M. TO 5:30 P.M. DAILY   PHONE: 357-2700

It is little short of miraculous that this building, born out of controversy, works at all, architecturally. L'Enfant's plan reserved this site as a "shrine to American heroes," but it never saw that use. After the old patent office burned, in 1836, this largely vacant lot was selected as the site for its fireproof replacement. Another of Washington's innumerable design competitions ensued, won by the consortium of Davis, Town, and Elliot; but President Andrew Jackson liked Mills and, notwithstanding the results of the competition, made him supervising architect "to aid in forming the plans, making proper changes therein from time to time, and seeing to the erection of said buildings in substantial conformity to the plans hereby adopted." One can hear Davis et al. grinding their collective teeth. Somehow the south wing got built (completed c. 1840), but then Mills started complaining that he wasn't being shown interior plans or structural specifications. Elliot in turn alleged that Mills had been, to put it politely, free-and-easy in his bookkeeping. A congressional inquiry exonerated Mills—but only *just*.

Mills gave the city some of its finest columned monuments, so, while precise documentation is lacking, it was probably he who designed the patent office's superb Doric portico, purportedly an exact copy of the Parthenon's, rendered in Virginia freestone. One wonders if James Fenimore Cooper had Mills in mind when he wrote *Home as Found* (1836): "The public sentiment just now runs almost exclusively and popularly into the Grecian school. We build little besides temples for our churches, our banks, our taverns, our court houses, and our dwellings. A friend of mine has just built a brewery on the model of the Temple of the Four Winds."

Mills died in 1855, and many, many other architects had to be called in to complete what he had begun. When work was finally finished, in 1867, the result was the largest office building in Washington. It was a busy place, too; over the years clerks issued 500,000 patents to the likes of Alexander Graham Bell, Cyrus McCormick, and Thomas Edison. During the Civil War these halls were made over into a hospital; one of the ministering nurses was Walt Whitman, who based his poem "The Wound Dresser" on his experiences here. Lincoln's second inaugural ball was held in the Patent Office, and apparently a good time was had by all except the *New York Times* correspondent, who complained that "the supper was a disaster." After the war, the Bureau of Indian Affairs moved into this building. Whitman reappeared, this time working as a clerk for the bureau until 1867, when the manuscript of *Leaves of Grass*, discovered in his desk, got him sacked as "injurious to the morals of the men."

This century has proven just as busy for the marble and sandstone masterpiece: for a while the Civil Service Commission kept its offices here, then those bureaucrats moved out and the building sat abandoned for several years. Demolition seemed inevitable until President Eisenhower intervened and offered the building to the Smithsonian, which now maintains the rambling structure as the National Portrait Gallery.

---

7   Tariff Commission (Old Post Office)

7th and 8th Streets between E and F Streets, N.W.

1839–1842   Robert Mills
1855–1860   Thomas U. Walter; Montgomery C. Meigs, superintendent of construction

Robert Mills (1781–1855) has secured his spot in history as the first great American-born professional architect. (Latrobe was born in England; Jefferson was an amateur.) His work, moreover, makes a fascinating mini-history of the evolving profession and of the Republic, for his projects include all the structures necessary to a new nation—capitols, courhouses, universities, jails, hospitals, office buildings, and, of course, monuments. Indeed, Mills's stature in the profession was such that President Jackson appointed him as official federal architect, a job he held for 16 years, until illness forced him to resign.

Mills designed three neoclassical government buildings in Washington: the Patent Office, the Treasury Building, and this post office. Perhaps the least known of the trio, the post office occupies the site of Blodget's Hotel (c. 1793). That earlier structure had festered as an infamous eyesore: in 1810 Latrobe complained of its occupants, "[They] keep hogs and commit nuisances in the house which render it offensive . . . and, indeed unwholesome," so no one cried when the hotel burned to the ground (accidentally) in 1836. The fate of the hotel made fire prevention a paramount concern when a new post office was proposed for the site, and Mills designed a building with double-loaded masonry vaults and thick marble walls. The solid structure is an aesthetic success as well. Mills based its noble lines on Palladio's drawing of the Temple of Jupiter Stator, and the graceful creation has won praise from sources as varied as historian Talbot Hamlin, who applauded the building's "power and simplicity of . . . design," and Charles Dickens (of all people), who blessed it as "very compact and very beautiful."

8   Gallery Row

401–413 7th Street, N.W.

1979 Hartman-Cox
Architects; Oehrlein &
Associates Architects,
preservation architects

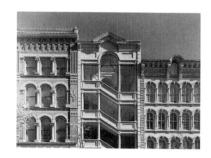

Infill need not be bland to be
good! Hartman-Cox and
Oehrlein took five disparate and derelict 19th-century commercial buildings, shored them up, and built a dazzling new link (409 7th Street) to create what is arguably the city's slickest and most successful center for the
creative arts.

Gallery space and painters' studios are a far cry from the row's use a
century ago, when this block (and its neighbors) were filled with a somewhat random assemblage of small shops, businesses, and residences. Architect Thomas U. Walter lived at 614 F Street; the *National Era* (an abolitionist newspaper) was published at 427 F Street; the improbably named
Mr. Croissant led the city's temperance drive from his Holly Tree Hotel at
518 9th Street; and Samuel F. B. Morse tinkered with his new-fangled tele-
graph in a since-demolished building that stood on 7th Street between E
and F. The 20th-century architects captured this lively history in 409 7th
Street's somewhat mannerist exterior; inside, the new unit's four-story
rotunda acts as a lobby and a pivot for the entire project.

---

9   Superior Court of the District of Columbia (Old City Hall)

451 Indiana Avenue, N.W.

1820–1850 George Hadfield

Emphatically terminating a short axis laid
out perpendicular to Constitution
Avenue, this was the first public building
erected by and for the District's municipal government. After the seemingly obligatory funding crises (a "grand National Lottery" was but one of
several unsuccessful schemes to raise the cash), the mayor laid the cornerstone in August 1820 for what he proclaimed as "an edifice devoted to
municipal purposes, to be the seat of legislation and of the administration
of justice for this metropolis." Displaying powerful Ionic temple forms
typical of the embryonic Greek revival and sheathed in Indiana limestone,
the earliest section of the building also boasts recessed window arches wor-

thy of Sir John Soane at his best. Additions arrived quickly as the District government grew: the east wing dates to 1826, the west to 1849, and further sections appeared in 1881 and 1916.

10 U.S. Tax Court Building

400 2nd Street, N.W.

1973 Victor A. Lundy; Lyles, Bissett, Carlisle & Wolfe, associated architects

Almost elegant on its west (3rd Street) façade, this building's 2nd Street entrance is impressively uninviting. And why not—who wants to go to tax court? The structure's angular black minimalism makes a nice foil to the gleaming neoclassicism of Hartman-Cox's nearby Georgetown University law library.

11 Courthouse of the District of Columbia

500 Indiana Avenue, N.W.

1978 Hellmuth, Obata & Kassabaum, PC

A little sign by the information booth in the courthouse's main lobby reads "Consider Alternatives to Litigation." This somewhat forbidding building encourages one to do just that, for the vast, off-putting pile seems to symbolize the grim, inexorable grindings of the legal system.

12 John Marshall Park

4th Street and Pennsylvania Avenue, N.W.

1983 Carol R. Johnson & Associates

Planned since the 1920s, this park creates one of the most successful cross-axes in the city, one that works from as far away as the south side of Independence Avenue. From that distant spot, one's eye meanders slowly and expansively over the Mall, becomes a bit more focused at 4th Street and the park, and finally comes to rest on the red bulk of the Pension

Building. The park's honoree, Chief Justice John Marshall, lived in many buildings in Washington, including a rooming house on Pennsylvania Avenue that, ironically, was one of dozens of structures demolished to make way for this green space.

13 Canadian Embassy

501 Pennsylvania Avenue, N.W.

1989 Arthur Erickson Architects

Given one of the most important sites in the District—a few
hundred yards from the Capitol
and right across Pennsylvania
Avenue from the National Gallery—Erickson managed to embrace both
neoclassical and modernist principles to create a building that is an aesthetic success in itself and that is congenial with its neighbors. Erickson, a
recipient of gold medals for design from the Royal Architectural Institute
of Canada, the French Académie d'Architecture, and the AIA, achieved
these admirable ends through several devices. First, he acknowledged the
skins of Washington's venerable monuments by sheathing the embassy in
smooth marble. Second, he showed himself familiar with the District's
fondness for numerical symbolism by giving the building's Rotunda of the
Provinces 12 columns, one for each of Canada's provinces and territories.
(The rotunda's dome obviously creates a dialogue with Walter's and Pope's
creations.) Finally, and in a modernist vein harmonious with the National
Gallery's East Wing, Erickson positioned the embassy's three wings and
six freestanding, 50-foot columns to create a beautiful minimalist courtyard.

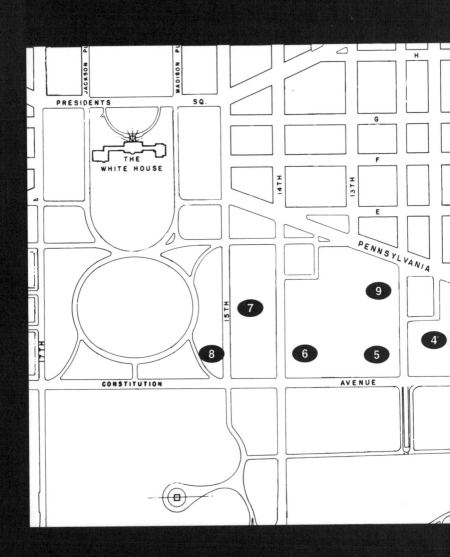

The Federal Triangle

Frederick Law Olmsted, Jr., argued in 1900 that "great public edifices must be strongly formal . . . if the total effect is to be consistent." He certainly would have been delighted with this monstrous project, for here is the center of big bureaucratic government in all its pompous—and *formal*—officialdom. The sheer immensity of the planned development makes it an undeniably powerful element in the cityscape. Like it or not, the Federal Triangle is simply too big to ignore.

The Federal Triangle in the 1920s, swaggering towards completion.

While most of the Triangle's buildings came from different architects' drawing boards, they were conceived as a single monumental composition and were guided to completion by a coordinating committee headed by Edward Bennett, architectural advisor to Andrew Mellon. Using different architects presented an element of chance, but Bennett managed to achieve Olmsted's yearning for consistency while avoiding repetition. For example, while most of the structures stand six full stories tall, Bennett saw to it that his teams used the full panoply of academic devices to obscure the uniform height. Anyone who doubts that Bennett achieved a certain artistic unity need only look inside the buildings, where the plans fulfill the prophecy, evident from without, of uniform, endlessly intersecting corridors.

Much pleased with his work, Bennett stated in 1929 that he viewed the Triangle as "a tribute to order, a human order, the product of centuries of civilization." Nor was he alone in his smugness; at a superbly self-congratulatory dinner, when the Triangle was well under way, Congressman Richard Elliott boasted that "the 69th and 70th congresses [which had funded the project] will go down in history as doing more in a constructive way for the remaking of the National Capital . . . than all the preceding congresses had done in this behalf." Many today agree, and the Triangle is now enjoying a good deal of favorable press. It has even spawned imitators at home and abroad—just glance down Pennsylvania Avenue to Market Square; and what is London's Canary Wharf but an elephantine Federal Triangle?

One is tempted to dissent. First, compare this project's orderly history, which seems a bit totalitarian, with the messy and contentious—and democratic—histories of the Capitol and the Washington Monument. Second, it is at least arguable that the Triangle disappoints as a work of art. Two contemporary projects, San Francisco's Civic Center (completed c. 1931) and New York's Rockefeller Center (a whistling-in-the-dark show of faith begun during the Depression) to some eyes possess greater finesse and excitement than the somewhat stolid Triangle.

1 Federal Trade Commission

6th Street and Constitution Avenue, N.W.

1937 Bennett, Parsons & Frost; Chaim Gross and Michael Lantz, sculptors

The massive and monolithic façades of this building oddly evoke its agency's original purpose, namely busting massive and monolithic trusts. The FTC and the more playful Mellon Fountain form the apex of the Federal Triangle. From this point, the buildings in the complex grow ever more massive as they march westward.

2 National Archives

Constitution Avenue between 7th and 9th Streets, N.W.

1935 John Russell Pope; Adolph A. Weinman, James Earle Fraser, and Robert Aitken, sculptors

10:00 A.M. TO 9:00 P.M. DAILY
PHONE: 501-5000

Of all the buildings in the Federal Triangle, perhaps only this one achieves individual success; what success the others enjoy is dependent on their cumulative effect. This may be because Pope, who clearly enjoyed the Archives project, gave the limestone-sheathed building a wonderfully appropriate form: he treated it as a mausoleum—freestanding and of great scale—the perfect shell for the final repository of tons of paper and mounds of microfilm. Actually, this is Pope's second giant mausoleum in the District; a few years earlier he designed the wonderful Masonic Temple on 16th Street.

3 Department of Justice

Constitution Avenue between 9th and 10th Streets, N.W.

1934 Zantzinger, Borie & Medary

Three-story pilasters, pedimented pavilions, and a nifty art deco main entrance combine to make the Constitution Avenue façade of the Justice Department a slightly syncopated version of the standard Triangle component. The cheerful interior courtyard also deserves note.

4 Internal Revenue Service

1111 Constitution Avenue, N.W.

1930–1935 Louis Simon

This was the first of the Triangle's neo-classical piles; it is also where the stuff that fuels the government is gathered, something one is reminded of by Oliver Wendell Holmes's maxim, carved over the Connecticut Avenue entrance, "TAXES ARE WHAT WE PAY FOR A CIVILIZED SOCIETY." In addition to 1040 forms, one finds other curiosities here, including a copper still that allegedly belonged to George Washington in pleasanter times before spirits were taxed.

5 Interstate Commerce Commission

12th Street and Constitution Avenue, N.W.

1935 Arthur Brown

Brown designed this three-unit behemoth to house the ICC, the Departmental Auditorium, and the Labor Department.

6 Department of the Treasury (Customs Services)

14th Street and Constitution Avenue, N.W.

1935 Arthur Brown

A two-story rusticated basement adds some interest to the otherwise plain five-story façades, just as the series of porticos and the aggressive cornice add a hint of rhythm to the predictable planar Triangle massing.

7 Department of Commerce

14th Street between E Street and
Constitution Avenue, N.W.

1932 York & Sawyer

Scored walls and a range of pedimented
windows give a somewhat— *somewhat*—
Italianate feeling to this building's 1,000-
foot-long 15th Street façade. When new,
Commerce's 1,000,000 square feet of
floorspace made it the largest office structure in the country.

8 Capitol Gatehouses

Constitution Avenue at 15th Street and
17th Street, N.W.

c. 1814 Charles Bulfinch

Created in rusticated Aquia Creek sandstone, these structures show that
Bulfinch, a normally correct and
restrained New Englander, had a whimsical streak. With square plans of roughly
15 feet to the side, the flat-roofed, one-
room gatehouses sport arched entrances
with flanking Doric columns, entablatures with guilloche friezes, and para-
pets with rinceau panels. Originally located near the Capitol, the gatehouses were moved here in the 1870s; otherwise they certainly would have
perished when Frederick Law Olmsted relandscaped Capitol Hill (see A-2
and A-5).

9 Ariel Rios Building

Pennsylvania Avenue
and 12th Street, N.W.

1934 Delano & Aldrich

Sophisticated seems the *mot
juste* here, reluctant as one may
be to use a word like that to

describe any building in the Federal Triangle. But, then, Delano and Aldrich, who formed one of the most genteel architectural firms of their day, were no strangers to European-influenced design. They gave this building a *piano nobile* and used fasces as window lintels, they draped a delicate belt course between the fourth and fifth stories, they bedecked the interior walls with superb WPA murals, and they built a full arcade that virtually transforms the 12th Street façade into the rue de Rivoli.

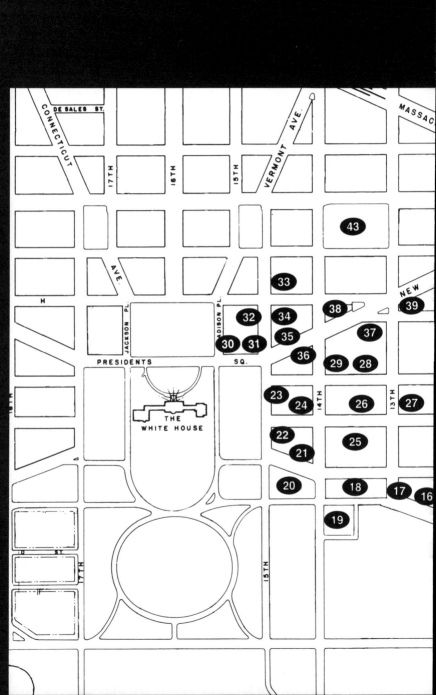

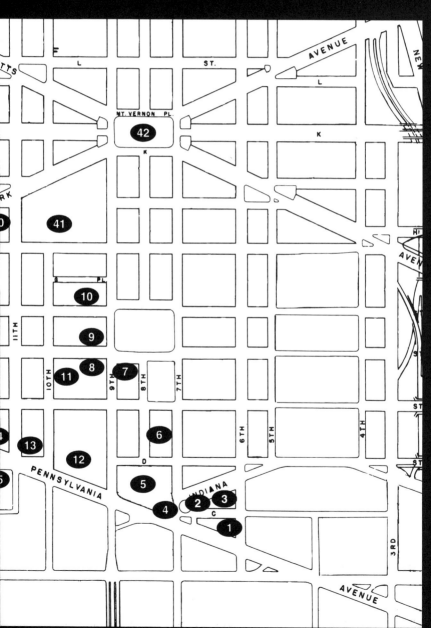

Pennsylvania Avenue has long been dubbed "America's Main Street"; the accuracy of such a notion—even its desirability—is for the moment moot. According to tradition, the avenue got its name as a sop to the keystone state's politicians, who became disgruntled when Congress selected the new city on the Potomac, not the old city on the Schuylkill, as the national capital. Some consolation! One early-19th-century congressman described Pennsylvania Avenue as "a deep morass covered with elder bushes," and, despite Thomas Jefferson's attempts to beautify the thoroughfare by planting flanking rows of Lombardy poplars, that description remained valid for much of the first half of the century.

Then, during the Civil War, Pennsylvania Avenue's sidewalks, especially between 7th Street and 14th Street, were covered with more than elder bushes, for the neighborhood became the favorite haunt of the thousands of ladies of the night who were drawn to Washington, in venerable tradition, by the city's hundreds of thousands of soldiers. General Joseph Hooker tried to get the freelancing entrepreneurs to confine their activities

The twin towers of the then-new Central National Bank building (distant right) are about all that remains from this c. 1890 image of Pennsylvania Avenue at 10th Street. One hopes that the riders were stepping to the strains of the "Washington Post March" (Sousa was born in the District in 1854), since the newspaper was headquartered in the light-colored building at the left. Across a now-closed D Street from the Post building, the elegant mansard roof and well-articulated windows of the Trader's National Bank rise in Second Empire splendor. (This is the present site of the FBI Building.) Looming over the Post, the hooded ventilator (note the fan) of the Ward's Dairy building strikes an oddly pastoral note in this urban scene.

to one small zone, but the ladies complained about governmental regulations and, according to one story, coined the pejorative nickname "Hooker's Army," later shortened to "hookers." (There are other stories about the origin of both terms.) That phase of the avenue's history ended when the District outlawed brothels in 1914.

In addition to fretting about the street's appearance, Jefferson, perhaps unwittingly, began another honored tradition when he walked down Pennsylvania Avenue to the Capitol for his inauguration in March 1801. Since then, except perhaps for New York's Fifth Avenue, Pennsylvania Avenue has witnessed more parades for more different organizations and causes than any other thoroughfare in the nation.

During much of the District's history, Washington's midtown lay north of Pennsylvania Avenue. These acres contained a mélange of buildings of every conceivable use—banks and boarding houses, churches and photographers' studios, open-air markets, libraries, and theaters. Possessed of a certain grubby charm, they formed what the compilers of the first and second editions of this guide called "Washington's forgotten architecture . . . off the beaten path." Well not any more! For a variety of reasons and spurred on by the Pennsylvania Avenue Development Corporation, which Congress created in 1972, developers swooped in and, during the 1970s and '80s, transformed the "forgotten" buildings beyond recognition, rehabbing some and replacing many more. While a venal few were, no doubt, motivated solely by favorable changes to the tax laws, the sheer architectural energy in the air along Pennsylvania and New York Avenues from 7th to 15th Streets suggests that most builders simply got caught up in the excitement of it all and, like the soldiers and young ladies 130 years ago, just decided to go out and have a good time.

1 Sears House (Apex, Brady, and Gilman Buildings)

625–633 Pennsylvania Avenue, N.W.

1859–1860 Brady Building: architect unknown
1887 Apex/Central National Bank Building: Alfred B. Mullett
1984–1985 Geier Brown Renfrow Architects; restoration: Hartman-Cox Architects; John Milner Associates

This delightful eccentric, which seems blissfully unaware of any disapproval emanating from the overly polite Federal Triangle nearby, must rank high on everyone's list of favorite Washington buildings. Actually, one is looking at not one but three buildings: the familiar twin-towered Central National Bank (ashlar with granite belt courses and trim) and the more restrained double building to the rear. Mathew Brady, the great Civil War photographer, kept his studio and office in the back building until, maintaining a long tradition of District entrepreneurial failures, he went bankrupt in 1873.

2 Temperance Fountain

7th Street and Pennsylvania Avenue, N.W.

1882 sculptor unknown

This fountain, now dry and decorative rather than dripping and demonstrative, was presented to the city by temperance crusader Henry D. Cogswell, a San Francisco dentist. Dr. Cogswell, who specialized in false teeth, made his real fortune in Bay-area real estate and California mining. He spent much of his wealth building fountains such as this in any community that asked for one. The version he gave Washington is granite, about seven feet square, with an elaborate central sculpture topped by a bronze heron. Dr. Cogswell picked a good site from which to launch his local anti-vice crusade, since for most of the 19th century this block marked the eastern boundary of the city's large red light district.

3 Argentine Naval Building (National Bank of Washington, later Riggs Bank)

630 Indiana Avenue, N.W.

1889 James G. Hill
1979 P. T. Astore (interior)
1982 renovation: Vlastimil Koubek

Built of rock-faced marble ashlar with smooth tooled trim on a granite base, this polygonal fortress is everything one would want in a great late-19th-century bank building. Yet Hill was artist enough to use Byzantine-style stone carvings, clustered colonnettes, and ornamental window grilles to relieve the stolidness. Koubek ably adapted the interior spaces, among the finest of their kind in the city, to new uses.

4   Navy Memorial

Pennsylvania Avenue between 7th and 9th Streets, N.W.

1990   Conklin Rossant; Stanley Bleifeld, sculptor

Nestled in the embrace of Hartman-Cox's Market Square, this paved plaza, brace of masts, and solitary bronze sailor pay an understated, moving tribute to the men and women who have served in the United States Navy.

5   Market Square

Pennsylvania Avenue between 7th and 9th Streets, N.W.

1990   Hartman-Cox Architects; Morris ★ Architects, associated architects

Adopting a baroque mien rare for the firm, Hartman-Cox achieved a number of estimable results here. The columned quadrants, heroic in scale and flawless in execution, prove the perfect neighbors for the Federal Triangle, holding their own against the huge 1930s complex through mass and motif. Further, the quadrants' neoclassical dignity makes them the perfect players in the dramas that make Pennsylvania Avenue "America's Main Street." Yet, while Market Square (which *Post* architecture critic Benjamin Forgey has dubbed "nonmarket, unsquare") is grand, it is anything but dull; and, indeed, the quadrants are among the few new buildings in town to show that *neoclassical* need not necessarily equal *pompous*. Finally, the project accomplishes the crucial task of guaranteeing a suitably monumental vista from Pope's Archives building up 8th Street to Mills's multi-porticoed Portrait Gallery. This view is possible only because of the space left between the quadrants, but, and more subtly, Hartman-Cox encouraged such gazing by stepping back the quadrants' upper stories, a trick that causes even the most unobservant pedestrian to look northward.

6 The Lansburgh

420–424 7th Street, N.W.

1991 renovations and additions: Graham Gund Architects

This must rank as one of the more ambitious projects in a neighborhood where ambitious projects are almost common-place. Developers rescued the shells of several adjacent structures, including Kresge's (7th and E Streets) and the Bush Building (710 E Street), and recycled them into commercial, residential, and general office space. Gund's expansive new brick building, with its polychrome brick walls and complex roofline, not only visually and functionally links the many once-disparate spaces but also suggests the block's somewhat convoluted history.

The developers even found room to create a new 447-seat theater (enter at 450 7th Street) within the project. This splendid room has caused the sometimes staid *New York Times* to gush that "there is not a bad seat or an uncomfortable one" in "the handsome oval auditorium." The theater now forms the permanent home of the city's formerly peripatetic Shakespeare Theater troupe.

7 Le Droit Building

8th and F Streets, N.W.

1875 A. L. Barber and Company; James H. McGill

Here's an oddity—one of the few remaining large office structures in this or any other city not to have an elevator. The Le Droit Building is also notable for its large, northward windows—necessary to provide steady, gentle work light in that prefluorescent era. The windows have made the building a favorite for artists' studios in more recent times. Artists who admire the texture of objects doubtless also derive pleasure from the building's vigorous Italianate trim (Corinthian entrances, mullioned display windows, bracketed cornice, brick window hoods), although the peeling paint and general shabby condition add perhaps more texture than most people really desire.

8 Riggs National Bank

9th and F Streets, N.W.

1891 James G. Hill
1926 addition to west end: Arthur
Heaton

The exterior bearing walls of this nine-story granite and brick tower have a close functional kinship with such architectural landmarks as Louis Sullivan's Auditorium Building and H. H. Richardson's Marshall Field Warehouse, although many critics feel that the Riggs building lacks the bold changes of scale and willful roughness characteristic of those masterpieces. In addition to its illustrious evocations, Riggs's soaring verticality plays an undeniably important and ennobling role in the generally tawdry urban landscape of this neighborhood. Solid at street level, with a U-shaped plan above, the building contains one of the town's more exciting commercial spaces, the Corinthian-columned main banking room.

9 Old Masonic Hall

9th and F Streets, N.W.

1868 Cluss and
Kammerheuber

The polychrome stone and cast-iron veneers applied to the brick walls of this Italian

Renaissance palazzo offer some of the more eye-catching façades in town. When new, the building exemplified the mixed use of space so characteristic of late-19th-century, pre–zoning code urban architecture: shops jostled one another on the ground floor, and the Masonic Hall filled the space above. President Andrew Johnson, himself a loyal Freemason, laid the cornerstone and led the gala parade that celebrated the start of construction.

In its prime the hall witnessed much Gilded Age gaiety: Washingtonians feted the Prince of Wales here in 1876 at a centennial banquet, and for decades society matrons fought for the honor of having their daughters' debutante parties here.

But the building fell on hard times in the 20th century. The masons and the ingénues moved out in 1908, to be replaced in 1921 by Lansburgh's Furniture Store, which remained until the late 1970s. Then for years the noble building stood abandoned, reeking of urine, with its tattered fliers for long-past professional wrestling matches flapping in the wind. Restoration now seems imminent.

---

10 Martin Luther King Memorial Library

901 G Street, N.W.

1972 Office of Mies van der Rohe

9:00 A.M. TO 9:00 P.M. MONDAY THROUGH THURSDAY, 9:00 A.M. TO 5:30 P.M. FRIDAY AND SATURDAY, 1:00 P.M. TO 5:00 P.M. SUNDAY

This traditional Miesian package is the great man's only work in the District. That the commission came from the city government rather than from a private client, coupled with the fact that giants such as Wright, Gropius, and Le Corbusier are completely unrepresented in town, says much about the low architectural aspirations of mid-20th-century corporate Washington.

11 Ford's Theater

511 10th Street, N.W.

1863 James J. Gifford
1968 Macomber & Peter; restoration:
William Haussman

9:00 A.M. TO 5:00 P.M. DAILY
PHONE: 426-6924

Entrepreneur and impresario John T.
Ford arrived in town in 1861, flush from
a string of successes at Baltimore's
Holliday Street Theater. He built this
theater in 1863 and seemed destined to repeat his Baltimore Triumphs.
But after Booth murdered Lincoln here on April 14, 1865, Ford's business
dried up, and he sold the building to the federal government in 1866.
Now, after a period of hostile neglect—a century ago, enraged citizens
demanded that the government raze the building—the entire structure has
been meticulously restored to its original condition and the stage lights
glow once again. The government still owns the theater and maintains,
through the National Park Service, a small museum of Lincolniana in the
basement; it also maintains the Peterson House, directly across 10th Street
at #516, the house where Lincoln died.

12 J. Edgar Hoover Building (FBI Headquarters)

Pennsylvania Avenue between
9th and 10th Streets, N.W.

1974 C. F. Murphy &
Associates

Brutalism on a grand scale, this
massive pile minces no words
and its concrete walls state un-
equivocally, "Here I am." According to material published by the FBI,
the building was designed to reinforce "the idea of a central core of files."
Since files and information were, as we now know, the eponymous
Hoover's specialty, the building must be deemed a success.

13 1001 Pennsylvania Avenue, N.W.

1987 Hartman-Cox Architects; Smith Segreti Tepper, Architects/Planners, associated architects

All the adjectives one associates with Hartman-Cox—*urbane, polished, distinguished*—apply here. The architects managed to fit the huge structure gently into the streetscape and keep it stylistically respectful of its landmark neighbors, such as the *Sun* and *Star* buildings. And while it does not dominate the smaller structures to the north, it manages to hold its own with the nearby FBI Building. In other words, this gentlemanly project is kind to the weak and fearless of the local bully. The building's workable main floor plan, suggestive of the National Gallery down the street, consists of two marbled concourses that traverse the block and meet perpendicularly in a central rotunda.

14 Evening *Star* Building

1101 Pennsylvania Avenue, N.W.

1898 Marsh and Peter
1988–1989 Skidmore, Owings & Merrill

When this ten-story Beaux-Arts building first opened, the *Star,* pleased with its new digs, ran a full-page story to announce its "architectural triumph." Continuing, the article stated that the paper's publisher had decided to make the District "notable in an artistic sense" and thus chose to erect "such a building as would be harmonious with that future and an inspiration to its speedy attainments." What a pity such corporate sentiments are not more widely shared today. Founded in 1852, the *Star* wasn't known for its timid prose: the publisher stated in the first issue that his paper would "fearlessly" expose "all the Corruptions of Government, and every attempt to defraud the public Treasury." What a pity those sentiments too are not more widely shared today.

The *Star* continued its many crusades from this building until 1955 (it published from a different location for another generation). The building's future was uncertain until the Pennsylvania Avenue Development Corporation coaxed Skidmore, Owings and Merrill onto the scene, and the architects created a vast addition, carefully repeating many of the architectural and decorative motifs the paper trumpeted so proudly in 1898.

15 Old Post Office/The Pavilion

12th Street and Pennsylvania Avenue, N.W.

1899 Willoughby J. Edbrooke
1982 restoration: Arthur Cotton Moore/Associates P.C.

The granite walls and spire of this marvelous Romanesque revival building stick out like a sore thumb in the midst of an otherwise exclusively, and a bit oppressively, neoclassical Federal Triangle. Or perhaps sore *tooth* might be better, since the 315-foot-tall clock earned the building the nickname, "old tooth." Controversy has swirled around the post office, the first major steel-framed structure in town, since its completion, when the *New York Times* sniffed that the new building looked like "a cross between a cathedral and a cotton mill."

The Post Office abandoned the wonderful building in the 1930s, and threats of demolition hung over the place for a half-century simply because it was deemed out of step with its neoclassical neighbors. Finally, in the early 1970s, a spirited band of preservationists hired Moore to restore the building. He did an exemplary job of creating a stylistic bridge between the Triangle and the picturesque downtown commercial structures to the north, and the post office's impressive atrium, measuring 99 by 190 feet and 160 feet high, is now filled to the brim with seven solid stories of offices and three of retail shops.

16 1201 Pennsylvania Avenue, N.W.

1981 Skidmore, Owings & Merrill

Atriums became a virtual cliché in 1980s Washington. This massive building, however, contains one of the better—certainly one of the more dramatic—examples of the breed.

17 Pennsylvania Building

1275 Pennsylvania Avenue, N.W.

1987 Smith, Segreti, Tepper, McMahon, Harned, Architects & Planners, PC

Try to picture the Federal Triangle—or, rather, one element of the Triangle— done on a small scale with elegance, finesse, and understatement. The Pennsylvania Building would be the result. Scored masonry, clearly articulated arches, even the red-tile roof all suggest the earlier grouping; but *suggest* is the key word, for the Pennsylvania Building might be viewed as a fond evocation, not an obvious imitation. The superb T-plan lobby, with its bank of hushed elevators, is one of new Washington's more soothing spaces.

18 Freedom Plaza (Western Plaza)

Pennsylvania Avenue between 13th and 14th Streets, N.W.

1980 Venturi, Rauch & Scott Brown; George E. Patton, landscape architect

Among the most successful of Washington's new parks, this open space gives continuity to the most important stretch of Pennsylvania Avenue, the axis formed by the White House and the Capitol. It does so while displaying all the wit and style one associates with the names Robert Venturi and Denise Scott Brown. The garden, laid out on a large, raised terrace, renders L'Enfant's plan in black and white stone, framing the giant map with paving stones incised with quotes about the District: some are serious; some less so. It is therefore a great place for a tourist to get a sense of the city's street pattern. Typically, these architects filled their creation with complex implications and hidden meanings. They once stated that the plaza's form is, like the city's, controlled by two "orders"—not the conventional Doric and Ionic but the "giant" or diagonal and "minor" or rectangular-grid. The architectural theatricality of the garden blends well with the dramas and musicals of the splendid Warner Theater project (1992; 13th and E Streets, Shalom Baranes and Pei Cobb

Freed and Partners). Landscape architect Patton's grasses and seasonal plantings set the whole thing off and tie it in nicely with adjacent Pershing Park.

19 District Building

1350 Pennsylvania Avenue, N.W.

1904 Cope & Stewardson; Adolfo De Nesti, sculptor

One gazes in wonder at the swaggering, Corinthian-columned District Building, half expecting a long-vanished political boss, vest-thumbing and bespatted, to stride through the doors. In fact, only recently has it come to be regarded as an endearing eccentricity rather than as an embarrassing monstrosity, which adds proof to novelist Anthony Powell's statement that "time's slide rule can make unlikely adjustments." (But one does wonder what to make of all that attic-level statuary.) Surfaced in marble, over granite structural walls, the building has a U-shaped plan above the first floor to guarantee light and air for the city's workers.

20 Pershing Park

Pennsylvania Avenue between 14th and 15th Streets, N.W.

1981 M. Paul Friedberg; Jerome Lindsay, associated architects

Built under the aegis of the watchdog Pennsylvania Avenue Development Corporation, Pershing Park strikes most viewers as a somewhat more traditional urban open space than its neighbor to the east, Freedom Plaza. Together the two parks form pleasant, stepped front gardens for both the Willard and National Place. Pershing Park's botanical interest begins with azaleas and spring-flowering bulbs and continues right through the chrysanthemum season; an outdoor skating rink guarantees winter activity as well.

21 Willard Hotel

14th Street and Pennsylvania Avenue, N.W.

1901 Henry Hardenbergh
1979–1986 conceptual design:
Vlastimil Koubek with Hardy Holzman
Pfeiffer Associates; restoration: Stuart
Golding; Oliver Carr Company,
managing partner

Without doubt the best-known hostelry in
town, the present twelve-story Willard is
the last in a succession of hotels that have stood on this site since about
1816. In that year, John Tayloe, builder of the Octagon, acquired the six
"two-story and attic houses" standing on this lot and leased them to Joshua
Tennison, who established Tennison's Hotel. In 1847 Tayloe's son, Benjamin Ogle Tayloe, paid to have the hotel refurbished and hired 25-year-
old Henry Willard to run it. Willard and his brother Edwin bought the
structure outright in 1850 and renamed it Willard's, which it has illustri-
ously remained.

During the Civil War, Julia Ward Howe wrote the "Battle Hymn of the
Republic" in her room at the Willard and the building played host to so
many luminaries that Nathaniel Hawthorne, covering the war for the
Atlantic, observed, "This hotel . . . may be more justly called the center of
Washington and the Union than either the Capitol, the White House, or
the State Department." On a less exalted level, the Willard also witnessed
the birth of the term *lobbyist,* coined to honor the men who prowled round
and round the lobby, peering through cigar smoke and potted palms in
search of the mighty.

The present building was begun in 1901 and completed in 1904 to the
specifications of Henry Hardenbergh, who also designed the 1907 Plaza
Hotel in New York. Cynics believe that Hardenbergh gave this hotel its
mansard penthouse to evade the city's height restriction; others suggest he
designed the upper level so it would form a stylistic link between the
Willard and the existing grand hotels, such as the old Waldorf-Astoria.

Good times and the Willard remained synonymous until World War II,
when the entire neighborhood took a nose-dive. (One of the hotel's few
bright postwar moments came in 1963, when Dr. Martin Luther King
penned his "I Have a Dream" speech in a room upstairs.) Boarded up and
threatened with demolition, the Willard was finally saved through the
intervention of the Pennsylvania Avenue Development Corporation and,
after a lengthy restoration, reopened its opulent doors in 1986 as the

Willard Inter-Continental Hotel. Its public rooms—the main lobby, with its 35 different types of marble; Peacock Alley, a block-long promenade of elegant shops (in which FBI operatives learn how to "shadow" people); and Round Robin Bar, which boasted a sign during Carrie Nation's heyday proclaiming "All Nations Welcome Except Carrie"—must rank among the grandest such spaces in the country.

22 Hotel Washington

15th Street and Pennsylvania Avenue, N.W.

1917 Carrère & Hastings
1985 Pennsylvania Avenue Development Corporation; Mariani and Associates, preservation consultants; Ivan Valtchev, materials conservator

The District's oldest hotel in continuous use, the nine-story (plus roof garden) Hotel Washington possesses one of most familiar silhouettes in town. Carrère and Hastings, who gave America such masterpieces as the main New York Public Library on Fifth Avenue, sheathed this steel-frame structure in veneers of pale, smooth stone below the third story and in similar-hued brick above; the liver-colored sgraffito decorations around the upper floors' windows, and the building's main frieze, which incorporates images of American presidents, form an appropriately eye-catching crown for the landmark. The building became more eye-catching when Washington's first electric street light was placed at the corner of Pennsylvania Avenue and 15th Street in October 1881.

23 Metropolitan Square

613–627 15th Street, N.W.
1986 Skidmore, Owings & Merrill, with Vlastimil Koubek

While some of the old façades still stand, this mixed-use megabuilding now looks inward to focus on a marble-floored atrium and lion-studded fountain. The ambitious project incorporates some of the city's more notable Theodore

Roosevelt–era structures, including the National Metropolitan Bank Building (1905–1907, B. Stanley Simmons; and Gordon, Tracey and Swartout) and the Albee Building (1911–1912, Jules Henri de Sibour).

24 Julius Garfinckel and Company

14th and F Streets, N.W.

1930 Starrett and van Vleck

Now abandoned, in its prime this big downtown department store was filled, one likes to imagine, with thousands of matrons bedecked in white gloves and pearls and hats with veils and stockings with seams. For years Garfinckel's (and Woodward and Lothrop at 11th and F) valiantly battled both the suburban shopping centers and the hucksters who turned F Street's sidewalks into veritable Middle East bazaars, but in the end it proved too much for Garfinckel's clientele, and in 1990 the store went out of business. Myrna Loy would not be pleased.

25 National Place and National Press Building

E to F Streets and 13th to 14th Streets, N.W.

1984 Mitchell/Giurgola Architects; Frank Schlesinger Associates

Nearly 100 shops fill this rambling series of structures, where history oozes from every brick. The project incorporates the National Theater—which *was* big-time theater in Washington's pre–Kennedy Center days—and the 1927 building that housed the National Press Club, an institution Eric Severeid described as "the Westminster Hall, . . . Delphi, . . . Mecca, . . . Wailing Wall [for] everybody in this country having anything to do with the news business."

26 Baltimore *Sun* Building

1317 F Street, N.W.

1885–1887 Alfred B. Mullett
1983 Abel & Weinstein; Jeffrey Morris,
project architect

At the *Sun* building one observes Mullett
working on a small scale— "small," that
is, compared to his Executive Office
Building. Still, his enthusiasm for the act
of building comes through loud and clear
in the *Sun*'s five-story oriel windows,
arcaded first and second stories, lion's-head frieze, and rear wing with
convex, copper-covered mansard roof. Many Washingtonians proudly
assert that the nine-story structure, built to house the Washington bureau
of the Baltimore *Sun,* wins the prize as America's first skyscraper; as the
Post remarked when what it called the "exquisite tower" marked its 100th
birthday in 1987, "although New York and Chicago are normally associated with skyscrapers, the oldest example is in neither city but rather in
Washington."

27 Homer Building

601 13th Street, N.W.

1913–1914 Appleton P.
Clark, Jr.
1990 Shalom Baranes
Associates

This immense, 12-story beige
brick and glazed tile structure,
which stretches the entire block
of 13th Street between F and G, uses Clark's 4-story block front as a start-
ing point. Then it takes off—but only in scale, not in spirit, since Baranes
took pains to design something properly deferential to the older buildings. Indeed, Baranes's work here suggests William Lawrence Bottomley,
responsible for some of America's most elegant buildings in the 1920s and
'30s, who once remarked that he always tried to preserve the idiom of the
past but to design within it in a fresh, new way.

28 Church of the Epiphany

1317 G Street, N.W.

1843–1844 John Harkness
1857–1890 various remodelings
1920 addition

Stark white stucco without, this cruciform church is one of the city's crispest,
coolest exercises in Gothic revival. Inside
one finds conditions a bit cozier and, with
the elevated chancel and glorious organ,
the church regularly plays host to some of
Washington's more memorable lunchtime musical programs.

29 Colorado Building

1341 G Street, N.W.

1922 Ralph S. Townsend
1990 restoration: KressCox
Associates, PC

The decoration here forms a
veritable architectural garden—
with eagles and lions standing
guard. If that metaphor lacks
appeal, how about thinking of
the building as the work of a
Viennese pastry chef who slathered the ten-story yellow brick pile with
every conceivable form of contrasting stone trim? The thoroughly joyous
structure leaves one humming tunes from *The Mikado*— "a source of
innocent merriment, of innocent merriment." Inside also, the building
provides a wealth of visual treats, particularly in the lobby, where an intricately patterned marble floor competes for attention with a voluptuously
gilded ceiling.

    Thomas Walsh, the building's original owner, intended to use steel
framing to brace the structure, but the construction industry could not
provide enough steel for the job. Or, perhaps Walsh refused to grease the
right palms; a contemporary account in the *Architects and Builders Journal*
slyly notes that "it is claimed by some contractors that if they are willing to
pay what is considered a fancy price they can have their orders promptly

filled." *Plus ça change . . .* In any event, Walsh (who lived in what is now the Indonesian Embassy) made do with masonry bearing walls.

The whole great big, overblown, joyous mess has just undergone a painstaking restoration, and, in at least one respect, KressCox improved a bit on the original. While revamping the mechanical systems, workers uncovered a smallish hole that ran from the second story to the roof. A little investigation revealed that the hole was part of the building's early form of air conditioning, in which huge blocks of ice were hauled up to the roof and fans blew the cooled air down the chute and through the building via a complex system of ducts and holes. Cooling in the building is more up-to-date today.

On a more serious note, the building stands as a monument in the decades-long struggle for racial equality. Thompson's Restaurant, once located on the ground floor, maintained the District's usual whites only policy until a group of activists, led by 90-year-old Mary Church Terrell, brought suit in 1950; in 1953 the Supreme Court declared Washington's Jim Crow laws unconstitutional and ordered the restaurant to serve Ms. Terrell.

30 Riggs National Bank

1503 Pennsylvania Avenue, N.W.

1902 York & Sawyer

This and the adjoining American Security Bank visually combine their massive columns with those of the Treasury Building to give Washington's financial district a solid ambiance appropriate to the gray-flannel world of banking. It all brings to mind a famous passage in Louis Sullivan's *Kindergarten Chats* (1918): "How did the hard common-sense man come to think of a Roman temple [for a bank]? . . . Why, easy enough. His architect made a picture of what he thought was a Roman temple, and showed it to the banker, telling him on the side that Roman temples were rather the go now for banks, and the banker bit."

31 American Security and Trust Company

15th Street and Pennsylvania Avenue, N.W.

1905 York & Sawyer

"Above all he had an uneasy distrust of bankers," wrote Henry Adams of himself in *The Education of Henry Adams* (1904). This granite building must have made Adams, who lived nearby on Lafayette Square, particularly uneasy, since it could not house anything but bankers. It looks like a little granite cash box, where piles of money and mortgages sit, seemingly secure behind rusticated walls and iron bars.

32 Union Trust Building (First American Bank)

15th and H Streets, N.W.

1906 Wood, Donn & Deming
1983 renovation and expansion: Keyes Condon Florance Architects

When partnered with Edward Donn, Jr., and William I. Deming, Virginia-born Waddy Wood's pen traveled along opulent, neoclassic paths. (Wood on his own often behaved altogether differently—see the whimsical house he designed for Alice Pike Barney at 2306 Massachusetts Avenue.) The trio's partnership lasted from 1901 to 1912 and produced, in addition to this Corinthian bank, the Masonic Temple at New York Avenue and 13th Street. Here Wood used a simple visual trick to lighten the somewhat ponderous structure, and the dark metal walls and window frames make the walls seem to melt away, leaving only the colonnade.

33 Southern Building

805 15th Street, N.W.

1912 Daniel Burnham and
Associates
1988 restoration and
addition: Shalom Baranes
Associates

Careful alignment of cornices
and belt courses gives a continu-
ity to this structure, while pure *schlag* trim makes it a fitting neighbor to
the Colorado Building. Viewers should take care not to be misled by all
these confectionery allusions, for the Southern Building is solidly framed
in steel. Its winged massing—designed to give light and air—typifies plans
of large office and apartment buildings in turn of the 20th century Washington. Research has revealed that the building as constructed was two stories shorter than the building as designed—an oversight Baranes gently
corrected by adding two deferentially unornate levels to Burnham's exuberant creation.

34 Folger Building and Playhouse Theater

725–727 15th Street, N.W.

1906 Folger Building: Jules Henri de
Sibour; Playhouse Theater: Paul Pelz
1985 addition: Mariani & Associates

One wonders, as the world plods on
towards standardization, if there will ever
again be room for swashbuckling Folger
Buildings? Its huge Beaux-Arts mansard
roof makes a delightful and worthy com-

panion to several nearby coverings, such as those of the Renwick and Corcoran galleries and the Willard Hotel. The 1980s addition built over the
old theater entrance pays homage to de Sibour's work: its marble suggests
the Folger while the stepped back roofline defers to the Folger's proud
crown. Stockbroker and banker W. B. Hibbs hired de Sibour to design the
Folger; the architect must have been pleased with the results, for he moved
his own offices here in 1908.

35 Crestar Bank (National Savings and Trust Company)

15th Street and New York Avenue, N.W.

1888 James Windrim

Juxtaposed with its "banker's classic" neighbors just across 15th Street, this red brick and terra-cotta fantasy provides another welcome example of the strong crosscurrents that keep the architectural observer in Washington on his toes. The successful additions to the west face, progressively less and less elaborate but all well done, also bear study.

36 Bond Building

14th Street and New York Avenue, N.W.

1901 George S. Cooper
1986 addition and renovation: Shalom Baranes Associates

In renovating one of Washington's most vigorous façades, with bricks laid in an amazing variety of angles and arches, Baranes felt little need to add to the old structure, so he simply retained most of the old office space and gently spruced up the exterior walls. But he did add a few touches of his own, most notably, two tall "book end" sections, some three-level infill, and a ground-story, marbled rotunda lobby that houses what must be the District's definitive column collection. In all, as the magazine *Architecture* observed, Baranes turned the Bond Building into an endearing "friendly-looking hodgepodge."

37 Inter-American Development Bank

1300 New York Avenue, N.W.

1985 Skidmore, Owings & Merrill

Robert Mills's Treasury Building continues to repercuss a century and a half after its completion. Note how Skidmore, Owings and Merrill bent this façade just enough to allow a view down New York Avenue to Mills's masterpiece. They embellished the new bank with a rhythmic series of columns, which in dual fashion provide further allusions to the Treasury Building and relieve the bank's undeniably imposing façade from austerity.

38 New York Avenue Presbyterian Church

1313 New York Avenue, N.W.

1950 Delos H. Smith

This may be the most withdrawn, stand-offish church in town. Well, how else could one describe a temple whose main level is placed a story above the sidewalk? The present restrained brick structure, a replacement and slightly larger version of an earlier church, became necessary when two once-separate congregations merged.

39 National Museum of Women in the Arts (Masonic Temple)

New York Avenue and 13th Street, N.W.

1907–1908 Wood, Donn & Deming; Waddy B. Wood, architect in charge
1987 renovations: Keyes Condon Florance Architects

10:00 A.M. TO 5:00 P.M. DAILY,
NOON TO 5:00 P.M. SUNDAY
PHONE: 783-5000

Waddy Wood's restrained limestone and granite trapezoid has, during its 90-year history, managed to fill the needs of two seemingly divergent groups—masons and devotees of women's history. To take the groups in chronological order, the masons originally housed themselves in a temple at 9th and F Streets, but when their growing numbers rendered that building inadequate, they hired Wood to design this much-larger structure. They were happy in their new temple, its exterior embellished with stone callipers and other Masonic motifs, until it, too, became too small and had to be abandoned.

The building then faced an uncertain future until far-sighted officials from the National Museum of Women in the Arts saw it and recognized its potential. Founded in 1981 through the largesse of Wilhelmina and Wallace Holladay, the museum required several distinct areas: public spaces for galleries, quiet spaces for a library and offices, and, since the new organization was short of cash, a few large rentable spaces. Thanks to the renovation architects' careful modifications, the old temple now meets all those needs perfectly.

---

40 1100 New York Avenue (Old Greyhound Bus Station)

1939–1940 William S. Arrasmith
1991 Florance Eichbaum Esocoff King Architects

A *bus* station? Yes, near the heart of trendy Washington, Manulife Real Estate chose to build this half-million-square-foot office structure around the old Greyhound station. They could have done far worse. The station's sleek exterior has long been valued as one of the city's more important art deco monuments. The architects created a series of small-scale forms, carefully massed so as not to overwhelm the 1930s jewel; they also used pale gray granite and limestone and panels of fluted aluminum to cover most of the new façades, and the varied materials create wise-cracking dialogue worthy of *It Happened One Night*.

41 Washington Convention Center

900 9th Street, N.W.

1983 Welton Becket

It is probably better to regard this 9.7-acre monster as a city planning tool than as an individual piece of architecture, for the center's four exhibition halls and forty meeting rooms are intended to draw free-spending convention-eers into a neighborhood that had been a bit, uhh, down-and-out. On those terms, the project must be rated an enormous success, a judgment supported by the sky-rocketing prices of nearby real estate.

42 Central Library

Mount Vernon Square (8th and K Streets, N.W.)

1902 Ackerman & Ross

The Beaux-Arts smugness of the old library's New York Avenue main entrance overpowers many viewers. But all that is necessary for relief is a quick walk around to the north façade, where the functional demands of the library within break through all the marble. Suddenly and surprisingly one sees a sight that might be called proto-deco: the book stacks within required lighting, and the light-holes took the form of a bold series of rhythmic slots. Now a part of the University of the District of Columbia, the building, one of scores throughout the nation donated by Andrew Carnegie, served as the District's main public library from 1902 until the late 1960s.

43 Franklin Square

13th to 14th and I to K
Streets, N.W.

Quiet for a century, the Franklin
Square area now bustles, as one
fine building project succeeds
another. Some represent new
construction; some are restora-
tions; all are admirable. The
square is dominated by the Franklin School, completed in 1868 to the
design of Adolph Cluss. A model of advanced design in its day, and the
scene of Alexander Graham Bell's first wireless message, the Franklin
School won design honors both abroad and at home. Cluss noted in 1870,
"What forms the main notable feature in this school building is that the
huge ventilating flues, which generally form unseemly protuberances, have
been grouped symmetrically on the four corners and shaped so as to form
the most prominent part of the decoration." He also observed that he had
avoided "monotony" in the three-story structure "by the little interrup-
tions of alternating the mass of red bricks by courses of stones of the warm,
light complementary color." Oehrlein and Associates has recently restored
the highly important school, joining it to a splendid new office structure by
Hartman-Cox. Oehrlein has been involved in another commendable
restoration—simply turn to see and admire the Almas Temple project.
Finally, Johnson Burgee's new office structure at 1300 I street should be
pointed out, in case there is anyone who might miss it. So, while much that
was good in the neighborhood has come down (Frances Hodgson Burnett,
author of *Little Lord Fauntleroy,* lived in a house, since demolished, at 1219
I Street, and the fabulous 1926 Capital Garage stood at 1312–1320 New
York Avenue), many admirable structures remain and many more are
being added.

Midtown

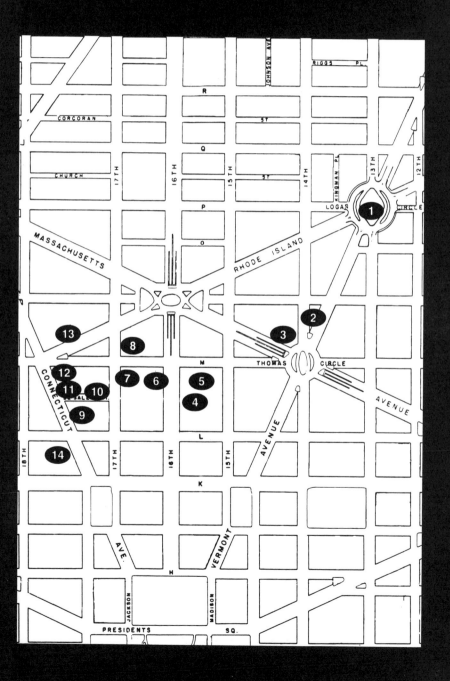

Connecticut Avenue, one of Washington's grand thoroughfares and the core of this tour, promenades through the city from Lafayette Square to Chevy Chase, Maryland. Midtown, once a fashionable residential area, is now primarily a center of mega-institutions such as the National Geographic Society, venerable churches such as St. Matthew's Cathedral, and new office buildings such as Hartman-Cox's Sumner School project. A few houses have managed to endure, prevailing over skyrocketing property values, but of this brave band nearly all have been put to official use, in the manner of the Russian Embassy, which occupies the old Pullman mansion. The neighborhood's shops and hotels, traditionally among the finest in the city, suffered some stormy times when the city's subway system was under construction, but, partially because of their innate chic and partially because of their enviable locations, most have rebounded and now strut with as much swank as they ever did.

Connecticut Avenue and the Mayflower Hotel c. 1920. J. Edgar Hoover regularly dined within while streetcars jangled without.

1   Logan Circle

1875–1900   various architects

Proof that neglect is often the handmaiden of preservation, this eight-block enclave presents scores of virtually unchanged Victorian and Richardsonian town houses. Nearly all were built during a 25-year period from c. 1875 to c. 1900 to house the District's powerful and wealthy, such as John A. Logan, prominent Civil War general and, later, senator from Illinois, who lived at 812 12th Street. Logan originated the idea of Memorial Day. The government named this circle for him in 1930 notwithstanding his efforts to have the national capital moved to St. Louis. (Perhaps as vengeance, city officials allowed his house to be destroyed for a parking lot.) In the early 20th century, Washington's fickle society folk abandoned the neighborhood for Dupont Circle, and Logan Circle entered a deep sleep. But it proved a healthy, time-defying snooze; recently roused by developers, the façades look exactly as they did a century ago.

2   Luther Place Memorial Church

1226 Vermont Avenue, N.W. (Thomas Circle)

1870   Judson York
1952   addition: L. M. Leisenring

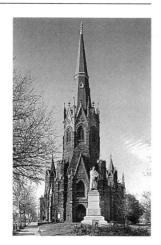

Built as a gesture of thanksgiving for the end of the Civil War, this red sandstone, neo-Gothic church contrasts sharply with the neoclassical National City Christian Church across the circle. The result is somewhat like a family reunion, with dotty great-aunts jostling each other to grab the young folks' attention.

3 National City Christian Church

14th Street and Massachusetts Avenue, N.W. (Thomas Circle)

1930 John Russell Pope
1952 addition: Leon Chatelain, Jr.

Christopher Wren, James Gibbs, and just about every American colonial church you've ever seen are all invoked here—but at a larger-than-life scale. (Just compare Pope's bell tower with the one at St. John's in Georgetown.) Pope placed his new building on a small mound, to ensure that it completely dominated the then-genteel circle.

4 Russian Embassy (Pullman House)

1119–1125 16th Street, N.W.

1910 Wyeth and Sullivan
1933 adaptation to embassy use: Eugene Schoen

The architects of this fine, Beaux-Arts mansion seem to have had two things on their minds: first, to make certain passers-by noticed the house's huge mansard roof and second, to emphasize, through pediments and columns, the house's locally rare *piano nobile* organization. They succeeded in both. Mrs. George Pullman, wife of the inventor of the sleeping car, built this splendid *petit palais*. Mrs. Pullman, one of the horde of midwestern tycoons to flock to town during Washington's giddy *Belle Époque,* purportedly never actually lived in her grand house but sold it shortly after its completion to the czarist government. It has filled its embassy role splendidly ever since.

5 Metropolitan A.M.E. Church

1518 M Street, N.W.

1886 Samuel G. T. Morsell

9:30 A.M. TO 3:30 P.M. WEEKDAYS

Architecturally significant as a superior
example of red-brick Gothic revival,
this granite-trimmed church, sometimes called the National Cathedral
of African Methodism, also played an
important role in the American civil
rights movement; for that matter, as the building's landmark plaque notes,
the entire site "possesses exceptional value in commemorating the Religious Life of the Negro in the United States of America." Organized in
1822 as the Union Bethel A.M.E. Church, its worshipers formed the
largest 19th-century black congregation in the country.

6 Hubbard Memorial Library

1146 16th Street, N.W.

1902 Hornblower and
Marshall

Somehow this granite and pale
brick structure seems more
inviting than do many other repositories of books. Perhaps it is the sweeping entrance stairway that creates this impression of welcome.

7 National Geographic Society Headquarters

17th and M Streets, N.W.

1902 Hornblower & Marshall
1964 Edward Durrell Stone
1984 Skidmore, Owings &
Merrill
1987 renovation of 1902

building: Keyes Condon Florance Architects

9:00 A.M. TO 5:00 P.M. MONDAY THROUGH SATURDAY,
10:00 A.M. TO 5:00 P.M. SUNDAY   PHONE: 857-7700

To walk around in this labyrinth is to undergo a virtual crash course in the history of 20th-century American architecture, from the curvaceous Beaux-Arts lines of the original building to the angular modernism of Skidmore, Owings and Merrill's M Street ziggurat. Of all the specimens, it is, of course, Stone's ten-story tower that makes the dominant impression. Or, rather, impressions: on one hand its lid roof, recessed top floors, and close fence of vertical shafts make it a descendant of Frank Lloyd Wright's Press Building in San Francisco, while at the same time its marbled dignity aligns it with Washington's neoclassic officialdom. In other words, it is, as Ada Louise Huxtable observed, "a commendable exercise in appropriate architectural footwork."

8 Sumner School

17th and M Streets, N.W.

1871–1872 Adolph Cluss
1986 restoration and additions: Hartman-Cox Architects; Navy, Marshall, Gordon, with RTKL Associates Inc., associated architects

Sumner, its whimsical clock tower restored and ticking, is a double landmark: it is an important survivor of the city's more advanced 19th-century school architecture, and it forms a showcase of 20th-century restoration techniques. Somewhat unusual among his peers, architect Cluss believed that how a building *worked* was as important as how it looked. At his schools, for instance, he innovatively used hallways and closets to isolate classrooms and minimize external noise. His work at Sumner won the "Medal for Progress" in school design at the Vienna World's Exposition of 1873. Yet, as serious as all that sounds, many of Sumner's decorative details, such as the tower, the tiny dormers with their spiky finials, the delicate cast-iron roof crown, and the superb Romanesque arched windows that face 17th Street, suggest that Cluss was not averse to an occasional bit of fun.

The school, named for abolitionist Charles Sumner, was a center of black education during the scores of years when Washington's schools were segregated. Ironically, with integration came neglect, and Sumner School sat, largely ignored and rapidly decaying, until Hartman-Cox, working with the District's Board of Education, restored it. They also added a nine-story office tower to the rear of the lot; in addition to helping pay for the restoration of the old school, the new building, with its gray curtain wall, acts as a suitably unobtrusive backdrop to Sumner and its neighbors, the Magruder School (also from the 1870s) and the Jefferson Hotel (1923, Jules Henri de Sibour).

9 Mayflower Hotel

1127 Connecticut Avenue, N.W.

1924 Warren & Wetmore; Robert S. Beresford

Built in the American hotel style of the twenties with French appliqué, the Mayflower is exactly what a bouncy, big-city, luxury hotel ought to be. When it first opened its doors to an awed public— just in time to house Calvin Coolidge's inaugural ball—the Mayflower is said to have boasted more gold leaf than any other building in the country except the Library of Congress. Recently spruced up and dusted off, the rambling lobbies and hallways are just plain fun, with their Aubusson carpets, Chippendale chairs, mirrored columns, and piped-in Strauss waltzes—but then what would one expect from a hotel with a clientele that included FDR, Huey Long, J. Edgar Hoover (who had his dinner here virtually every evening), a nest of Nazi spies (who surrendered to the federal government in room 351), and Gene Autrey, who once galloped around the main banquet room mounted on Champion.

10 ABC News Washington Bureau

1717 DeSales Street, N.W.

1981 Kohn Pedersen Fox Associates, PC

Gazing at this interesting transitional building causes one to wonder if it is Washington's last modernist structure or one of the first postmodern ones. Whichever, its cool metal and blue-glass bands are quiet and restrained. While that seems to belie the newsroom frenzy within, the ground-story columns do manage to create an appropriate bit of architectural tension.

11 1133 Connecticut Avenue, N.W.
1987–1988 David M. Schwarz;
Vlastimil Koubek, associated architect

Among the most deferential of the city's
newer structures, this strapping young
building relates to its dowager neighbor,
the Mayflower, much as a debutante's
escort might to the young lady's grand-
mother. Schwarz accomplished this trick
by retaining time-tested motifs and massing but executing them with a
fresh, new twist: for instance, the building's conventional three-part
façade is traditional at the base (two pilastered limestone stories) and attic
(also two stories) but gains a little fillip in the center shaft, a highly contemporary, seven-story curtain wall. It is a bit like a young man in flawless
formal attire—with a pony tail.

12 Demonet Building
M Street at Connecticut Avenue, N.W.

1880 John Sherman, owner-builder
1901 Totten and Rogers
1984 addition and renovation:
Skidmore, Owings & Merrill

God may or may not always be "in the
details," but most people would agree that
God was certainly hanging around when
Skidmore, Owings and Merrill's architects designed this nine-story enveloping
addition, for everything in the new structure works to flatter Sherman's 3
1/2-story, corner-lot dwelling. If pressed to single out one feature for special praise, one might mention the new tower's attic corbels, clearly created
to echo those on Sherman's town house.

13 St. Matthew's Cathedral

1725 Rhode Island Avenue, N.W.

1889 Heins and LaFarge

A study in contrasts: does one concentrate on the frankly delicious interiors, with their pastoral mosaics and flamboyantly gilded Corinthian capitals, or on the clear geometry and plain brick surfaces of the exterior?

14 Washington Square

1050 Connecticut Avenue, N.W.

1982 Chloethiel Woodard Smith & Associates

The crisp, cool lines and clearly articulated massing of Smith's work here is so good, so true to itself, so unabashedly modern, that it ought to make the architects of certain of its more frivolous neighbors blush.

White House/
Lafayette Square

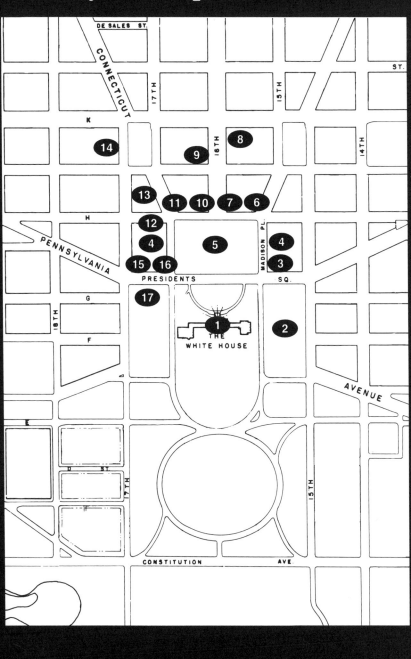

According to Henry Adams, who lived on Lafayette Square longer than anyone has, "Beyond the square, the country began." Adams also wrote that when he moved to the capital city, "no literary or scientific man, no artist, no gentleman without office or employment, had ever lived there. It was rural and its society was primitive. . . . The happy village was innocent of a club. . . . The value of real estate had not increased since 1800, and the pavements were more impassable than the mud. All this favored a young man who had come to make a name."

When L'Enfant selected the site for the President's House and next to it what he called the "President's Park," a flourishing orchard filled the acreage. Construction on the Executive Mansion began in 1792, and President and Mrs. John Adams (Henry's great-grandparents) moved in to the semihabitable dwelling in November 1800. Jefferson, who succeeded Adams in March 1801, wrote, "we find this a very agreeable country residence . . . free from the noise, the heat, . . . and the bustle of a close-built town," which suggests just how urban Washington was in 1801!

The White House, sporting its new north and south porticos, and Blair House and the Treasury Building are all more or less recognizable in this c. 1850 drawing of Lafayette Square. But there's no Jackson statue; Madison and Jackson places are but spottily occupied; and Mullett's new State, War, and Navy Building (which later became the Executive Office Building) hadn't yet replaced the E-plan headquarters of the War and Navy Departments, designed to make an appropriate neoclassical bookend to the Treasury Building.

Jefferson, an inveterate gardener, also redesigned the President's Park; L'Enfant had hoped that the grassy sward could serve as an extension of the White House grounds, but the democratic Jefferson felt that he did not really need a seven-acre lawn, so he had Pennsylvania Avenue laid out so as to divide the grassy space in two, creating Lafayette Square. The new park, named in 1824 to honor the visiting Lafayette, has served in a variety of egalitarian ways ever since. Soldiers bivouacked in the park during the Civil War; in 1829, when Andrew Jackson won election over Henry Adams's grandfather, he held boisterous inauguration festivities in the square and brought in opened kegs of whiskey to delight his coonskin-capped constituents; in the 1870s Ulysses S. Grant started a small zoo here and presented to it his favorite pet prairie dogs. (Their stench caused their immediate removal.) Andrew Jackson Downing had drawn up plans for landscaping the park as early as 1851, but planting was not completed until the turn of this century. The fountains and brick walk date to 1970; the protective barricades between park and White House are a product of the nervous '80s.

With the White House for a focal point, lots around the square soon became the favored location for court residences. Decatur House and the Cutts-Madison House began the trend around 1818; H. H. Richardson's houses for Henry Adams and John Hay (now the site of the Hay-Adams Hotel), built in 1885, ended it. By the Adams/Hay era, fashions had changed; "the country" no longer began at Lafayette Square, and Massachusetts Avenue, Kalorama, and other elegant purlieus had become the residential areas of choice.

---

1   The White House

1600 Pennsylvania Avenue, N.W.

1792 James Hoban, Benjamin Henry Latrobe, and others
1902 McKim, Mead & White
1948 Lorenzo Winslow

10:00 A.M. TO NOON, TUESDAY THROUGH SATURDAY   PHONE: 456-7041

With the federal city a reality—at least on paper—President Washington and Secretary of State Jefferson organized design competitions for the new nation's two most important buildings, the Capitol and the President's House. Jefferson entered—and lost—both competitions, under a gentle-

Amateur architect James Hoban used an Anglo-Irish villa as the inspiration for this 1792 design for the President's House, a building Thomas Jefferson dismissed as "big enough for two emperors, one Pope, and the grand Lama."

manly pseudonym. In July 1792 the judges awarded James Hoban, an Irish architect practicing in Charleston, South Carolina, the commission for the President's House; they also presented him with a gold medal and with the deed to a city lot.

Hoban apparently drew inspiration for his somewhat conservative design from Leinster House, Dublin, and from other English and Irish country houses shown in James Gibbs's *Book of Architecture* (1728). Construction began in the fall of 1792, but the building's Virginia sandstone walls were still unfinished when the government moved to the District from Philadelphia in November 1800. President and Mrs. John Adams were the first to take possession of the house—which Abigail Adams felt a rather hollow honor. She wrote her daughter complaining: "There is not a single apartment finished. . . . We had not the least fence, yard, or other convenience, without, and the great unfinished audience-room [the East Room] I make a drying room of, to hang up the clothes in." Mrs. Adams, rock-ribbed Yankee to her bones, also used the building's incomplete state as a chance to take a shot at the slow pace of southern workmen: "If the twelve years, in which this place has been considered as the future seat of government, had been improved as they would have been if in New England, very many of the present inconveniences would have been improved."

Thomas Jefferson displaced the grumbling Adamses in 1801, but the Virginian wasn't overly enamored of the building, either. Or perhaps it merely rubbed his democratic principles the wrong way, for he groused that it was "big enough for two emperors, one Pope, and the grand Lama." (The Irish journalist Isaac Weld agreed and in his *Travels through North America* [1799] dismissed the "ridiculous" building as "too large and too splendid for the residence of any one person in a republican country.") A diligent amateur architect, Jefferson designed low terrace-pavilions for either side of the main building, thinking they would soften the structure's grandiloquent impression. He worked in association with his favorite professional architect, Latrobe, on these and other projects, and the latter's correspondence suggests that it was not an altogether happy collaboration. The president's well-meaning daubs began to grate on Latrobe, who wrote his clerk in 1805, "a post or two will bring you the President's colonnade. I am sorry I am cramped in this design by his prejudices in favor of French books, out of which he fishes everything—but it is a small sacrifice to my personal attachment to him to humor him and the less so, because the style of the colonnade he proposes is exactly consistent with Hoban's pile—a litter of pigs worthy of the great sow it surrounds." Jefferson also removed the house's leaky slate roof and replaced it with one of sheet iron.

Jefferson's eight years in the Executive Mansion allowed him ample time to indulge in another favorite avocation, landscaping. He built on the grounds a pair of earthen mounds (all the rage at the time), laid out tree-lined axes from the house, planted formal flower beds south towards the Mall, built a circular carriage drive to service the mansion's north entrance, and encircled it all with a folksy post-and-rail fence. Fashions change, and in 1849 Andrew Jackson Downing drew up plans to relandscape the grounds, and the gardens' present appearance owes much to his thinking, although virtually every chief executive has added a tree, a bush, or a shrub of his own (the official *White House Guidebook* explains which presidents planted which trees).

Torched by the British in August 1814, the White House was saved from total destruction by a violent thunderstorm, which quenched the flames. After the fire, James and Dolley Madison borrowed the Tayloe family's town house, the Octagon, and brought in Hoban to oversee the Executive Mansion's restoration. Incidentally, the building was first painted white at this time, to cover charring from the fire; it is not known who first used the term *White House*, but when Theodore Roosevelt made the name official in 1901 he was merely giving formal sanction to long-standing common usage.

Hoban was still lingering on the scene in 1824 when President Monroe hired him to add the semicircular South Portico, a Latrobe/Jefferson pastiche. Five years later, in 1829, Hoban built the North Portico, again following Latrobe's Jefferson-sanctioned plans. Technological advances brought mechanical changes to the mansion throughout the 19th century, most notably gas lighting (1848), city water (1853), bathrooms (c. 1878), and electricity (c. 1890).

With the 20th century came several schemes to expand and alter the

White House. All of them were sluffed aside, more or less politely, until 1902, when Theodore Roosevelt discovered that the mansion was unsafe for habitation. TR moved his boisterous family into a house across Lafayette Square and brought in the leading architects of the day, McKim, Mead and White, to remodel the original building, remove a run of Victorian conservatories, and add the East Gallery and Executive Office wing.

All remained quiet for 40 years. Then investigations during Harry Truman's administration revealed that the White House was again structurally unsound—*thoroughly* unsound. Although the exterior walls, which were, in Truman's memorable phrase, "standing up purely from habit," were salvageable, nothing else was, and the entire building had to be gutted. Steel replaced the crumbling stone framing and the original paneling, trim, and decorations were removed, repaired, and reinstalled. And, of course, Truman added his famous balcony to the South Portico—a nice, American touch to the grand Lama's palace.

---

2 Treasury Building

1500 Pennsylvania Avenue, N.W.

1836 Robert Mills
1855–1864 Thomas U. Walter
1855–1860 Ammi B. Young
1865–1869 Alfred B. Mullett

TOURS ALTERNATE SATURDAY MORNINGS AT 10:00, 10:20, AND 10:40   (RESERVATIONS REQUIRED) PHONE: 622-2000

President Andrew Jackson did the site planning for this, the oldest of the government's departmental buildings: he stated, "Build it here!" and thus in one stroke obliterated L'Enfant's magnificent "reciprocity of view" down Pennsylvania Avenue from the White House to the Capitol. With a bulk that covers five acres, Treasury stands as the largest Greek revival structure in the world, the fitting symbol of our bloated federal financial system.

But it hasn't always been thus; indeed, in its original state, the building ranked as one of the new republic's few genuine architectural masterpieces, with an Ionic colonnade (made up of 30 36-foot-tall monoliths) so powerful it set the tone for the District's entire financial neighborhood. Work on what has been called a "temple to the deified dollar" stretched out over a generation. It began in the 1830s with Jackson's favored architect, Robert Mills. Born in Charleston, South Carolina, in 1781, Mills arrived in the capital city in 1830. The first American-born professional architect, Mills relied on his own considerable imagination and talent for his designs; he had no use for the bookish amateurism that had previously dominated high-style American building, and once wrote that "books are useful to the student, but when he enters upon the practice of his profession he should lay them aside, and only consult them upon doubtful points or in matters of detail, or as mere studies, not to copy buildings from."

Mills designed three buildings for the federal government, this, the Patent Office, and the original post office. All are masterpieces of up-to-the-minute technology, but Treasury stands as his crowning achievement. William Pierson, one of the country's leading architectural historians, has suggested that, except for Latrobe's 1804 Baltimore Cathedral, "no other building in America at that time was conceived and executed with such an overriding integration of structure and form" as the Treasury Building. In somewhat typical Washington fashion, Mills was dismissed from this job, in 1851, the victim of political squabbling, and a series of other architects eventually completed the immense structure.

---

3 Treasury Annex

Madison Place and
Pennsylvania Avenue, N.W.

1919 Cass Gilbert

The promulgators of the 1902 McMillan Plan called for a series of neoclassical palaces to surround Madison Place and pay stylistic homage to Mills's Treasury Building. That recommendation was not altogether followed, but a trio of columned structures did pop up. This, the middle one chronologically, may be the best architecturally; the other two are the Chamber of Commerce Building, also by Gilbert, and the Veterans Administration Building (1918, James A. Wetmore). The profusion of columns—these and the ones that brace the façades of the Riggs and American Security banks to the east—indicate just how powerfully Mills's Ionic temple influenced design in the capital's financial enclave.

4 Lafayette Square Reconstruction: West— New Executive Office Building; East—U.S. Court of Claims

H Street, Madison Place, and Jackson Place, N.W.

1968 John Carl Warnecke & Associates

Lafayette Square, the pride of 19th-century Washington, lost several of its greatest treasures to 20th-century wrecking balls. A scheme to raze row houses on the square surfaced in 1961, but President Kennedy, attentive to architectural beauty and integrity, asked architect Warnecke to devise a plan that would both save what remained of the square and make economic sense. In Warnecke's solution—high towers placed in the center of a block and framed by the older row houses—the tall buildings are perhaps more dominant than one might wish, but Lafayette Square was saved.

This approach has obvious applications elsewhere and has spawned a thousand imitators from Boston to San Francisco, but that doesn't mean it is easy to do. Just see the disaster that fills the 2000 block of I Street, where a looming glass bulk reduces the "saved" older buildings to a joke, a mere Hollywood stage set. At Lafayette Square, however, architect and contractor took pains to ensure that everything worked, down to details such as painting the new masonry and mortar red to match the older houses' brick.

5 Jackson Statue

Lafayette Square

1853 Clark Mills

Cannon captured by Andrew Jackson in the War of 1812 supplied the bronze for this, the first equestrian statue designed by an American and cast in America. Sculptor Mills, a stickler for authenticity, trained a horse to remain in a rearing position so he could study how the animal balanced its great weight. He then created the Jackson statue, a remarkable fusion of artistic merit and engineering prowess. Jackson's *joie de vivre* emanates from every square inch of the piece, which impressed even Henry James. The expatriate novelist recorded his thoughts about his native country in *The American Scene*; he liked Lafayette Square generally because of its "rich sense of the past," but he saved special praise for this statue, "the most prodigious of all Presidential effigies, Andrew Jackson, as archaic as a Ninevite king, prancing and rocking through the ages."

6 St. John's Parish Building (Old British Embassy)

1525 H Street, N.W.

1836 Mathew St. Clair Clark, owner-builder

1853 and c. 1870 remodelings: architects unknown

Also called Ashburton House, in honor of Lord Alexander Ashburton, a mid-19th-century British minister to America, this building has seen a number of distinguished personages come and go, each of whom, it seems, felt the urge to make modifications to the original brick dwelling. Mathew Clark, clerk of the House of Representatives, began the building in 1836; he soon went bankrupt and sold the house to the British government. Ashburton took up residence in 1842, and he and Daniel Webster negotiated the Webster-Ashburton Treaty in the house's parlor. (The treaty settled the burning issue of the Maine–New Brunswick boundary.) Ashburton and his ministerial successor, novelist Edward Bulwer-Lytton, made minor alterations to Clark's design. The house received its final remodeling, the present dashing Second Empire shell, in the 1870s.

7 St. John's Church

16th and H Streets, N.W.

1815 Benjamin Henry Latrobe
1881–1890 James Renwick
1919 McKim, Mead & White

PHONE: 347-8766

Latrobe designed a Greek cross plan for this building, "the church of the presi-

Latrobe's 1816 sketch of St. John's Church shows the building's pure Greek-cross massing; it also shows that the White House still bore wounds from the War of 1812 (note the collapsed wall).

dents," and intended thereby to show how classical forms might be modified to fit the needs of Protestant worship. His intentions have been obliterated on the exterior, hidden beneath an extended nave, a portico, and a steeple. One can, however, sense the original plan within if one sits in a pew beneath the saucered dome's lantern. The church served the District's second Episcopal parish. (The first was housed in Christ Church on Capitol Hill.) Latrobe, who had been in Pittsburgh, returned to the capital in June 1815; he met with members of the St. John's vestry, made some sketches, and posted an ad in the July 22, 1815, edition of the *National Intelligencer* newspaper calling for bids from all "mechanics" who wished to work "agreeably" on the building, "to the plan and specifications, which will be shown by B. Henry Latrobe, Esq. the Architect, at his office at the Capital." The cornerstone was laid September 14 and work was completed the following June.

The results much pleased Latrobe, a not uncommon sensation for an architect, but few architects would—or could—do what he did, namely write a hymn of praise to the structure and then play the tune on the organ at the celebratory opening.

Every president since Madison has attended services at St. John's, and Latrobe wrote his son, Henry, "I have just completed a church that made many Washingtonians religious who have not been religious before." By tradition, pew 54 is set aside for the current chief executive and family.

8 Sheraton-Carlton Hotel

16th and K Streets, N.W.

1926 Mihran Mesrobian

One of the undisputed grand hotels in the city, this elegant structure earns particularly high marks for its hushed public spaces. Although the eight-story building presents a rather austere front to 16th Street, its baroque third- and seventh-story windows and its porte-cochere add a sparkle of humor that saves it from sinking to the level of a grand dame caricature.

For an equally successful mix of styles and moods, turn around and gaze at the quite wonderful Moreschi Building (1599 I Street; Eggers and Higgins), which may be the only office structure in the world that combines Stalinist massing and gilded rococo trim.

9 Third Church of Christ, Scientist, and the Christian Science Monitor Building

910 16th Street, N.W.

1970 I. M. Pei & Partners

SERVICES WITH TOURS AFTERWARD: NOON AND 8:00 P.M. WEDNESDAY, 11:00 A.M. AND 5:00 P.M. SUNDAY

Perhaps best thought of as an octagonal sculpture at architectural scale, this is one of a number of complexes Pei has designed for the Christian Science church throughout the nation. Although the plaza on 16th Street has been criticized as unnecessary, the tension created among tower, wall, and octagon make this perhaps the most satisfying of Washington's many similar groupings.

The church is a model of workmanship, too, and the team that sculpted Pei's simple forms in exposed, textured concrete single-handedly voided the often-heard complaint that skillful craftsmen are a vanished breed.

10 Hay-Adams Hotel

800 16th Street, N.W.

1926–1927 Mihran
Mesrobian

Who can quarrel with this
proper and dignified building?
The hotel replaced the adjoining houses H. H. Richardson
designed for John Hay and
Henry Adams in 1885. It's too bad the houses are gone, but certainly the
hotel respects their *gravitas*. (Actually—and it isn't widely known—bits of
Adams's 1885 house have endured, for some canny scavenger hauled away
two of its Romanesque arched openings and incorporated them into a
house at 2618 30th Street, N.W.)

11 Chamber of Commerce Building

1615 H Street, N.W.

1925 Cass Gilbert

The history of this building
reflects the vagaries of taste.
This and the Treasury Annex
are the only completed portions
of a plan to unify the architec-
ture of Lafayette Square in the be-columned manner of the older Treasury
Building. The plan was made, two buildings were built, and the plan was
then quietly scrapped. This particular structure, polite and dignified,
replaced a brace of houses owned by men of more than passing interest:
Daniel Webster lived at the corner of H Street and Connecticut Avenue,
and the adjacent house was home to John Slidell, antebellum congressman
from Louisiana, Confederate minister to France, and one half of the
Mason-Slidell controversy, which nearly brought the British Empire into
the Civil War on the side of the South.

12 Decatur House

748 Jackson Place, N.W.

1818 Benjamin Henry Latrobe

10:00 A.M. TO 3:00 P.M. TUESDAY
THROUGH FRIDAY, NOON TO 4:00 P.M.
WEEKENDS   PHONE: 842-0920

Latrobe gave Commodore Stephen
Decatur, scourge of the Barbary Pirates, a
house that 20th-century architects admire
for the harmonic proportions of its interi-
ors and for the elegant restraint of its façades. Actually, if one seeks
Latrobe's memorial, just look around Lafayette Square, for Decatur
House, the White House, and St. John's Church form a compact mini-
museum of his work. Ironically, within a year of completion of this superb
house, Latrobe died of yellow fever and Decatur was killed in a duel.

The house then endured an aimless series of owners, residents, and
uses: several British, French, and Russian diplomats lived in the place, as
did Henry Clay, Martin van Buren, and the Confederate financier and secretary of state, Judah P. Benjamin. Western explorer Edward Fitzgerald
Beale and his wife, Mary, bought the house in 1872. (It was Beale, then
based near San Francisco, who in 1848 galloped east to announce that gold
had been discovered at Sutter's Mill.) The Beales left the house to their
son, Truxton, whose widow, Marie, bequeathed it to the National Trust
for Historic Preservation in 1956. The Trust maintains the property as a
distillation of two eras: the ground story is pure federal-Decatur while the
upstairs is boisterously Victorian-Beale.

13 816 Connecticut Avenue, N.W.

1987 Shalom Baranes Associates

Art deco is alive and well in Washington! Indeed,
one can, of an evening, squint at this slender,
elegant building, its surface all sleekly polished,
and see Gertrude Lawrence slink onto the scene
in a shimmering white Molyneux gown. Strange
how potent cheap imagery is.

14 Barr Building

910 17th Street, N.W.

1930 Stanley Simmons

Clearly expressed window modules and
structural bays should have been enough,
yet Simmons added flourishes of gray
neo-Gothic ornament to the Barr Building's façade, and the additions do little but
blur the otherwise crisp organization.

15 Renwick Gallery (Old Corcoran Gallery and U.S. Court of Claims)

17th Street and Pennsylvania
Avenue, N.W.

1859 James Renwick
1967–1971 exterior restoration: John Carl Warnecke
& Associates; interior
restoration and remodeling: Hugh Newell Jacobsen

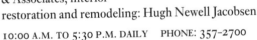

10:00 A.M. TO 5:30 P.M. DAILY   PHONE: 357-2700

Renwick designed this wonderful creation to house the art collection
amassed by William Wilson Corcoran (1798–1888), financier and
cofounder of the Riggs Bank. The architect clearly enjoyed the commission. Following Latrobe's lead at the Capitol he Americanized classical
Corinthian capitals by turning acanthus leaves into corncobs; his sandstone pilasters, too, are a joy to behold, as are the niches with their busts of
Utrillo and Rubens. Renwick affixed these delights to one of America's
earliest Second Empire shells, designed to be seen from only two sides.

Notwithstanding the building's manifold success, Corcoran had some
trouble settling in to it. Just as his gallery neared completion, the Civil War
broke out, the government borrowed the structure, and Corcoran, a Confederate sympathizer, found it desirable to wait out the war in Europe. He
returned to America in 1869, retook possession of the building, and
opened it as a gallery—the District's first—in 1870, the same year the
Metropolitan Museum of Art opened in New York. Renwick's splendid
creation eventually became too small for Corcoran's ever-growing collection, which included the then-shocking nude statue "The Greek Slave."

The larger Corcoran Gallery, on 17th Street, was constructed following the financier's death.

After a regrettable interval when the building was altered to house the court of claims, the gallery's interiors, once again plushy and be-palmed, have been returned to their original function. Hugh Newell Jacobsen, who oversaw the meticulous restoration, said of Renwick and the gallery, "The guy was awfully good. He picks you up on the street, takes you into the building, there's that roll of drums on the stairs, and then you're up there—in the great space." Enjoy the trip.

16 Blair House and Lee House

1651–1653 Pennsylvania Avenue, N.W.

1824 Blair House: architect unknown
c. 1860 Lee House: architect unknown
1931 restoration: Waldron Faulkner

The scored stucco façades of these two elegant buildings, and the rooms contained therein, were purchased by the federal government in 1942 for use as presidential guest quarters. Eleanor Roosevelt, purportedly, insisted on some sort of guesthouse, because she had grown tired of having foreign potentates overrunning the White House. (According to widely repeated tradition, one morning at 6:30 she encountered a pudgy, pajama-clad figure roaming the hallways, cigar in one hand and snifter of brandy in the other. "To see Franklin," was his response when asked, "Winston, where are you going at this hour?" The first lady—again according to rumor—said, "No you're not. You kept him up half the night as it is. Let him get some sleep.")

The original Blair House was built by Surgeon General Dr. Joseph Lovell; its name came after Francis Preston Blair, a Kentuckian who made a fortune in Washington real estate, bought it in 1837. Blair, a rabid advocate of Jacksonian Democracy, founded the *Washington Globe* in 1830 and used that newspaper to vent his pro-Jackson sentiment. The house was later inherited by his kinsman, Montgomery Blair, an attorney who represented Dred Scott and served as postmaster general under Lincoln.

The great Lee family of Virginia owned the adjacent house, and it was here that scion Robert E. was offered and refused command of the Union forces at the start of the Civil War. Lee later recalled the scene: "I declined . . . stating as candidly and as courteously as I could, that although opposed to secession and deprecating war, I could take no part in an invasion of the Southern states."

17 Old Executive Office Building (Old State, War, and Navy Building)

Pennsylvania Avenue and 17th Street, N.W.

1875 South Wing
1879, 1882, 1888 other wings: all Alfred B. Mullett; Richard von Ezdorf, sculptor

TOURS SATURDAY MORNINGS, BY APPOINTMENT ONLY
PHONE: 395-5895

Reviled at its inception, when Henry Adams dismissed it as "Mr. Mullett's architectural infant asylum," and still unloved 70 years later when Harry Truman shuddered at "the greatest monstrosity in America," the ten-acre building's gray Virginia granite exterior, with its 900 projecting and superimposed Doric columns, bewilders many passers-by even today. Those who find their way inside are greeted with still more surprises: a spiraling cantilevered stairway at each corner and, buried within the vastness of the interior, a pair of libraries that have been well described as perforated fantasies of cast iron.

The building's unpopularity—architect Mullett committed suicide in 1890—has spawned several plots to have its exterior remodeled to match the critically sanctioned Treasury Building nearby. The latest such scheme came in 1929: that year, President Hoover groaned that Mullett's "architectural orgy" was, of all the buildings in town, the one "we regret most." He asserted, "For a comparatively modest sum we can strip it of its function to represent the different types of architecture known to man and bring it back to the sound classic lines of the Treasury." Congress went so far as to hire architect Waddy Wood to do the deed, but the Depression intervened, making the expenditure of even a Hoover-esque "modest sum" politically impossible. While one deeply rejoices that such plans got aborted, the concept is not all that far-fetched, since the original early-19th-century structures matched and since the present buildings, Treasury and the Executive Office Building, do have strikingly similar floor plans beneath their totally dissimilar façades.

One historical and architectural postscript: when Douglas MacArthur served as building superintendent, he designed some of the extant street-level planters.

Foggy Bottom/West End

A neighborhood of schizophrenic sensations: to stroll beneath the arching boughs of 17th Street's ancient elms is to experience one of the pleasantest sojourns the city can offer, but to negotiate the careening and largely unmarked hairpin turns necessary to drive to the Kennedy Center is an exercise in sheer terror.

No one has ever given a definitive account of the neighborhood's curious name. Some say it commemorates the mingled fumes spewed forth from a triumvirate of now-defunct industries—the Heurich brewery, the city gas plant, and a glass factory; others insist it refers to Potomac-spawned fogs. Then again, "Foggy Bottom" may connote an even more unpleasant past. During the first half of the 19th century, the Tiber Canal bisected the neighborhood. By the time the Civil War broke out, the canal had degenerated into an open sewer, swarming with flies and mosquitoes. Horses and mules grazed on what is now the Ellipse, and between the canal and the mules, the stench got so bad it often forced

Foggy Bottom from the air today. Forested Theodore Roosevelt Island lies in the foreground and the Watergate and Kennedy Center on the far shore of the Potomac, with Rawlins Park and the Interior Department complex a bit beyond and the Ellipse in the distance.

Lincoln to flee the White House and seek breezy refuge in upland, suburban cottages.

Now, however, Foggy Bottom, with its Renaissance-style splendors facing the shaded expanse of the Ellipse, is probably the best spot in town from which to see that L'Enfant's and Jefferson's dreams of Washington as a city of white monumental buildings mounted in green, park-like settings really has come true.

---

1 Winder Building

604 17th Street, N.W.

1847–1848 architect unknown

1975 restoration: Max O. Urbahn Associates

It may not look it now, but when new, this building was little short of revolutionary, for it pio-

neered the use of central heating and steel beams. The original restrained façade has been altered, but that does not diminish the engineering and historical importance of the building. Not only were its mechanical systems and framing avant garde, the structure itself pioneered a hardy Washington breed—cheap, speculative office space built to be leased to the federal government.

---

2 Resolution Trust Corporation (Liberty Plaza)

17th and G Streets, N.W.

1977 Max O. Urbahn Associates

Much of Washington's 1970s and '80s architecture strikes the viewer as overly obsessed with

the notion of fitting in, of seeking to escape an uncertain present by resurrecting the reassuring values of the past. While the excesses of most of the postmodernists are to be regretted (since so few postmodernist architects really *know* their history), now and then someone does create a truly valuable, artistically stimulating dialogue between times past and times present. Such is the case here. At first glance it seems as if Urbahn designed a totally contemporary concrete building, which would have been fine; but closer examination reveals something more complex, something even finer. The new structure's rambling, eccentric façade, ornamented by what might be taken for pilasters and columns, *suggests*, in a respectful manner, Alfred Mullett's rambling, eccentric, pilastered Executive Office Building directly to the east across 17th Street.

---

3   1801 F Street, N.W.

c. 1825   Tench Ringgold, owner-builder
c. 1860   architect unknown
c. 1911   Jules Henri de Sibour
c. 1985   various architects

Tench Ringgold played a leading part in the embryonic District's political and social life: a scion of several old Maryland families, Ringgold, in addition to his many other responsibilities, formed one-third of the three-man team that oversaw restoration of the buildings the British had burned during the War of 1812. His daughter inherited the house on his death. Times were not as flush for her, and she, like so many "distressed gentlefolk," felt obliged to take in paying guests. Among her sometime tenants one could find Martin van Buren, Major General George McClellan, and John Marshall, chief justice of the Supreme Court from 1801 until his death in 1835.

In the Ringgolds' eras, this dignified structure stood two stories tall; the present dimensions, and main entrance, were added to meet the needs of the building's best-known 20th-century owner, noted Washington hostess the Countess of Yarmouth. A cautionary tale: architect de Sibour designed superb additions for the countess, but she must have told her construction crew to cut costs, and today most passers-by notice not the additions' perfect proportions but the sloppy brickwork.

4 The Octagon

1799 New York Avenue, N.W.

c. 1800 William Thornton
1989– restoration: Mesick Cohen
Waite Architects

10:00 A.M. TO 4:00 P.M. TUESDAY
THROUGH SUNDAY   PHONE: 638-3105

4a American Institute of Architects Headquarters

1735 New York Avenue, N.W.

1973 The Architects Collaborative
1989– interior renovation: Malesardi
& Steiner/Architects
1993 library expansion: The Architects Collaborative; Malesardi & Steiner

PHONE: 626-7300

Still proudly standing, the Octagon provides an object lesson in the art of nonrectangular planning, provoked in this case by one of L'Enfant's oblique intersections. The brick house was built by Col. John Tayloe, III (1771–1828), a polished product of Eton and Christ Church, Cambridge, and one cog in a family prominent among the Virginia upper crust since the 17th century. Architect William Thornton created for Tayloe one of the most influential residences ever built in the city.

The plan is an exercise in pure spatial geometry. It consists of two equal-sized rectangular wings which radiate from a circle; the resulting interstitial triangle contains service rooms and passageways. What could be simpler or purer—a circle, two rectangles, and a triangle? And what could be a better way to use an awkwardly shaped lot? Apparently nothing, since that basic scheme has been reused again and again—and never improved upon (see, for example, the offices of the National Trust, 1785 Massachusetts Avenue). Moreover, the inspired use of geometry marks a dramatic improvement in the skills of the heretofore rankly amateur Thornton. One suspects that the learned client provided much of the intellectual inspiration for the building. (Thornton's other truly great Washington building, Tudor Place in Georgetown, also involved clients of more than routine polish.)

Legend maintains that, on the whole, Tayloe would rather have been in Philadelphia, a much larger and more sophisticated city, but he settled in the District at the urging of his friend George Washington. Events, however, conspired to keep the Tayloe family from spending much time here. During the War of 1812 the French minister was allowed to take over the Octagon, which somehow escaped the British torch. He was delighted and called it "the best house in town." In 1814 James Madison requisitioned the Octagon, and he and Dolley lived here while workmen repaired the charred White House. History doesn't record where the poor, displaced Tayloes lived during all this.

By 1855 the family had had enough of the Yankee capital and retrenched themselves back across the Potomac. The AIA leased the house in 1899, purchasing it outright in 1902, to use as a headquarters. The AIA moved into newer, larger headquarters in the 1940s and the American Architectural Foundation now maintains the Octagon as a house museum. Wrapped around the site of the older residence, the newest and current headquarters building acts as a buffer, shielding the venerable brick house from the modern development going on to the north and east.

5   Rawlins Park

E Street between 18th and 19th Streets, N.W.

1938 John Kirkpatrick, landscape architect
1973 statue: A. Bailey, sculptor

Particularly when the magnolias are in bloom, forming billowy clouds of pink and purple and white, this urban park sets a standard to which all such spaces should aspire. In spring and summer the park becomes popular as well as beautiful, and its straightforward promenade, offset by the cool grays of tree bark and pools, is filled with lunchtime brown-baggers.

John A. Rawlins, for whom the park is named, served in Grant's cabinet as secretary of war.

---

6   Corcoran Gallery of Art

17th Street and New York Avenue, N.W.

1897 Ernest Flagg
1927 Charles Platt

10:00 A.M. TO 9:00 P.M.
THURSDAY, 10:00 A.M. TO 5:00
P.M. FRIDAY THROUGH MONDAY AND ON WEDNESDAY (CLOSED TUESDAY)

The clear articulation of each block, the uncompromising elevations, and the magnificent interior atrium galleries and splendid rotunda show the Beaux-Arts tradition at its best. This is actually the second Corcoran Gallery, and was built to replace the out-grown original (now called the Renwick Gallery) on Pennsylvania Avenue. But this building also proved too small for the growing collection and had to be enlarged to the west in 1927 so it could receive the paintings and sculptures left to the Corcoran by Montana senator William A. Clark.

---

7   American National Red Cross

17th Street between D and E Streets, N.W.

1913–1917 Trowbridge & Livingston, architects; Boyle-Robertson Company, builder
1929 Goodhue Livingston
1933 R. Tait McKenzie, sculptor (Nurses' Memorial)

President Wilson laid the cornerstone in 1915 for what was to be a memorial "to the heroic women of the Civil War"; and while additions and expansions have produced a vast, full-block complex, the original building's 11-bay, Vermont-marbled façade remains easily discernible. Within that structure's Corinthian-columned walls, one finds some of the city's most endearingly eccentric treasures, such as a trio of Tiffany windows that depict nurses ministering to fallen soldiers, the whole cast glamorously draped in medieval garb.

8 Constitution Hall

1776 D Street, N.W.

1939 John Russell Pope

10:00 A.M. TO 2:30 P.M. WEEK-
DAYS PHONE: 879-3254

This hall is architecturally
notable without for its triple
frontage, which affords excel-
lent circulation and permits
entrances on three sides, and within for the promenade that connects the
various entrances in one grand sweep. The Daughters of the American
Revolution built the place to house public concerts. Famed violinist Efrem
Zimbalist opened the building with a recital. That event, however, was
completely overshadowed by a concert that never took place, or, rather,
that never took place *here*. Incredible as it seems in the 1990s, in 1939 the
DAR hierarchy were fully within the law when they refused to allow singer
Marian Anderson, a black woman, to perform here, because of her race.
The outcry was loud and immediate: Eleanor Roosevelt resigned her DAR
membership, and then she and Chief Justice Charles Evans Hughes
headed up a committee to organize an alternative concert. What a concert
it must have been, too, when on Easter Sunday 1939 some 75,000 people
massed in front of the Lincoln Memorial to hear Ms. Anderson sing. The
incident helped focus attention on the evils of racial segregation and is
memorialized in a mural in the Interior Department. The DAR has since
revised its policy towards integrated concerts.

9 Organization of American States (Pan-American Union)

17th Street and Constitution
Avenue, N.W.

1910 Albert Kelsey and Paul
P. Cret; Gertrude Vanderbilt
Whitney, sculptor

9:00 A.M. TO 5:30 P.M.
WEEKDAYS PHONE: 458-3751

Funded in part by a $750,000 gift from Andrew Carnegie, this marbled
building, headquarters of the world's oldest international organization,

was intended to symbolize the peaceful spirit that pervades relations among the nations of North, South, and Central America. Actually, the building fuses many themes: 1) it combines two qualities that usually are mutually exclusive, that is, imposing formality and inviting elegance; 2) its neoclassical façades make it an amiable neighbor to the White House and the Corcoran; 3) the tropical patio within, built around Whitney's fountain representing Mayan, Aztec, and Zapotecan art, suggests the unity of the Americas. (One wonders if the statue of the Aztec god Xochipilli, which presides over the garden, was a mistake: Xochipilli was the god of flowers, which seems pleasant enough, but in other moods he dabbled in hallucinogenic drugs and human sacrifices.)

The building stands on the site of the fabled Van Ness mansion. Completed c. 1816 to the designs of Benjamin Henry Latrobe, the house boasted innovative features, such as hot and cold running water, which earned it the reputation of being the costliest private residence in the nation. The house deteriorated and had to be demolished c. 1907. The stuccoed stable (also by Latrobe) has, however, survived; it stands at 18th and C Streets and may be glimpsed through the trees and shrubs.

---

10 Department of the Interior

18th to 19th Streets between C and E Streets, N.W.

1935 Waddy B. Wood

8:00 A.M. TO 5:00 P.M.
WEEKDAYS (MUSEUM)
PHONE: 208-4743

Waddy Wood's vast superblock
takes a middle ground: it wears its neoclassicism more lightly than the contemporaneous Federal Triangle does, yet it does not begin to approach, in subtlety and grace, what Paul Cret and Jules Henri de Sibour were up to just around the corner at the Federal Reserve Building and the Interior Department South (Constitution and 20th), respectively. A mural near the entrance at C and 18th depicts Marian Anderson's landmark 1939 concert at the Lincoln Memorial. The department's museum, opened in 1937 and essentially unchanged since, is among the funkier places in town.

11 Federal Reserve Building

Constitution Avenue and 20th Street, N.W.

1937 Paul P. Cret

Typical of Cret's stripped classicism, this building, neither modern nor revival, along with his Folger Library and the nearby Pan American Union, shows off 1930s academic style at its best. The government held an architectural competition for the new Reserve building, and the guidelines stated that the proposed structure should "have the central location in a group of five . . . which, with their appropriate landscape treatments, [will] make a frame for the Lincoln Memorial." The judges selected Cret's design partly, they said, because it reminded them of the architecture of Robert Mills. Eleanor Roosevelt, however, had reservations and noted in her February 3, 1938, "My Day" newspaper column that she "was assured rather apologetically that the space taken up by the . . . staircase could not have been utilized in any other way."

12 National Academy of Sciences

2101 Constitution Avenue, N.W.

1924 Bertram G. Goodhue

Goodhue's boiled-down Beaux-Arts palace is the eighth of nine neoclassical monuments that march, in L-formation, down 17th Street and then swing to the west along Constitution Avenue. The procession begins with Flagg's Corcoran Gallery and ends with Pope's Pharmaceutical Association building. It is hard to think of another formation of such structures that works as well.

13 American Pharmaceutical Association

23rd Street at Constitution Avenue, N.W.

1933 John Russell Pope

Pope originally designed this structure as a shell to house Abraham Lincoln's natal log cabin, but for various reasons he decided to use it here for bureaucrats, and it does fit in nicely with the other marbled palaces that front the Ellipse and Mall. (Pope whipped up another neoclassical reliquary for Lincoln's birthplace.)

14 Pan American Health Organization

525 23rd Street, N.W.

1964 Roman Fresnedo-Siri, design architect; Justement, Elam, Callmer & Kidd, architects

With its complementary curved tower and circular conference center this building group suggests a workable, if unorthodox, solution to the usual bane of Washington builders—the city's many narrow, triangular sites. Fresnedo-Siri, a Uruguayan architect, won the international competition for the project; an established Washington firm assisted in the actual construction.

15 John F. Kennedy Center for the Performing Arts

2700 F Street, N.W.

1971 Edward Durrell Stone Associates; Edward Durrell Stone, Jr., landscape architect

TOURS 10:00 A.M. TO 1:00 P.M. BY APPOINTMENT
PHONE: 416-8341

Despite criticism of its location, scale, and form, the Kennedy Center has undeniably succeeded in bringing a much richer cultural fare to the nation's capital. But even amongst the slings and arrows of outraged columnists, some of the building's features have drawn praise, particularly the acoustics of the performing halls, the grandeur of the entrance plaza, and the willow-shaded terrace along the river façade, the last of which can transform a routine intermission stroll into a magical and memorable event. Inside and out, the building displays myriad gifts from other nations, including marble from Italy, bronzes from West Germany, crystal from Sweden, Austria, and Norway, mirrors from Belgium, and silk from Japan.

16 The Watergate

2500–2700 Virginia Avenue, N.W. and 600–700 New Hampshire Avenue, N.W.

1964–1972 Luigi Moretti and Mario di Valmarana; Corning, Moore, Elmore & Fischer, associate architects

The convolutions of the overall plan have a certain inner and outer logic—the outer logic is evinced in the restless form that fills the oddly shaped site and that manages to reduce the aggregate bulk of the buildings; the inner logic appears in the succession of partially enclosed courts and in the great variety of aspects and views enjoyable from within the apartments. Some of the detailing borders on the eccentric, but it is generally consistent with the baroque quality of the whole complex. In all, the project successfully accomplishes the architects' stated purpose, namely to bring some softening curves into the otherwise linear and angular cityscape.

Many wonder about the name: in the 1930s some enterprising folk hatched a plan to construct a ceremonial water gate to the city near the Lincoln Memorial. (Visions of Cleopatra stepping off her dhow are inappropriate and should be squelched.) Nothing much came of the idea, although during World War II a barge, anchored nearby, provided the site for a popular series of summer concerts.

17 St. Mary's Episcopal Church

730 23rd Street, N.W.

1887 Renwick, Aspinwall and Russell

Originally housed in a relocated Civil War barracks on this same site and originally called "St. Mary's Chapel for Colored People," St. Mary's represents a landmark episode in black ecclesiastical history, since its congregation formed the first black Episcopal church in the city of Washington. Morning Prayer was first said here on June 9, 1867; the congregation grew and prospered, making necessary a larger church—the present Gothic revival structure. Worshipers and visitors alike often comment on the church windows: made in France, the painted-glass panes depict St. Cyprian, the African bishop and martyr, as well as St. Simon the Cyrenian and St. Tryphoena. Outside, between Renwick's church and the 1881 Sunday school building, one finds the Herbert Files garden, dedicated in 1971 and perhaps the most charming and peaceful of Washington's many small, tucked-away green spaces.

18 George Washington University Law Library

718 20th Street, N.W.

1970 Mills, Petticord & Mills
1984 expansion: Keyes Condon Florance Architects

Confronted with a seemingly impossible task—to give coherence to a wildly disparate block—Keyes Condon Florance achieved remarkably successful results. The site contained a late-Victorian town house at 20th and I, a somewhat modernist 1970 library, a 1922 neo-Georgian academic structure known as Stockton Hall, and a 1930s apartment building. KCF recognized that the cumulative effect of these structures far outweighed any of their individual merits, for the block represents the sort of stylistic jumble so characteristic of urban America. Thus, the architects decided to make the most of the block's variety: note the monochromatic colors and sculptural profile of the new building (read: "1930s apartment"); note how the new brick and sandstone matches the Victorian town house neighbor, how the false new "attic dormers" complement actual dormers nearby, and how KCF's porte-cochere suggests the Massachusetts Avenue mansions—with their porte-cocheres—just around the corner. Not obvious to the passer-by but functionally important is a series of doors and halls that links the once-separate structures and increases their usefulness.

19 International Monetary Fund

1700 19th Street, N.W.

1973 Vincent G. Kling & Partners, in association with Clas Riggs Owens & Ramos

1983, 1993 additions: The Kling/Lindquist Partnership

9:00 A.M. TO 5:00 P.M. DAILY (INTERIOR LOBBY ONLY)

A massive and magnificent interior courtyard provides light for the inward-looking offices and a 110-by-120-foot, air-conditioned plaza for receptions and exhibitions. The architects showed some whimsy on the exterior by using projecting, concrete-framed windows to emphasize, of all things, the building's attic.

20 World Bank, Building J

1818 H Street, N.W.

1987 Hellmuth, Obata & Kassabaum, PC

These ordered and rational façades seem highly appropriate for housing such an organization as the World Bank— regularity helps assure nonbankers that the people inside really do know what they're doing.

21 National Permanent Building

1775 Pennsylvania Avenue, N.W.

1977 Hartman-Cox Architects

Can this building really be approaching its second decade? One of the city's few truly epochal structures, since its completion this monument has influenced virtually all subsequent (intelligent) design in the District. The work of Hartman-Cox has always evinced the partners' awareness of how important it is that individual pieces fit into the city's aesthetic continuum. Yet, in the manner of Paul Cret, the firm eschews copy-book phoniness and remains thoroughly of the present. Neither George Hartman nor Warren Cox is likely to weigh a sentence down with a word like *contextualism*, but the minute their National Permanent Building appeared on the streetscape, all of the city's lesser lights suddenly became aware of how important things like context are in this town.

Both Cox and Hartman are Lutyens scholars; both can (and do) quote verbatim from Lutyens's 1925 letter to his wife in which he said that he liked the District's architecture but that the city wanted "tidying up and pulling together." With that in mind, it is hard to imagine that Hartman-Cox did not design this building to tidy up and pull together midtown Washington. Its wisp of a mansard roof suggests Hardenbergh's Willard Hotel, Mullett's Old Executive Office Building, and Renwick's gallery, and its exterior concrete columns and exposed ducts make obvious reference to the 900 Ionic columns that strut across Mullett's masterpiece.

22 Republic Place

1776 I Street, N.W.

1987 Keyes Condon Florance Architects

Almost overnight, before anyone could stop it, the blocks between Lafayette Square and George Washington University got filled with some of the most banal of banal 1970s ribbon-windowed office towers. And if Wilkes and Faulkner's jewel-like Brewood Building offers one small island of relief, KCF sought to achieve a more substantial visual oasis here. By and large, they succeeded. Republic Place, with its modulated façades, certainly evokes the best of what one might call 1930s American office building classic, while its ornamental brickwork reads like "Broadway Boogie Woogie" on the largest possible scale, adding color and cheer to an otherwise dreary streetscape. One further distinction between Republic Place and its neighbors: generally speaking it's hard to find the front door of most 1970s buildings, but one can't miss the entrance here, for it forms the base of an eye-catching engaged octagonal tower. The tower seems to have been devised as a bow to the art deco Hecht Company warehouse at 1401 New York Avenue, N.E., a 1930s masterpiece .

---

23 International Square

1850 K Street, N.W.

1985 Vlastimil Koubek

Washington's famous building height restrictions often make it difficult for buildings—particularly along this stretch of K Street—to stand out. Koubek, however, employed a variety of devices, such as broken massing and heroic-scale entrances, to ensure that his building staked its claim on the streetscape. Of course, taking up virtually the entire block helps.

---

24 1915 I Street, N.W. (Princess Apartments)

1917 Frank Russell White
1982, 1988 Kerns Group Architects PC

Two ambitious remodelings have quadrupled the floorspace of one of the city's more beloved early-20th-century apartment buildings. The additions behave themselves: they echo the "Dutch gable" roofline of the 1917 structure and they step back to avoid overpowering the streetscape.

---

25 Arts Club

2017 I Street, N.W.

1802–1806 Timothy Caldwell, owner-builder
1988 façade restoration: Davis Buckley

Caldwell stated that he wanted to build "the handsomest house in the capital city." Towards that ambitious end, he gave the main block of his new building stone window lintels of splayed voussoir and keystone design and a wealth of finely carved interior woodwork. Such genteel touches shot construction costs way over budget, and he had to sell the house shortly after its completion. But Caldwell bided his time and managed to buy the place back in 1813. James Monroe lived here briefly in 1817; later, photographer Frances Benjamin Johnston proved a longer-term tenant, as did meteorologist Cleveland Abbe. (Now largely forgotten, Abbe pioneered the concept of issuing daily weather forecasts.) The Arts Club took over the building in 1916 and has made its home here ever since.

---

26 Brewood Building

1147 20th Street, N.W.

1974 Wilkes and Faulkner Associates

A dignified gem in a neighborhood of ribbon-wall horrors, this structure recalls the distinguished residences and shops that once filled Washington's "Golden Triangle" (west of the White House between the Mall and Pennsylvania Avenue). Wilkes and Faulkner gave the Brewood bold elements that add punch to its diminutive scale and enable it to hold its own visually with the behemoths.

27 The Grand Hotel and Office Building

2300–2350 M Street, N.W.
1984 Skidmore, Owings & Merrill

Although it is hard to imagine Greta Garbo or John Barrymore striding through this lobby, the building's name is nonetheless important, for it tips one off to the developer's aspirations, namely, to construct a "grand hotel" for the 1980s. In case one harbors residual doubts about motive, just note the building's fenestration, massing, and rusticated ground story, all of which pay homage, in no uncertain terms, to the Hay-Adams and other of the city's truly grand hostelries.

28 1250 24th Street, N.W. (B and W Garage)

1925 Peter Reinsen, Fred Drew Construction Company, designer-builder
1988 renovation: Hisaka & Associates Architects

Those who view adaptive use projects warily, fearing the results will be neither fish nor fowl, ought to wander through this building: conversion to the cause will immediately ensue. Hisaka worked closely with the developer, Kaempfer Company, to produce a highly sensible product wherein past and present blend happily. The garage's large open spaces, whose original use remains clear, now contain some of the District's lightest and most cheerful offices. Some adaptive use seems contrived; this was inspired.

29 U.S. News and World Report Complex (Carnegie Foundation)

24th and N Streets, N.W.

1983 Skidmore, Owings & Merrill

People said all the best sites had been taken, but these long twins managed to stake out a nearly unobstructed view up the sinuous valley of Rock Creek Park. The architects' neobaroque-cum-neofederal effort invites comparisons with Hartman-Cox's purely neobaroque Market Square on Pennsylvania Avenue.

Dupont Circle

A round the turn of the century, a cross-section of the nation's plutoc-
racy built more than 100 grand mansions along Massachusetts and
Connecticut Avenues and around Dupont Circle itself, making this once-
quiet section of the city suddenly the rival of New York's upper Fifth
Avenue as *the* place in the nation to live. One recalls what Henry Adams
wrote in 1904: "The American wasted money more recklessly than any
one did before; he spent more to less purpose than any extravagant court
aristocracy; he had no sense of relative values, and knew not what to do
with his money when he got it, except to use it to make more, or throw it
away." Later, the Dupont Circle phenomenon prompted Phillip Wylie to
use his 1942 book, *Generation of Vipers,* to attack "every sullen, rococo,
snarling, sick, noxious and absurd form of vainglorious house . . . [built

*Dupont Circle around 1921, shortly after the du Pont family replaced the original
small bronze statue of Admiral Samuel du Pont with the present large marble fountain. McKim, Mead and White's gleaming and multi-skylighted Patterson House,
now the Washington Club, at the corner of P Street, is shown here* (left of center, on
the circle), *as is the porticoed and even larger mansion (destroyed c. 1947) of dry-
goods millionaire L. Z. Leiter, built in 1891 between 19th Street and New Hampshire Avenue* (at right).

here] to assuage the cheap pretensions of the middle class and the Middle West."

The evolution of the little park in the circle certainly sets the tone. In 1882 Congress decided to commemorate Admiral Samuel Francis du Pont (1803–1865), a Civil War naval hero, and did so by naming this new circle for him (the neighborhood had been known as "The Slashes") and by placing a small bronze statue of him in the center. That wasn't enough for the du Ponts, who, in good Gilded-Age style, decided to circumvent the federal government: working on their own, the gunpowder magnates hired the team that gave the city the Lincoln Memorial—architect Henry Bacon and sculptor Daniel Chester French—to build the present, far grander, memorial.

The Great Depression and World War II rendered the neighborhood's excesses more than a little politically incorrect, and by the 1950s many of the buildings here had been converted to boarding houses. Beginning around 1970, however, interest in Dupont Circle began to grow again: the area was recognized as a historic district, many of the city's young professionals restored and moved into the neighborhood's side-street row houses, and many of the grand old mansions were converted again, this time to high-style shops, private clubs, and art galleries.

---

1   Euram Building

21 Dupont Circle, N.W.

1970 Hartman-Cox Architects

Vigorous, dramatic, and featuring a surprising open inner court, this contemporary office building may rank as this generation's most original addition to the circle. Post-tensioned concrete beams span the length of the glazed façades and spring from masonry piers at the corners, while the overall massing and plan creates a modern twist on precedents set one century ago at the Patterson House and two centuries ago at the Octagon.

2 Historical Society of Washington, D.C. (Heurich House)

1307 New Hampshire Avenue, N.W. (at 20th Street)

1892 John Granville Myers

NOON TO 4:00 P.M. WEDNESDAY
THROUGH SATURDAY
PHONE: 785-2068

Knotty, apprehensive, and bristling with gargoyles, the brownstone and brick façades of this house are unmatched in Washington as examples of what historian Richard Howland called "beer-barrel baronial" Victorian grandeur. In addition, the house claims two District firsts: the town's first poured-concrete walls and the first residential fireproofing. The shadowy interiors, intact and original, form a museum of their time and attest to the taste of the house's builder, German immigrant Christian Heurich (1842–1944). Heurich, whose company's slogan was "Beer recommended for family use by Physicians in General," brewed himself a vast, bubbly fortune and made no bones about using the house to acknowledge the source of his wealth. The breakfast room in the basement is representative of the *gemütlich* spaces. Its walls are covered with murals depicting the virtues of beer-drinking interspersed with appropriate sayings such as *"Raum ist in der kleinsten Kammer für den grossten Katzenjammer"* ("There is room in the smallest chamber for the biggest hangover").

3 Sunderland Building

1320 19th Street, N.W.

1969 Keyes, Lethbridge & Condon, Architects

Foursquare and relatively small, this professional office building, with its buff-colored, poured-in-place concrete walls, stands out in Dupont Circle as a rare example of a good thing in an understated package. Recessed windows punctuate all façades; the architects innovatively flanked the openings with columns and duct enclosures that are angled to enlarge the view in one direction and simultaneously shield the glass from the hot summer sun.

4 1818 N Street, N.W.

1984 David M.
Schwarz/Architectural
Services, PC; Vlastimil
Koubek, associated architect

This building has been called
"façadism with finesse." Perhaps more seriously, 1818 N
Street marks the end of a series
of highly successful Washington infill projects. The line stretches back to
Warnecke's fine, pioneering work at Lafayette Square. One thing that dis-
tinguishes Schwarz's work from similar endeavors is his evident serious-
ness about design and history. When hired to construct this infill, he
looked hard at the five diverse N Street town houses that would remain
and anchor the project; he studied their heterogeneous mix of pediments,
domes, and windows; then he playfully reinterpreted the elements in a new
red brick building. On paper, it sounds simple enough, but others have
failed where the talented Schwarz succeeded.

5 1752 N Street, N.W.

c. 1890 architect unknown
1983 Martin & Jones, Architects

If one enjoys turn-of-the-century architecture for being enthusiastically larger
than life, for throwing together the most
unlikely combinations and really not giving a damn about "correctness," the
façades of this restless brick pile will produce feelings akin to ecstasy. There probably isn't another building in town that so
rambunctiously incorporates such a mix: Sullivanesque brownstone
details, classical thermal windows, attic dormers that suggest Bruges or
Antwerp, and an onion-domed corner turret straight from Minsk or
Pinsk. It's more than a little surprising—and quite a relief—to walk
through the arched entrance, which itself suggests H. H. Richardson, and
discover that behind those vigorous walls Martin and Jones created some
of the most restrained office space in the city.

6   Peruvian Chancery (Wilkins House)

1700 Massachusetts Avenue, N.W.

1909 Jules Henri de Sibour

Echoing the Thornton-Tayloe Octagon house built a hundred years earlier, the French-born de Sibour showed that a good designer can triumph over L'Enfant's tapering corner lots and radial avenues. In addition, de Sibour gave the limestone-faced Wilkins House several distinctly European, and distinctly successful, touches, such as a restrained mannerist façade and a *piano nobile* organization. The 17th-century English interiors—lots of dark, carved wood—are, perhaps, less of a triumph. Emily Wilkins, widow of Ohio congressman Beriah Wilkins, commissioned de Sibour to design the polite dwelling; in addition to his congressional duties, her late husband had owned a large block of stock in the *Washington Post* company and at times actually edited the paper.

Jules Henri de Sibour (1872–1938) did as much as any single individual to improve the quality of Washington's early-20th-century architecture. Born in Paris, the son of an American mother and an aristocratic French father (a vicomte in the diplomatic corps), de Sibour got his early education at St. Paul's in Concord, New Hampshire, and at Yale before returning to France to attend the École des Beaux-Arts. He appeared in Washington around 1900, leading the wave of Paris-trained architects who brought the Beaux-Arts style to Massachusetts Avenue. De Sibour remained in the District for several years and produced an oeuvre notable for quality of design and for suitability to upper-class American lifestyles. In addition to improving District millionaires' housing, he accepted a few corporate commissions. The best-known of these may be his clubhouse for the Chevy Chase Club (1910); de Sibour, a gifted athlete, became a fixture at the club, where his skill with bat and glove made him the perennial star of its baseball team.

7 Benjamin T. Rome Building of the Johns Hopkins University (Forest Industries Building)

1619 Massachusetts Avenue, N.W.

1961 Keyes, Lethbridge & Condon, Architects

The ordered restraint of the light-colored concrete frame and the deep-set, contrasting wood windows give a dignity and three-dimensional quality to this structure's façades. The building's recessed entrance court is thought to have been the first in town and has been much copied.

8 Carnegie Institution of Washington

1530 P Street, N.W.

1908–1910 Carrère & Hastings
1937 William Adams Delano

In 1902 Andrew Carnegie gave funds to establish this "institution dedicated to the discovery of knowledge," and Carrère and Hastings's headquarters building, a three-part Beaux-Arts palazzo fronting on 16th Street, soon followed. The institute grew quickly into one of the world's premier centers for advanced research in the physical and biological sciences, and the many Nobel recipients drawn here made the original temple bulge at the quoins. Thus the need for an addition, Delano's restrained rear wing. Ever polite, Delano designed his wing so it perfectly matches the older section in window treatment, overall scale, and materials.

9 Swedenborgian Church of the Holy City

1611 16th Street, N.W.

1895 Herbert Langford Warren

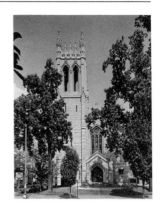

Construction of this restrained French Gothic structure was overseen by Paul Pelz, who was simultaneously working on the main Library of Congress building; try as one might, it is difficult to see any connections between the two very different creations. The charming chapel and baptistry to the south, now the home of St. Hilda of Whitby Anglican Catholic Church, may be a greater aesthetic success than Warren's somewhat off-putting main building.

10 The Cairo

1615 Q Street, N.W.

1894 Thomas Franklin Schneider
1973–1974 restoration: Arthur Cotton Moore/Associates P.C.

The Cairo is a double landmark. The tallest building in 1894 Washington, its 165-foot height so shocked city residents that they pushed Congress to establish height limitations for buildings in the District. Also, it was one of the first residential towers in America to employ steel-frame construction. Even before it opened, the Cairo's first promotional brochure touted it as "the largest and most luxurious apartment house in Washington" and "the most thoroughly equipped establishment of this nature south of New York." The flyer also acclaimed the establishment's bakery, two billiard rooms, and rooftop garden complete with tropical plants and electrically powered fountains "bubbling here and bursting forth there."

11 Schneider Row Houses

1700 block of Q Street, N.W.

1889–1892 Thomas Franklin
Schneider

Built by Thomas Schneider of Cairo
hotel fame, these three-story brown-and
greenstone row houses enliven the street
with a robust mix of turrets, projecting
bays, tiled mansard roofs, and Richardsonian Romanesque decorative detailing.
The Washington *Evening News* profiled
Schneider, "the young Napoleon of F Street," on November 5, 1889:
" 'Why it's just a few years ago that I was going to school with him, playing
"Old Man" and buying a cent's worth of taffy, which we divided at recess,'
said an acquaintance. And it was just last Saturday that the young
Napoleon paid $175,000 for a row of lots on Q Street, occupying the whole
front of the square between Seventeenth and Eighteenth Streets. He is a
young looking man, with a slight moustache, and a modest retiring air, but
he certainly is what the Westerners call a 'hustler.' "

12 Thomas Nelson Page House

1759 R Street, N.W.

1897 McKim, Mead & White

When Stanford White set out to design
the Page House for the famous southern
author (or, actually, for his wife), he
decided to work in the federal revival
style, and thus made a clean break from
the Loire Valley châteaux and Parisian
palaces then so popular with Washington's architects and their clients. Page set
most of his stories in antebellum Virginia, so perhaps White, in invoking
Jefferson and Madison and Monroe, simply wanted to acknowledge the
locales of these best-selling novels. For all that, the house's two main
façades could not be more different from each other: the R Street wall
(illustrated here) is solemn and restrained while that facing New Hampshire Avenue seems relaxed to the point of informality.

13 Belmont House (Order of the Eastern Star)

1618 New Hampshire Avenue, N.W.

1908 Étienne Sansom; Horace Trumbauer

With its Louis XIV prow and Palladian motifs, this building gains much from its direct, not to say head-on, way of dealing with a triangular site. The builder, diplomat Perry Belmont, was a grandson of Commodore Matthew Perry. He imported Sansom, a fashionable French architect, to design the $1.5 million house and brought in Trumbauer, himself no stranger to grandees' commissions, to guide the Frenchman through the District's baleful labyrinths of red tape and triplicate forms—yes, even back then.

14 Women's National Democratic Club (Weeks House)

1526 New Hampshire Avenue, N.W.

1892 Harvey Page

A large cape of a roof—from which peers an occasional attic window—drapes down over the angles of this house's turreted façade. Composed and detached, the brick building's great and sympathetic personality sets it apart from its flashier neighbors and has caused even the cynical Philip Johnson to proclaim it an "architectural masterpiece." Sarah Adams Whittemore, a cousin of Henry Adams, built the house, which may explain its reserved Yankee correctness. Its eponymous and best-known owner, banker John C. Weeks, was another New England transplant; a congressman and senator, Weeks also served as under secretary of war for presidents Harding and Coolidge.

15 Washington Chapter/AIA

1777 Church Street, N.W.

c. 1900 architect unknown
1970 renovations: Hartman-Cox
Architects

In a fine example of what might be called
minimalist adaptive use, the Chapter
bought this three-story brick town house
in 1968 and then gently modified it to suit
modern office needs. Long-time District
residents still remember 1777 Church
Street as the home of Mr. and Mrs. L. Morris Leisenring, who bought the
building in 1917 and lived here for a half-century. Leisenring, chief architect for the army quartermaster corps and the man responsible for the initial Washington Architectural Registration Act, did a bit of adapting himself, adding a studio for himself and his wife, a distinguished sculptor. The
studio is now the board room. The chapter house gains enormously from
having the flowery vest-pocket garden and attractive ruins of St. Thomas
Church (1893) right across the street.

16 Embassy of Iraq (Boardman House)

1801 P Street, N.W.

1893 Hornblower & Marshall

The imposing arched entryway
of this substantial house
strongly suggests that Hornblower and Marshall were influ-
enced by H. H. Richardson, whose Lafayette Square houses for John Hay
and Henry Adams were much admired in the city's architectural community. The house is also architecturally notable for its orange Roman bricks:
their thinness requires a greater number of courses than is usual to create a
house of this height, and the extra courses combine with the splayed jack
arches over the windows to give élan to the otherwise staid façades. Mabel
Boardman commissioned the fine building. Well known for her work with
the Red Cross, Boardman also cofounded the Sulgrave Club, whose members met here until 1932, when they were able to buy and remodel their
present headquarters building nearby.

17 National Trust for Historic Preservation (McCormick Apartments)

1785 Massachusetts Avenue, N.W.

1915 Jules Henri de Sibour

TOURS BY APPOINTMENT
PHONE: 673-4000

Chicago-based Stanley McCormick, heir to the McCormick reaper millions, commanded de Sibour to create "the most luxurious apartment house in Washington." The architect did just that. The limestone edifice contained just one unit per floor and quickly became among the most sought-after residences in the city, attracting such tenants as Lord Duveen, Pearl Mesta, and Andrew Mellon. (The armies of servants who looked after these nabobs lived in tiny 8 1/2-by-10-foot rooms crowded onto six mezzanine levels.) In addition, the building's siting and plan, which reflect its irregular lot, create an interesting variation on the axis/cross-axis/corner-pivot theme that William Thornton devised for the Octagon a century earlier. The building has been adapted for office use.

18 1746 Massachusetts Avenue, N.W.

1906 Jules Henri de Sibour

Clarence Moore, a West-by-God-Virginia tycoon, built this Louis XV *palais*, one of the finest houses ever erected in the city. He was able to enjoy it for only a few years, however, because he had the misfortune to book passage on the maiden voyage of the *Titanic* in 1912. (Moore, a noted horseman and master of the hounds at the Chevy Chase Club, had been to England on a dog-buying trip.) The light-colored Roman brick façades and remarkable interior paneling and hardware (note the satyr wall sconces and the iron balustrades with CM monogram) result in a somewhat more ambitious building than the nearby Wilkins House, also by de Sibour. Yet both structures display the restraint and good breeding that characterize de Sibour's work, qualities that become especially evident when one compares his buildings to most others in the neighborhood. The Canadian government acquired the property in 1927 and splendidly maintained it as a chancery until 1988, when embassy staff moved to their magnificent new quarters on Pennsylvania Avenue.

19 Sulgrave Club (Wadsworth House)

1801 Massachusetts Avenue, N.W.

c. 1900 architect unknown
1932 remodeling: Frederick Brooke

The tan press-brick walls and terra-cotta and stone trim of this fine building somehow seem quieter than those of its boisterous neighbors. But the house, when new, was anything but quiet. It was commissioned by Herbert Wadsworth, an engineer who also owned vast farms in the Finger Lakes region of New York State. Wadsworth liked portecocheres, and since space limitations imposed by the triangular site seemed to make such a feature impossible, the inventive Wadsworth ran the driveway through the first floor and then build himself a porte-cochere in the center of the house. Architect Brooke, hired to convert the house to club use, also worked as the local consulting architect for Lutyens's British Embassy on Massachusetts Avenue.

20 Washington Club (Patterson House)

15 Dupont Circle, N.W.

1901–1903 Stanford White

Built for Robert Wilson Patterson, publisher of the Chicago *Tribune,* this white marble Renaissance-style palazzo presents its own method of dealing with Washington's nonrectangular lots. Compare its outstretched arms with the thrust *back* arms seen at the Octagon and the McCormick Apartments. Patterson's redoubtable daughter, "Cissy," owner of the Washington *Times-Herald,* inherited the mansion in the 1920s, whereupon she and it Charlestoned their way into every international society column. Cissy's death in 1948 put an end to that feverish era. She left the building to the Red Cross, which sold it to the Washington Club in 1950.

21 Blaine Mansion

2000 Massachusetts Avenue, N.W.

1881 John Fraser

Brooding and grim, this craggy pile glowers at passers-by as if to express disapproval of the neighborhood's present commercial bustle. But brooding and grim may have been Fraser's architectural style, for his Union League Club, where the elite of Philadelphia gather, seems equally dour. The Washington house was built by James G. Blaine (1830–1893), a man known to his friends as "the Plumed Knight of American Politics"; to others he was "Slippery Jim." A Republican from Maine, he served in the House and the Senate, was Speaker of the House, and thrice ran and lost the race for the White House. The mansion eventually grew too expensive for Slippery Jim to maintain, so he leased it to more cash-laden contemporaries. His tenants included the likes of Levi Leiter, an early partner of Marshall Field and proud father of Mary Leiter, who became Lady Curzon and vicereine of India, and George Westinghouse, whose surname speaks for itself. Westinghouse liked the place so much he bought it outright in 1901 and lived here until his death in 1914.

22 The National Federation of Business and Professional Women's Clubs (Beale House)

2012 Massachusetts Avenue, N.W.

1898 Glenn Brown

Something of a tour-de-force, the Beale House's russet façades, although composed of two distinct materials, are quietly monochromatic, for the liver-colored brick perfectly matches the sandstone.

When new, the house's somber mien echoed an equally somber building to the east, the Litchfield House; unfortunately, the latter was demolished several years ago.

23 Indonesian Embassy (Walsh-McLean House)

2020 Massachusetts Avenue, N.W.

1903 Henry Anderson

TOURS BY APPOINTMENT

PHONE: 775-5306

Construction costs of $3,000,000+ made this the most expensive house in Washington. Created by Thomas Walsh, who embedded a slab of gold ore into the front porch to proclaim the source of his wealth, the 60-room house, according to Walsh's daughter, Evalyn Walsh McLean, "expresses the dreams my mother and father had when they were poor in Colorado."

A 19-year-old Irish lad, Walsh immigrated to America from County Tipperary in 1869. He went west and garnered his first fortune in 1876 during the Black Hills Gold Rush; his second came from Camp Bird Mine, among the thickest veins of gold in the world. In 1902 Walsh decided he'd had enough of mining, so he sold the Camp Bird Mine, for $43,000,000 plus a percentage of future yields, and moved his family to Washington. Determined to cut a social swath, he realized he needed a grand mansion. And here it is, a robust mix of an infinite number of styles. Walsh is known to have copied the three-story, galleried art nouveau stairwell from a favorite White Star ocean liner, but he gave the façades undulating walls and rounded corners that defy stylistic pigeon-holing. For a while, the good times certainly rolled, perhaps hitting their giddy peak during Theodore Roosevelt's administration: at one New Year's Eve party, reported the *New York Times*, Walsh's 325 celebratory guests downed 288 fifths of scotch, 480 quarts of champagne, 40 gallons of beer, 35 bottles of miscellaneous liqueurs, and 48 "quarts of cocktails."

But Walsh suddenly grew reclusive, and in 1910 he died in the house in virtual isolation. Alcoholism, pill-induced suicides, and car accidents fill most of the rest of the family saga. Daughter Evalyn Walsh inherited the house but refused to move into it, stating "it was cold, but its deepest chill lodged in my breast." She married publishing heir Edward Beale McLean (his family owned the *Post*), and the pair lived lavishly at their estate on upper Wisconsin Avenue. Lavishly indeed! According to James Goode's *Capital Losses*, the pair "managed to dissipate almost all of the vast McLean and Walsh fortunes, amounting to 100 million dollars." (She "dissipated" a relatively small amount of the money when she bought the Hope Diamond.) The Indonesian government purchased the mansion in 1951 for $350,000—1/10th of its original cost.

24 Society of the Cincinnati (Anderson House)

2118 Massachusetts Avenue, N.W.

1902–1905 Little and Browne

TOURS BY APPOINTMENT
PHONE: 785-2040

Several features distinguish this limestone-veneered mansion from its similarly sheathed peers and neighbors; most noticeable are the great, arched gates and dignified entrance court.

Boston architects Little and Browne designed this Italianate palace for career diplomat Larz Anderson, III, and his heiress wife, Isabel Weld Perkins. (The same firm designed the couple's country house, Weld, near Boston.) Likenesses of Anderson family heroes fill the cavernous interior. The three-dimensional ones include a bust of Nicholas Longworth, Anderson's maternal great-grandfather, remarkable as one of America's early vintners and as the first millionaire in the Northwest; murals depict other favored ancestors, including great-uncle Maj. Robert Anderson, at his command of Fort Sumter in 1861, and great-grandfather Col. Richard Wheeler, an aide-de-camp to Lafayette. For all their Americanisms, Larz and Isabel managed to find room for such furnishings as a set of Brussels tapestries originally woven as a gift of Louis XIII to Cardinal Barberini, papal representative at the French court. The mansion and furnishings were bequeathed to the Society of the Cincinnati, a benevolent organization George Washington established for his officers and their direct male descendants.

25 Phillips Collection

1600 21st Street, N.W.

1897 Hornblower & Marshall
1915 McKim, Mead & White
1960 new wing: Wyeth & King
1989 alterations to new wing: Arthur
Cotton Moore/Associates P.C.

10:00 A.M. TO 5:00 P.M. MONDAY
THROUGH SATURDAY, NOON TO 7:00 P.M.
SUNDAY   PHONES: 387-2151,
  387-0961

The quietly intimate rooms within this turn-of-the-century brownstone
contain one of the nation's most distinguished private art collections.
Duncan and Marjorie Phillips may have represented the perfect fusion of
intellect and cash. He was an art-loving heir to the Jones and Laughlin
steel fortune and she was a painter of no small skill. (There must have been
something in the air at Jones and Laughlin; see I. B. Laughlin's splendid
Meridian House.)

Young Phillips developed his avocation early on: while still a New
Haven undergraduate he wrote an article titled "The Need for Art at
Yale," and he called his first book, published when he was 28, *The Enchant-
ment of Art*. He began collecting around 1918 and, unlike most of his
mogul industrial peers, decided to concentrate solely on the works of contemporary artists. Phillips worked quickly (nothing like having good eyes
and pockets of limitless depth) and in 1921 opened two rooms in the house
for public tours.

This is thought to have been the first museum of modern art in
America. The Phillipses stated that they envisioned their collection as
"a joy-giving, life-enhancing influence." (They may have succeeded too
well, for swelling numbers of visitors made life in the house impossible
and the couple had to move elsewhere in 1930.) "This kind of collection,"
wrote John Canady of the *New York Times*, "bearing consistently the
personal stamp of one individual's special and highly cultivated taste, is
extremely rare, and the experience of seeing it in its natural setting—the
collector's own house, where he lived with it, rather than in a museum
atmosphere—is even more rare." Canady further characterized the
collection and the collectors as embodying "wit, grace, intellect and love
of life."

Those qualities were absent when a new marble wing was added in 1960,
but, happily, corrections have been made and that section's rooms now

approach the old brownstone's in beauty and serenity. Entrance to the new wing is through a door surmounted by a sculpture of a bird in flight. Interpreted from one of Mr. Phillips's favorite Braque paintings, the bird certainly symbolizes a visit to the Phillips, for an hour in this "life-enhancing" place causes the heart to soar.

26 Cosmos Club (Townsend House)

2121 Massachusetts Avenue, N.W.

1899–1901, 1904 Carrère & Hastings; Frederick Law Olmsted, Jr., landscape architect
1958 alterations: Horace W. Peaslee

This exemplifies the best of what Victorian-era railroad money, carefully directed, could produce. Richard Townsend's fortune came from the Erie Line and Mary Scott Townsend's from the Pennsylvania. The couple pooled their immense wealth and told Carrère and Hastings that they wanted a Washington château based on the Petit Trianon, a good choice, for the New York architects had a deep predilection for things French (Hastings even named his own Long Island estate Bagatelle). A bit quirky, the Townsends had the new house built *around* an older one, because a gypsy had once predicted that Mrs. Townsend was destined to die "under a new roof."

The couple's daughter, Mathilde, inherited the house in 1935; she had married Sumner Welles (1892–1961), a diplomat who played several crucial roles in FDR's administration. The Cosmos Club acquired the superb property in the 1950s. In adapting the place for its new use, Peaslee had to take away much of Olmsted's landscaping—parking lots do take up room—but he was able to maintain surprisingly large sweeps of Carrère's interiors. Thus, the structure, largely intact, forms a veritable museum of railroad-financed, Gilded Age grandeur.

27 1718 Connecticut Avenue, N.W.

1982 David M. Schwarz/Architectural Services, PC

One can confidently predict that in a quarter-century or so, when the saga of the District's post-1960s architecture is being written, historians will uniformly give this building landmark status, for it and Hartman-Cox's 1775 Pennsylvania Avenue are the first—and best—of the city's New Age, "contextual" structures. Mixing motifs from architects as varied as H. H. Richardson (the massing and the Connecticut Avenue façade) and Le Corbusier (the stuccoed alley front), the building's eclecticism cannot be denied. But why should it? Isn't that the point of contextualism? More importantly, Schwarz displays a sure grasp of Washingtoniana—for example, this building's large arch simply reinterprets Richardson's arches at Henry Adams's Lafayette Square house—and it is this knowing use of history that separates Schwarz from the pack, since so many contextual architects display their lack of education by glibly creating "references" that don't, in fact, refer to anything.

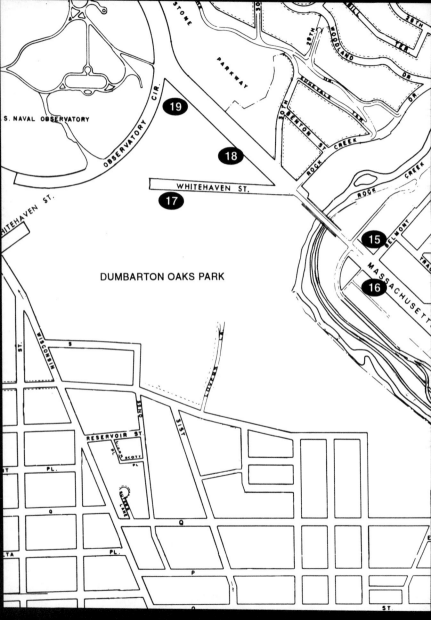

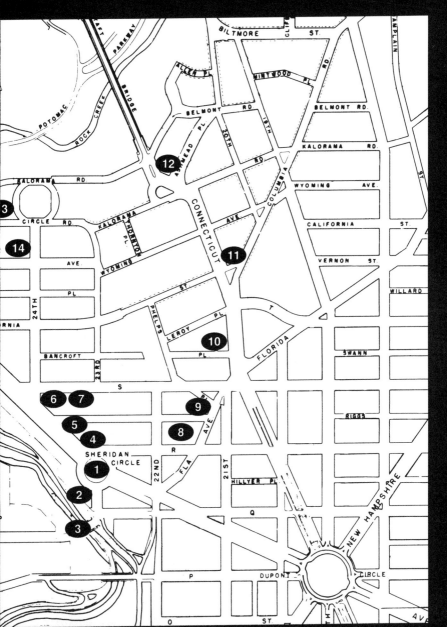

The word *kalorama* means "beautiful view" in Greek and is the fitting name that poet, liberal activist, and diplomat Joel Barlow gave to the estate he created on "the heights" above the new federal city and the older Georgetown. Barlow, among Thomas Jefferson's most trusted cronies, embraced whatever was new and advanced in any field—politics, literature, science—so long as it improved the condition of mankind. For him that urgently included improving the condition of the new United States: "My object is altogether of a moral and political nature," he wrote. "I wish to encourage and strengthen in the rising generation, the sense of the importance of republican institutions." Or, as he versified,

> But no more the patriotic mind
> To narrow views and local laws confin'd. . . .
> For realms and ages forms the general aim,
> Makes patriot views and moral views the same,
> Works with enlightened zeal to see combin'd
> The strength and happiness of humankind.

Barlow backed Robert Fulton's new-fangled steamboat, and many believe that Fulton built the first version of *Clermont* at Kalorama and tested it in Rock Creek.

If Barlow's house still stood, it would be on the corner of 23rd and Bancroft, but it was demolished around 1890, after which Kalorama

Cyril Farey's preconstruction (c. 1925) impression of the ambassador's residence at the British Embassy. (Architect Lutyens must have approved of the image, for he signed the watercolor.) Lady Lindsay, an American-born professional landscape architect, improved the straggly-looking gardens during the 1930s, when her husband served as ambassador.

Woods, as realtors originally called the neighborhood, quickly took on its present appearance, as the rich, famous, and powerful raced in to build mansions amidst the trees and plant gardens on the hills. While it is the rolling topography, as much as anything, that gives the area its distinctive appearance, architecture provides the tone that prompted Russell Baker to quip, "Kalorama has the quiet, slightly sinister atmosphere of the aristocratic quarter of a Ruritanian capital."

Life here changed perforce with the Great Depression. At most of the mansions, suddenly impoverished dowagers and debutantes slipped out the back door and diplomats from all over the earth strode in the front, and "Embassy Row" was born.

---

1 Sheridan Statue

Sheridan Circle and Massachusetts Avenue, N.W.

1908 Gutzon Borglum, sculptor

Gen. Philip H. Sheridan's eventful career included the scorched-earth Valley Campaign in Virginia during the Civil War and a series of particularly savage battles during the western Indian wars, during one of which he is said to have coined the phrase, "The only good Indian is a dead Indian." Thus, some may smile at the irony of the general's role here, a pigeon-plagued policeman, silently and forever reduced to directing traffic from downtown, around the circle, and on to "Embassy Row." Sculptor Borglum showed what he could do on a larger scale when he created Mount Rushmore.

---

2 Turkish Embassy (Everett House)

1606 23rd Street, N.W.

1914 George Oakley Totten, Jr.

Totten's District commissions prove him nothing if not versatile: simply compare his "Pink Palace" on Meridian Hill, where he was as Venetian as a doge, or his proper Beaux-Arts Moran House (now the Pakistani Embassy) to this restless limestone-faced mélange, whose outside contains a more or less successful combination of Franco-Italian neoclassical motifs and exposed, "honest" California Arts and Crafts construction techniques and whose inside sports an Italianate ballroom, an English dining room, and a French drawing room. Then there are all the gold-plated doorknobs, the basement swimming pool, and the other gewgaws that gained for the place the sobriquet "San Simeon on the Potomac."

Edward Hamlin Everett, who commissioned this palace and moved here from his native Cleveland, was one of scores of late-Victorian and Edwardian industrialists who flocked to Washington, eager to be near the seat of governmental power. Everett derived some of his evident wealth from the usual sources, such as mining, oil and gas, and beer; but a sizeable chunk has more idiosyncratic origins—royalties from his invention of the fluted bottle cap.

---

3 Buffalo Bridge

23rd and Q Streets, N.W.

1914 Glenn and Bedford
Brown; A. P. Proctor,
sculptor

The Brown brothers built this
bridge to join Georgetown with
the then-developing Kalorama
area. Viewed from the Rock
Creek Valley, the span's massive battlements and great arches combine to form a single, powerful, Renaissance-derived image. From the roadbed, however, it is pure Americana; in addition to the bison from which its name derives, the bridge is embellished with a series of masonry heads modeled on the Sioux chief Kicking Bear. It's a bit like watching Buffalo Bill's Wild West Show trundle across the Ponte Vecchio. The Browns did more than design bridges, however, and to catch them in a domestic vein, see Joseph Beale's house at 2301 Massachusetts Avenue.

Actually, this section of Rock Creek is traversed by four large bridges. Each merits attention, each is different, and each says something distinct and important about building attitudes in the city. The others are the ornate 1906 William Howard Taft Bridge, which carries Connecticut Avenue over the creek (George Morison, architect; Roland Hinton Perry, sculptor), pure Washington à la Paris; Paul Cret's 1931 bridge (also on

Connecticut, but farther north, near the zoo), its single arch, stylized urns, and discreet railing politely suggesting the nascent modern movement; and the Calvert Street Bridge (see K-6).

4 Embassy of Haiti (Fahnestock House)

2311 Massachusetts Avenue, N.W.

1909 Nathan C. Wyeth

Designed and detailed in the 18th-century French manner, this building, commissioned by financier Gibson Fahnestock, harmoniously blends with the rows of similar *hôtels* that line the blocks around Sheridan Circle. Wyeth (not to be confused with N. C. Wyeth the illustrator) was a prominent and talented architect who practiced in Washington for nearly 50 years. The finely carved Corinthian pilasters and the restrained rusticated basement of Fahnestock House certainly show his mastery of Beaux-Arts detailing.

5 Embassy of Pakistan (Moran House)

2315 Massachusetts Avenue, N.W.

1908 George Oakley Totten, Jr.

Here is proof that there really was a unifying design aesthetic among most of the District's Gilded Age rich-rich. This building and its counterpart next door were commissioned by different plutocrats and designed by different architects. But, because the two structures employ similar materials, mansard roofs, cornice lines, pilasters, and detailing (notably the swags, cartouches, and be-figured panels), their limestone-faced fronts read as a single composition. The bold tower reads as an architectural exclamation point—and a highly successful one—that terminates one of the city's most opulent blocks.

6 Embassy of the Republic of Cameroon (Hauge House)

2349 Massachusetts Avenue, N.W.

1906 George Oakley Totten, Jr.

This romantic limestone château marks
the western end of Massachusetts
Avenue's great turn-of-the-century
Beaux-Arts residences, a procession
which begins with de Sibour's Wilkins
House at 17th Street. Christian Hauge, a
Norwegian diplomat, commissioned the
traceried delight shortly after he was appointed his nation's first minister
to the United States in 1905 (the year Norway gained its independence
from Sweden). Hauge died in 1907, while snowshoeing back in Norway,
but his Kentucky-born and quite rich widow stayed on in the house, holding sway as one of the city's more influential hostesses until her own death
in 1927.

7 Woodrow Wilson House

2340 S Street, N.W.

c. 1915 Waddy B. Wood

10:00 A.M. TO 4:00 P.M. TUESDAY
THROUGH SUNDAY BY APPOINTMENT
ONLY   PHONE: 387-4062

President and Mrs. Wilson occupied this
comfortable Georgian revival house, with
its center hall plan, Adamesque interiors,
and carefully designed details, from the end of his latter term as president,
in 1921, until his death in 1924. Mrs. Wilson particularly liked the place—
she called it "an unpretentious, comfortable, dignified house, fitted to the
needs of a gentleman"—and she continued to live here until 1961, when
she died. Interestingly, although the Wilsons did not commission the
house—they purchased it from its builder, businessman Henry Parker
Fairbanks—it is the only one the couple ever owned.

Waddy Butler Wood (1869–1944), from a First Family of Virginia,
enjoyed a successful career as one of upper-class Washington's favored
architects and designed more than 30 mansions in the Kalorama area
alone. He was a particular favorite of the Wilsons, perhaps because they
shared his deep Old Dominion roots, and they chose him to design the

inaugural stands for both of Wilson's inaugurations. In an unpublished essay, "Colonial—Now and Yesterday," Wood set forth his conservative beliefs, ideas which must have been reassuring to most of his clients. He firmly believed in a "rational, Anglo-Saxon-based style" and commented that "striving for originality for originality's sake has invariably been a failure because originality not based on evolution has to be based on revolution . . . with the inevitable result—Architectural Bolshevism."

Yet now and then Wood burst forth in an entirely different vein. One of his finest exotic forays was the nearby Alice Pike Barney residence and studio (2306 Massachusetts Avenue): all stucco and neo-Mediterranean and wildly romantic, it perfectly suited the temperament of its builder, an aesthetically minded Lady Bountiful. Barney once complained, "What is capital life after all? Small talk and lots to eat, an infinite series of teas and dinners. Art? There is none." To cure this, she painted and wrote plays, one of which was attended by Sarah Bernhardt, who arrived in a litter carried by four liveried footmen; a renowned musician as well, Barney received a commission from no less than Anna Pavlova to score a ballet for the great Russian dancer to use on her triumphant 1915 tour of America.

The National Trust now maintains the Wilson house; the Smithsonian acts as custodian for the Barney studio; and poor Waddy Wood is largely forgotten.

---

8   2145 Decatur Place, N.W.

1901   Ogden Codman

One of the city's most "proper" residences, this Flemish bond-brick house seems to withdraw behind its gilded iron fence in horrified disapproval of its flashier neighbors. That the building should be so prim—not to say prissy—is hardly surprising; Codman was Edith Wharton's collaborator on that classic book of architectural dos and don'ts, *Decoration of Houses* (1897), in which the authors purse their lips and take a firm stand against such modern horrors as the "electric light, with its harsh, white glare." (They encouraged their tasteful readers to rely on wax candles instead.)

The stairway just west of the house, connecting 22nd Street to S Street, is one of the District's hidden treats. Nicknamed "the Spanish Steps," it suggests a formal, east coast version of San Francisco's laid-back Filbert steps.

9 Friends Meeting House

2111 Florida Avenue, N.W.

1930 Walter H. Price; Rose
Greeley, landscape architect

Somewhat surprisingly placed
among the bombastic mansions
of Russell Baker's "Ruritanian
capital," this simple stone struc-
ture recalls the Quaker buildings that dot rural Pennsylvania. The meeting
house is faced with Foxcroft stone, a material once found in abundance
throughout the District but now unavailable. Greeley designed and
planted the informal, tranquil grounds to resemble a small private park;
she also produced a sundial for the upper terrace inscribed with the query,
"I mind the light, dost thou?"

10 St. Margaret's Church

1820 Connecticut Avenue,
N.W.

1895 James G. Hill
1900 James G. Hill
1913 Arthur B. Heston

Charmingly and thoroughly
quirkish, this brick church is
noted for its fragmented, exterior massing and, on the interior, for its
exposed roof trusses and glorious Tiffany windows. The parish prospered
early in the 20th century under the pastorate of the Rev. Dr. Herbert Scott
Smith, and most of the present structure may be read as evidence of his
fund-raising skills.

11 Lothrop Mansion

2001 Connecticut Avenue,
N.W.

1901 Hornblower & Marshall

Its splendid site, the prow formed
by the intersection of Connecticut Avenue and Columbia Road,
gives this Kalorama *palais* an

unrivaled vista down Connecticut Avenue to Dupont Circle. The grand, open façade shown here is the *rear* of the house, which looks across Columbia Road.

12 Woodward Apartments

2311 Connecticut Avenue, N.W.

1913 Harding and Upman

Crowned with a villa in the sky, this building ranks as one of the best of the many lavish apartment houses that appeared up and down Connecticut Avenue in the early 20th century (note 2101 Connecticut, famed for its gargoyles). Fortunately, it has been spared the heavy-handed remodelings that have defaced so many of its peers.

13 The Lindens

2401 Kalorama Road, N.W.

1754 Robert "King" Hooper, owner-builder
1934 Moved to Washington, D.C.
1935 restoration: Walter Macomber

This magnificent frame Georgian house correctly claims the title of oldest building in Washington, even though it wasn't built here. Its somewhat complex history begins with Hooper, a prosperous Yankee merchant, who erected the house in Danvers, Massachusetts. Now, fast-forward to 1934, when Mr. and Mrs. George Maurice Morris bought the building, dismantled it, moved it in sections, and reconstructed it on a sloping Kalorama lot, where it immediately seemed cozily at home amongst its eclectic neighbors.

The house's entrance pavilion, carried up three stories to the pedimented attic and partially defined by the flanking Corinthian pilasters, adds a surprising vertical thrust to the otherwise foursquare dwelling. Spruced up in 1988–89, the house's buff quoins and pilasters and pale pink rusticated wooden façades (the planks were sanded to resemble more expensive ashlar) now sparkle contentedly in the Washington sun.

14 Embassy of Oman (Devore House)

2000 24th Street, N.W.

1931 William Lawrence Bottomley

Bottomley, specialist of the new-old house, is perhaps best known for the James River Georgian brick villas he built in and around Richmond in the 1920s and '30s. But this limestone creation proves that there was nothing the least parochial about him: he worked gingerly within this somewhat alien, slightly Gallic idiom to produce his usual perfectly proportioned, well-bred masterpiece.

15 Islamic Center

2551 Massachusetts Avenue, N.W.

1949 Egyptian Ministry of Works; A. J. Howar, builder, with Irwin S. Porter and Sons

The religious center for all American Moslems, this steel-framed mosque could not be anything but what it is. Its architects sited the building so it faces Mecca and filled it with a dazzling array of Arabic art: Persian carpets cover the floors; the ebony pulpit is inlaid in ivory; stained glass sparkles in the clerestory; and verses from the Koran are rendered in mosaics around the entrance, throughout the front courtyard, and atop the 160-foot minaret. Still, the Egyptians did make a few concessions to the neighborhood, particularly in deciding to face the mosque in limestone, the favorite material of Massachusetts Avenue's château builders.

16 Japanese Embassy

2516 Massachusetts Avenue,
N.W.

1932 embassy: Delano &
Aldrich
1960 tea house: Nahiko Emori

Here are Delano and Aldrich at
their dignified best. The em-
bassy has a simple, pedimented Georgian revival façade that makes the
substantial structure seem quite modest by comparison with the architectural stage sets that dominate this stretch of Massachusetts Avenue. The
widely praised gardens contain an authentic tea house that was built in
Japan, taken apart, shipped to America, and reassembled on this site; the
charming little structure marks the 100th anniversary of diplomatic relations between the two nations.

17 Danish Embassy

3200 Whitehaven Street,
N.W.

1959 Wilhelm Lauritzen

Shaded by a wooded hillock,
Lauritzen's building stands cool
and white and crystalline. Un-
fortunately, much of this lovely effect is lost, for one must view the
embassy across a parking lot at the entrance. Nevertheless, the embassy
(built on land that had been part of the Dumbarton Oaks tract) and the
adjacent Center for Hellenic Studies form a quiet enclave, far removed
aesthetically from the Massachusetts Avenue bravado.

18 Brazilian Embassy
  (McCormick House)

3000 Massachusetts Avenue,
N.W.

1931 embassy: John Russell
Pope
1973 chancery: Olavo de
Campos

Built as the Washington lair of Chicago tycoon Robert S. McCormick, this house presents another variation on Pope's palazzo formula. Here the architect created a recessed entrance, derived from Peruzzi's Palazzo Massimi alle Colonne in Rome. To the north of the residence is the chancery, a mass of dark glass suspended from roof trusses that cantilever out beyond the interior columns.

---

19 British Embassy

3100 Massachusetts Avenue, N.W.

1927–1928 Sir Edwin Lutyens
1930–1939 gardens: Lady Lindsay

Lutyens, by any standard one of this century's truly important architects, came to the United States in 1925 to accept the AIA's Gold Medal and to begin negotiations concerning a new embassy for the British government. That was a busy year for Lutyens: he also designed a new gold and silver communion service for St. Paul's Cathedral, remodeled the massive façades of the Grosvenor House Hotel in Park Lane, and set to work planning buildings, roadways, and parks for the proposed city of New Delhi.

From America, the architect wrote to his wife, who had remained in England, that he was much impressed with building in the States—"the general character of the work is of a very high standard indeed, far higher than anything on the continent or in England." He magnificently met that standard. The plan is a particular triumph, for Lutyens hit on the idea of using the ambassador's study as a second-story link between the public chancery and the private residence. The great man may also have been having a bit of fun with J. R. Pope and company. As those earnest revivalists were sweating to create neoclassical references to an idealized (and largely fanciful) American past, Lutyens, who called architecture "the great game," impishly chose *colonial* American associations for the new embassy. The Massachusetts Avenue façade is a pastiche of Williamsburg—then very much in the news—and Sir Christopher Wren, while the garden façade, dominated by a giant Ionic portico, suggests Hollywood epics about the Old South.

The renowned embassy gardens were begun by the American-born wife of Sir Ronald Lindsay, the first ambassador to live in the new residence.

She devised a layout that perfectly set off Lutyens's masterpiece, and she chose plants that would thrive in Washington's difficult climate.

Despite Lutyens's and Lindsay's efforts to have the embassy fit into the American scene, somehow one leaves the complex with the definite impression that Rupert Brooke was right: there is indeed "some corner of a foreign field that is forever England."

Cleveland Park/Woodley Park/Rock Creek

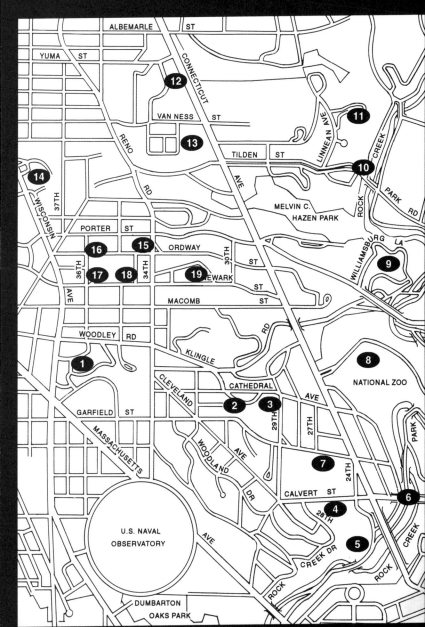

Watched over by its great cathedral towers and named after a brace of summer houses (President Cleveland's Red Top, now demolished, which was on Newark Street, and Woodley House on Cathedral Avenue), this charming neighborhood virtually defines the word benign. And how could it be otherwise in a place of elm-crowned streets and picket fences, where the two best-known landmarks are the National Cathedral and the National Zoo? But these monuments are truly *sui generis,* and by and large the neighborhood's considerable tone comes from its eclectic mix of stuccoed and shingled homes of the McKinley era, sprinkled with a few striking productions from contemporary talents. Whatever the vintage of the houses, though, they all seem just slightly shabby, with porches full of faded chintz and wicker in the summer and with air redolent of burning wood in the winter. One senses that denizens of the area are abuzz year-round with wholesome activities—looking for lost Redskins tickets or baking a casserole for a PTA covered dish supper or planning a Greenpeace rally. Sadly, recent outcroppings of stickers reading "Property Protected by XYZ Security" shatter these musings and jolt one back to a harsh late-20th-century reality.

In 1905, Easter Monday was a popular time for a stroll at the National Zoo.

1 Washington National Cathedral (Cathedral Church of St. Peter and St. Paul)

Massachusetts and Wisconsin
Avenues, N.W.

1906–1907 George Frederick Bodley
1907–1917 Henry Vaughan; Arthur B.
Heaton, superintending architect
1920–1942 E. Donald Robb
1920–1944 Harry B. Little
1920–1971 Philip Hubert Frohman
1971–1973 James E. Godwin,
superintending architect
1973–1981 Howard B. Trevillian, Jr., superintending architect
1981–1990 Anthony J. Segreti, superintending architect
1981–1993 Robert Calhoun Smith, superintending architect
1989 EDAW Inc., landscape architects, west front

Constructed largely according to medieval structural principles, this building, widely regarded as the most beautiful cathedral in America, proves to skeptics that a Gothic interior can still inspire awe.

The idea for a cathedral in Washington goes back to L'Enfant, who envisioned a "great church for national purpose . . . equally open to all"; but distrust of comingling church and state kept the project on hold until 1893, when President Benjamin Harrison yielded to congressional pressure and established the Protestant Episcopal Cathedral Foundation. A cathedral, of course, does not just happen; its existence is predicated on the jelling of a limitless number of complex factors and, in the words of the Rt. Rev. Henry Satterlee, an original mover and shaker here on Mount St. Alban, "the least work of a cathedral is that which is directly connected with . . . building."

It may seem curious, and prove instructive, to note that the District's most successful buildings—this cathedral, the Capitol, the White House, the Washington Monument—have all emerged from push-and-pull, compromise-filled histories. What else, after all, is possible in a nation based on democratic consensus? To get the cathedral going, the Episcopal hierarchy first had to do some politicking and create a new diocese, since Washington was then part of the Diocese of Maryland. Then ensued a years-long search for the right site, as Satterlee, by then Bishop of Washington, rejected one tract near Dupont Circle as "too expensive" and another near Chevy Chase as "utterly unfit." Then came design competitions, or, rather, a series of what the present Clerk of the Works, Richard Feller, calls "wranglings": the neoclassical City Beautiful movement held turn-of-the-century Washington by the throat, and church officials came within one vote of adopting Ernest Flagg's plans for a domed, Renaissance-style cathedral. (Flagg had given the city the wonderful Corcoran Gallery.) Satterlee, a devoted Gothicist, traveled to England to persuade the aged Bodley to come up with sketches for a Gothic building—and even then factions fussed with each other, since Bodley wanted "a good, soft-looking, . . . red stone" church while the Bostonian Vaughan, brought in to assist the older man, favored white limestone. Then Bodley died and someone had to be found to take his place, a struggle in which the largely untested Frohman narrowly beat out the distinguished John Russell Pope. *Then* came the inevitable fundraising, a process helped initially by Charles Carroll Glover, president of Riggs Bank, and still under way today, since cathedrals require considerable maintenance and perform many functions.

Finally, in 1907, Theodore Roosevelt tapped the cornerstone into place and cried "God speed the work!" Construction continued in spurts for 83 years until the building was essentially finished in the fall of 1990. Now, as the cathedral's former provost, Charles Perry, observed, "construction will never again dominate the life of the cathedral. The cathedral's use as a center of ministry and worship, as a house of prayer for all people, will be the focus of attention."

In its landscaping, the disciplined lines of the cathedral benefit from having the prodigal wilderness of Bryce Park, its neighbor to the southwest, for a foil; Bryce Park, in turn, benefits from the presence of the elegant St. Alban's Tennis Club (Hartman-Cox, 1971).

---

2 Maret School (Woodley House)

3000 Cathedral Avenue, N.W.

1806 Philip Barton Key,
owner–builder
1952 adaptation: architect
unknown

Woodley House crowns a gently sloping hill. Its stepped façade and general massing, which reflect the shaped rooms within, markedly resemble the better-known Oatlands near Leesburg, Virginia. Philip Barton Key was a lawyer, a member of Congress from Maryland, and an uncle of Francis Scott Key; he bought the land from his friend Gen. Uriah Forrest, who lived nearby at Rosedale.

3 Swiss Embassy

2900 Cathedral Avenue, N.W.

1959 William Lescaze

Is it possible that Lescaze concocted this unpretentious, well-crafted creation to reflect the thrifty virtues of its owners? It certainly seems likely. The expansive and informal rear gardens, visible from 29th Street, with their California-style pool and cabanas, create a completely different set of impressions.

4 Shoreham Hotel

2500 Calvert Street, N.W.

1930 Joseph Abel

"Expansive" perhaps most kindly describes the sensation this building's drives, entrances, and public spaces create in the viewer. The lobby steps down and opens out to present an exciting view of Rock Creek Park, a surprising visual reward for entering this otherwise unpromising complex. Many feel that the Shoreham makes an altogether more coherent impression than its near neighbor and spiritual twin, the Sheraton-Park, and perhaps they are right. Even so, this building is also decidedly duller.

5 Rock Creek Park
Established 1896

One of Washington's greatest natural features, Rock Creek cuts a deep, green gash
through the District, defining neighborhoods as it rushes southeastward to meet
the Potomac. The creek's dark mysteries
made it a favorite with impressionable visitors: in the 1830s, for example, Frances
Trollope marveled at the "dark, cold little
river . . . so closely shut in by rocks and
ever-greens, that it might serve as a noon-
day bath for Diana and her nymphs." But even those without a drop of
romantic blood must acknowledge that the valley's wildness and size are
unsurpassed by any other urban park in America, perhaps in the world.

In 1890, after much prodding by landscape architect Frederick Law
Olmsted, Sr., Congress voted funds to acquire and safeguard Rock Creek's
streambed, to create a "pleasuring ground for the benefit and enjoyment of
the people of the United States," and to "provide for the preservation . . .
of all timber, animals, or curiosities . . . in their natural condition." In
1924, Olmsted, Jr., got Congress to enlarge the park to include, so far as
was practical, the creek's tributaries as well.

Now sprawling over some 1,800 acres, Rock Creek Park forms the
largest element in the National Capital Parks system. It is but one segment
in a chain of parks that line the creek. Park and creek begin miles beyond
the Beltway, near the wilds of outer Rockville, and then gradually meander
their way into the city. Once within the District boundaries, the creek
abuts the relatively high ground of the National Zoo; then in sequence
come Dumbarton Oaks Park, Montrose Park, Oak Hill Cemetery, and the
Rock Creek Parkway, which accompanies the waterway until it tumbles
down to meet the river near the Kennedy Center.

6 Duke Ellington Bridge (Calvert Street Bridge)

Calvert Street over Rock Creek, N.W.

1935 Paul P. Cret

One of several notable bridges in the area, this handsome span, with its wide side-walks and graceful concrete arches, car-ries motorists and pedestrians over Rock Creek, which gurgles along 120 feet below. Four pylons support the bridge, and Cret embellished these functional props with stylized 1930s sculpture sym-bolizing travel by air, rail, water, and highway.

7 Sheraton-Park Hotel (Wardman-Park Hotel)

2660 Connecticut Avenue, N.W.

1918 Mihran Mesrobian; Harry Wardman, builder

This sprawling, eight-story, red-brick hotel and its rambling acreage seem more suggestive of a Homestead-like resort than an urban hotel. Indeed, as Benjamin Forgey wrote in the November 11, 1989, *Washington Post,* all of upper Connecticut Avenue, with its ten-story apartments and hotels "set apart from one another almost like manor houses," is "at least as countrified as it is citi-fied." Potentially overpowering, the Sheraton, thanks in part to Mesro-bian's use of homey details such as bay windows and balconies, does not intimidate visitors but welcomes them, and one half expects to find a tray laden with stirrup cups just inside the doors.

   The building, which helped earn Mesrobian an award for excellence from the AIA in 1926, also helped set the highly agreeable tone of this stretch of Connecticut Avenue. Three generations of architects have lined the thoroughfare with the dozens of exceptional hotels and apartments alluded to above: the World War I–vintage Sheraton began the lively theme, which was picked up in the Astaire-Rogers era (note especially the Kennedy-Warren, 3133 Connecticut Avenue, built 1931, Joseph Younger, architect), and is now enjoying some vivacious modern reinterpretations, including David Schwarz's much-praised Saratoga at 4601.

8   National Zoological Park

3001 Connecticut Avenue, N.W.

1907 Hornblower & Marshall, and many others

APRIL THROUGH OCTOBER, 9:00 A.M. TO 6:00 P.M. DAILY; NOVEMBER THROUGH MARCH, 9:00 A.M. TO 4:30 P.M. DAILY

The zoo houses its appealing and exotic animals in a collection of endearingly fanciful buildings and accurately recreated wild settings. The best of the structures—and there are a good many that might be called the "best"—not only provide shelter for the zoo's animals but also elicit grins from the zoo's patrons. Note, by way of example, the whimsical Monkey House, clad in mossy stone and topped with a purple and green tile roof set off by bear cub, bobcat, and fox finials, and also the Reptile House (shown here), a Romanesque-Moorish fantasy with a stegosaurus-emblazoned fanlight.

9   Klingle Mansion

3545 Williamsburg Lane, N.W.

1823 Joshua Pierce, owner-builder

Established by a son of mill owner Jacob Pierce, this estate contains many details that suggest the family's Pennsylvania origins: note the beehive oven and the bank barn. Young Pierce, a noted horticulturist, created extensive gardens around the granite-walled, center hall–plan dwelling; and a few of his plantings have managed to remain, as has his two-story utility house with its built-in potting shed. The entire property lies within Rock Creek Park's original 1890s boundaries; the National Park Service restored the house and grounds in 1935.

10 Pierce Mill

2311 Tilden Street (at Beach Drive), N.W.

c. 1810 Isaac Pierce, owner-builder

9:00 A.M. TO 5:00 P.M. WEDNESDAY
THROUGH SUNDAY
PHONE: 426-6908

Rock Creek's powerful current once powered eight separate mills, grinding corn,
rye, oats, and wheat grown by local farm-
ers. Indeed, the 1932 *Washington Sketch-*
book observes that the creek "was originally a racing stream, deep enough where it flowed into the Potomac to anchor seagoing ships," but that "gradually the little harbor filled up." Simultaneously, changes in District land use spelled extinction for local amber waves of grain. Of those original eight mills, this one alone remains, and students of early industry particu-larly value the building for its rare under-shot wheel. Mill and acreage were absorbed into the park in 1890 and WPA workmen restored the industrial building to working order around 1935. Other survivors of the once-flourishing Pierce family compound include a distillery (c. 1811) and a stone springhouse (c. 1801) on this farmstead, and the adjacent Linnean Hill property.

11 Hillwood

4155 Linnean Avenue, N.W.

1923, 1955 architects
unknown
1955–1965 Perry Wheeler,
landscape architect
1985 Indian artifacts collection: O'Neil & Manion
Architects, PA
1986 café: O'Neil & Manion
Architects, PA

TUESDAY THROUGH SATURDAY BY APPOINTMENT ONLY
PHONE: 686-5807

Here follows the saga of cereal heiress Marjorie Merriweather Post, who moved to Rock Creek Park and lashed out to create grand living on the largest possible scale. She bought Arbremont, a red brick neo-Georgian mansion with 25 acres, in 1955, shortly after divorcing her third and penultimate husband, Ambassador Joseph E. Davies. She changed the estate's name to Hillwood and, for a while at least, making over the house and garden became the septuagenarian's all-consuming passion. Post took some measurements and decided that the original dwelling, built for a daughter of a Michigan lumber millionaire, was too pokey to house her collections, to say nothing of the movie room she wanted. So she started dismantling the place. With her favorite, Catherine the Great, as inspiration, and very much her own boss, she terrorized workmen for years, building and remodeling until her Hillwood achieved its present 40-room bulk. During one of her visits to the site, according to one typical story, recounted in WETA magazine, she declaimed that the roof was three feet too low. When the builder pointed out that he had followed her design exactly, she replied, "I didn't ask you how it was designed, I said it was too low." At the same time, she was commanding Wheeler, who had proved himself to her by designing the White House Rose Garden, to add a French garden, a Japanese garden, a Scots garden, etc., etc., etc. to the rolling grounds.

When Hillwood finally met her standards, she began to fill it with her treasures, including the predictable mogul-French *objets* as well as an astonishing tonnage of Fabergé eggs, icons, and other remnants of the Czars that she had persuaded Stalin to sell her in the 1930s, when Davies was our man in Moscow.

When Merriweather Post died in 1973 (after her fourth husband, she decided to resume use of her maiden name), she bequeathed Hillwood to the Smithsonian. Once the initial shock had worn off, that organization hired Sara O'Neil-Manion to design a structure that could accommodate Post's immense collection of American Indian artifacts, which she had also left to the institution. During the heiress's life, she had kept the blankets and pottery and baskets at her upstate New York camp, and O'Neil-Manion tactfully brought the rustic quality of the Adirondacks to Washington without the slightest trace of irony.

12　Van Ness Center

4250 Connecticut Avenue, N.W.

1983　Hartman-Cox Architects

Mention the 2000, 3000, and 4000 blocks of Connecticut Avenue and what comes to mind? Why, of course: beige-brick art deco apartment houses with colored tile trim. Those elements and that overall aesthetic clearly inspired this witty spec building. In addition, the architects politely acknowledged several buildings on the nearby campus of the University of the District of Columbia (Connecticut Avenue and Van Ness Street; Bryant and Bryant, John Chase, and others) as well as the superbly art deco Hecht Company warehouse across town at 1401 New York Avenue, N.E.

13　Intelsat Headquarters

3400 International Drive, N.W.

1987　John Andrews International, Ltd.; Notter Finegold + Alexander, associate architects

Suburbanites beware! The Emerald City has appeared near Chevy Chase. Perhaps one should simply point out the obvious—that this complex evinces a different design aesthetic than does the nearby Van Ness Center.

14 Friends' School Administration Building (The Highlands)

3825 Wisconsin Avenue, N.W.

1816–1822 Charles Joseph Nourse, owner-builder

One of the few remaining 19th-century stone houses in the area, this stately dwelling once presided over hundreds of acres of farmland. It still looks the part. Joseph Nourse, who more or less ran the Treasury Department around 1800, gave vast acreage here, extending east to Rock Creek, to his son Charles, chief clerk at the War Department, and daughter-in-law, Rebecca. Then, using stone quarried on the place, the couple built the house they called The Highlands. As Anne Hollingsworth Wharton observed in *Social Life in the Early Republic* (1904), "no house in the vicinity of Washington is more replete with associations of the past than The Highlands, where the Madisons, Thomas Jefferson, . . . and other distinguished people of the day were wont to congregate" and whose gardens boasted "shrubbery planted on the grounds by Thomas Jefferson." The square stone columns on the west front are comparatively recent additions.

15 3411 Ordway Street, N.W.

1962 I. M. Pei

A diminutive creation in gray brick, this house rests snug and secure behind its front wall. Crisp and clean, it demonstrates the heights that modern domestic architecture—*good* modern domestic architecture—could attain.

16 Winthrop Faulkner Houses at Rosedale

Ordway and 36th Streets, N.W.

1964–1978 Winthrop Faulkner

Partly to ensure compatibly modernist neighbors, Faulkner designed this group of hand-some contemporary houses including 3530 Ordway (1963), 3540 Ordway (1968), 3407 36th Street (1978), and 3411 36th Street (1978) to surround his own residence at 3403 36th Street (1978). The enclave, especially when the 36th Street house of Waldron Faulkner (Winthrop's father) is included, forms a body of work whose excellence of line and sureness of massing can hold its own with any grouping of similar scale in the District.

17 Waldron Faulkner House

3415 36th Street, N.W.

1937 Waldron Faulkner
1964 Lester Collins, landscape architect

This superb modernist urban villa—by any standard one of the finest houses of its time in America—is classically propor-tioned, symmetrical, and manages to maintain its quiet, scholarly reserve and still be a real part of its own clanging era.

Armed with three degrees from Yale, Waldron Faulkner (1898–1979) began his architectural career in New York in 1925. He moved to Wash-ington in 1934 and, in partnership with Slocum Kingsbury, embarked on a highly successful series of campus design projects at Vassar, American University, and George Washington University. A staunch supporter of the New Deal, Faulkner worked hard to fuse social reform and modern design, for he saw how clean lines and sturdy yet inexpensive materials might be used to improve the state of low-cost housing in the District. (He also served as president of the Washington Urban League and the

Washington Housing Association.) He was a prolific writer, and his book *Architecture and Color* (1972) remains a standard work on the subject.

Faulkner set forth his views about architecture and history in a piece he prepared for the AIA in 1945: "In the natural order of things, one art form follows its predecessor in continuous succession. Each generation resembles its ancestors and its descendants, with minor variations. . . . When a form of architectural expression passes its peak, it dies . . . and becomes archaeology. . . . When I refer to modern architecture, I mean architecture which reflects man's true nature at any given period and offers a solution to the basic needs of the day. . . . Fitness may be taken as the true test of modern architecture of any period."

Site planning and planting accentuates the symmetry of this house; Faulkner planted four *Magnolia grandiflora* trees to mark the building's corners and placed the well-articulated front door smack on axis with Norton Place. Waldron Faulkner also designed the guest house at 3419 36th Street, completed in 1940, for which Winthrop designed an addition, completed in 1992.

---

18 International Exchange—Youth for Understanding (Rosedale)

3501 Newark Street, N.W.

1793 Uriah Forrest, owner-builder

Gen. Uriah Forrest, a man hugely responsible for the creation of the District of Columbia, bought 1,000 rural acres north of Georgetown and built this delightful yellow clapboard farmhouse as a summer retreat. But within a few years he succumbed to the farm's charms and decided to abandon his M Street residence and live at Rosedale year-round. Even today, with a city of 4,000,000 grown up around it, the unaggressive building, set off by an immense sweep of front lawn and by stands of towering magnolias and hollies, retains a distinctly un-urban air. Only the ranges of new brick dormitories to the west give away the farmstead's new, academic use.

19 Highland Place

Between 34th and Newark Streets, N.W.

Middle to late 19th century various architects and builders

Tall, gnarled oaks lining the streets shade this collection of houses, which distill all that was good about 19th-century America. It is the architecture of the front porch, at once romantic and picturesque, and it evokes nostalgic sounds of children's laughter across backyards, player pianos, bats hitting balls, and the occasional, unmistakable bang of a screen door.

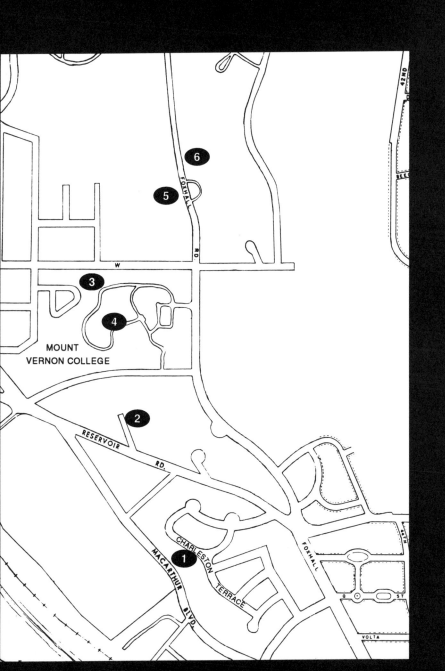

Perhaps the most desirable neighborhood in town at the moment (things move fast in the world of D.C. real estate), this area seems so thoroughly professional-class, so uniformly post–World War II suburban, that many are surprised to learn that not all that long ago it was open farm country. In the 1920s and '30s the grassy lawns of Mount Vernon College, now scene of promenading students, were the grassy meadows of Palisades Dairy Farm, then scene of grazing Jersey cattle.

The entire area takes its name from the Foxall (without an *h*) family farm, which was located near where Foxhall Road and P Street intersect. Henry Foxall, who established the farm, lived on 34th Street in Georgetown; he made a fortune in shipping, arms manufacturing, and banking, and, in quieter moments, played violin duets with Thomas Jefferson. The farm proved an impractical anachronism in the 20th century and was sold around 1910. Construction of Foxhall Village (with an *h*) began in 1927, and cocktail parties, station wagons, and bridge games quickly replaced the cattle, chicken coops, and orchards.

Saint-Mémin's early-19th-century profile captures a somewhat jowly Henry Foxall, industrialist, connoisseur of the arts, and mayor of Georgetown; a century later, Foxall's surname gained an h *when it came to be used to describe this new, suburban neighborhood.*

1 Montedonico House

4622 Charleston Terrace, N.W.

1986–1987 Cass & Pinnell Architects

Perched on a cliff overlooking the Potomac about one mile upstream from Georgetown, this modernist triumph takes full advantage of its steeply sloping site. The house somehow succeeds in being both open, with views of the river that can only be called panoramic, and private, a complex achievement for which Cass and Pinnell are to be heartily congratulated.

2 German Embassy Chancery

4645 Reservoir Road, N.W.

1964 Egon Eiermann

The chancery serves both to wall off the site and to link the embassy's residence on Foxhall Road above and the business entrance on Reservoir Road below. Mindful of the neighborhood's character, Eiermann stepped-down the ends of the building to reduce the bulk and bring the chancery close to the scale of the nearby houses.

3 Florence Hollis Hand Chapel, Mount Vernon College

2100 Foxhall Road, N.W.

1970 Hartman-Cox Architects

10:00 A.M. TO 5:00 P.M. SCHOOL DAYS.
INQUIRE AT GATEHOUSE AT OTHER TIMES.

On the outside, this highly imaginative college chapel addresses itself to the scale of the campus and its suburban environs. On the inside it creates an impressive volume by taking advantage of the hillside site, while the stepped clerestory roof, a brave detail that works, creates a gentle light that avoids uncomfortable contrasts. The architects have said that when working on this pure structure they kept American colonial churches, "with white walls, red carpet, wood floor and pews . . . very much in mind." It shows.

4   Dormitory, Mount Vernon College

2100 Foxhall Road, N.W.

1971 Hartman-Cox Architects

A confidently executed and carefully detailed expression of the materials used, the sweeping lines of this building produce an eloquent solution to the problem of a complex arrangement of many small units. At the same time, Hartman-Cox were well aware of the natural contours of the rolling land and gave the dormitories a wealth of balconies and arcades, which yield expansive vistas of woodland and river.

5   2300 Foxhall Road, N.W.

1931 Horace Trumbauer

Washington, a city where mansions are almost commonplace, has few dwellings that can match this building's restrained elegance. The Hôtel de Charolais in Paris supplied inspiration for the main façade, but the overall spirit is pure *Great Gatsby*. "There was music from my neighbor's house through the summer nights," Fitzgerald wrote. "In his blue gardens men and girls came and went like moths among the whisperings and the champagne stars."

6 David Lloyd Kreeger House

2401 Foxhall Road, N.W.

1967 Philip Johnson and Richard Foster

Johnson designed this veritable Roman villa to house the owner's extensive collection of art. Mr. Kreeger endeared himself to the city's building-design community by resolutely choosing to be a patron of creative architecture rather than merely a consumer of mass-produced construction.

Kreeger

202 338 3552

Tues + Sat.
10^{30} + 1^{30}

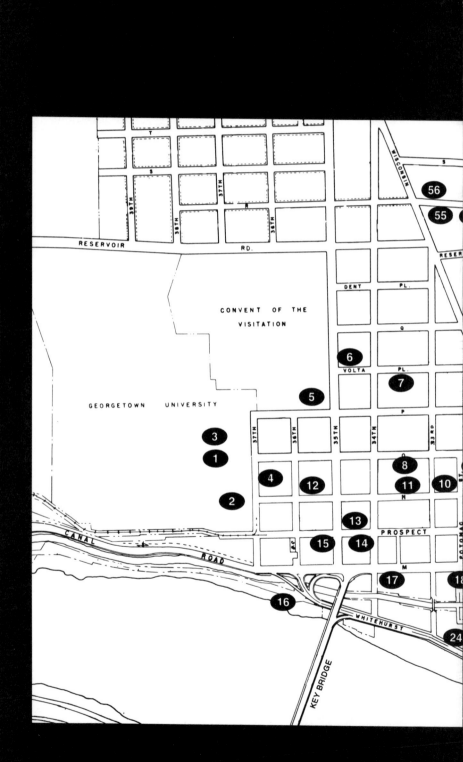

which Georgetown University was later built. Incorporated in 1789, Georgetown formed a discrete little entity with a mercantile economy based on exporting flour and tobacco and importing luxury European goods and West Indian rum.

It can be argued that Washington, D.C., owes its existence to Georgetown, whose mayor, Uriah Forrest, gathered the local elite in his M Street house so President Washington could persuade them to sell their land to the federal government. But most early residents of the "dirty little hole" had no use for the new capital city. President Jefferson, in turn, had no use for Georgetown's aloofness and planned a "good gravel road" to connect the stand-offish enclave with the President's House, Capitol Hill, and the Navy Yard. The road, Pennsylvania Avenue, got

"View of Georgetown D.C.," a lithograph published by Sachse and Company in 1853, shows a town no longer the "dirty little hole" Abigail Adams had dismissed a half-century earlier. Rock Creek can be seen entering the Potomac from the right in the middle distance. The bridge crossing the river (roughly at 36th Street) is the Potomac Aqueduct, a wooden superstructure on stone piers, designed by Benjamin Miller and built 1833–43 to carry C & O Canal traffic to and from Virginia.

built, but Georgetown remained a place apart. As late as 1826, one observer noticed that "the people of Georgetown . . . form a striking contrast to their neighbors in Washington, their minds being generally more cultivated. It is hardly possible to conceive how towns so near . . . should differ so widely."

Georgetown didn't fare too well during the rest of the 19th century: the river silted up; the C & O Canal, dug to lure the rich Midwest trade to the Potomac, proved no match for the B & O Railroad; and trade bypassed Georgetown's once-flourishing port in favor of Baltimore. The inevitable came in the 1870s when Georgetown, by then largely shabby, was quietly annexed into Washington; the community even lost its name, for the blocks along Wisconsin Avenue and M Street became legally known as "West Washington."

Georgetown then entered a period of quiescence that did not end until the New Deal, when the growth of the federal government—and the consequent rise in District population—brought about the rediscovery of "West Washington" as a choice place to live, convenient to the office buildings of Foggy Bottom and Capitol Hill. The pace of this rediscovery quickened after World War II until it began to look as if Georgetown might be spoiled by its success. To ensure the preservation of the architectural character of their town, residents lobbied the Old Georgetown Act through Congress in 1950. The act requires that plans for demolition, renovation, or new construction be approved by an appointed commission. Throughout all this, Georgetown has retained its unique quality: clearly distinct from other parts of Washington, the community and its residents add interest and variety to the capital's life. Now about parking . . .

---

1   Healy Building

Georgetown University
1879 Smithmeyer & Pelz

Bringing a touch of the Rhine to the Potomac, this baronial fantasy was designed by the stylistically ambidextrous architects of the Library of Congress building. The Potomac gneiss walls of the 4 1/2-story fortress and its 200-foot clock tower completely dominate the university's federal and neoclassical buildings, such as Old North. The interior of the Riggs Library, with its four levels of cast iron stacks, forms a wonderfully impressive space which a recent Georgetown undergraduate pithily described as "dynamite!"

2 Joseph Mark Lauinger Memorial Library

Georgetown University

1970 John Carl Warnecke & Associates

Known for his desire to be a good neighbor, a trait especially evident in his work at Lafayette Square, Warnecke gave this exposed-concrete library broken massing, a spiky profile, gray color, and a tiny tower in deference to the craggy façades of the nearby, massive Healy building. He also kept the new library low, to maintain the romantic view of the Healy tower from across the river.

3 Old North Building

Georgetown University

1792–1793 architect unknown

The earliest building in this oldest of American Jesuit institutions, Old North bears striking similarities to other simple, if elongated, brick Georgian or federal collegiate structures, such as Princeton's Nassau Hall. It also strongly suggests the residential blocks that once characterized domestic design in the District (see, e.g., Wheat Row–Harbour Square). The beneficiary of a recent face-lift, Old North now houses the university's business school.

4 Alumni Square and Leavy Center

Georgetown University

1983 Hugh Newell Jacobsen

Designing accommodations for 360 students in the midst of a nationally important historic district was no small task. Jacobsen rose to the challenge with a highly successful solution: he designed the Alumni Square complex as a U-shaped array of row houses resembling the 19th-century ones located just outside the university's 37th Street gates. Because the dorms lie in Georgetown, not on the campus proper, Jacobsen treated them as town houses, as part of the urban streetscape, not as huge dormitories. Although a few undergraduates have complained that this approach denies them the interaction so central to dorm life, it undeniably makes the project more compatible to its historic neighbors. The architect's well-known wit sparkles through in the details: note the vacuum-formed fiberglass cornices and the sandstone window lintels with their corner blocks inscribed "G" and "U."

As a contrast, Jacobsen designed the Leavy Center, a large, multi-use facility firmly within the campus on the other side of the gates, to harmonize with other university structures, particularly the Healy Building, whose stone gables and towers it reinterprets, with only slightly less swagger, in brick.

5 Convent of the Visitation

35th and P Streets, N.W.

1825 chapel: Joseph Picot de Clorivière
1857 monastery: architect unknown
1874 academy building: Norris G. Starkweather

Three different architectural styles combine here in a catalog of period design. They form a masonry crescendo, from austere federal, via the Gothic-classic stuccoed chapel, to the ornate Victorian 3 1/2-story brick

Academy Building with its mansard roof and elaborate entrance. Established by French nuns in 1799, Visitation is the second oldest convent in the United States. Its grounds are now dotted with more than 20 separate structures.

6 Volta Bureau

1537 35th Street, N.W.

1893 Peabody and Stearns
1948–1949 Russell O. Kluge

When Alexander Graham Bell invented the telephone, the French government awarded him the $10,000 Volta Prize; Bell turned around and used the money to establish the American Association to Promote the Teaching of Speech to the Deaf, an organization headquartered here. The building's 35th Street front looks like a yellow-brick temple, but the other elevations more accurately suggest its office use, particularly the rear or east façade, which is composed of a series of slit-windows suggestive of the old Central Library on Mount Vernon Square.

7 Pomander Walk

Volta Place, between 33rd and 34th Streets, N.W.

1885 architects unknown

Within the last 30 years this alley has changed from a slum to a small attractive center-block enclave; its 10 tiny houses display a light-hearted, almost fey, charm.

8   Bodisco House

3322 O Street, N.W.

1815   Clement Smith, owner-builder

Banker and land speculator Clement Smith built this massive brick dwelling. A bit later, the Russian legation purchased the place, evidently feeling that the building's height, sweeping double flight of stairs, and columned entrance made it imposing enough to house the Czar's emissaries.

One of the more colorful of those ministers, Alexander, Baron de Bodisco, gave his name to the house and caused one of the mid-19th century's more reverberant local scandals. Bodisco, who represented the Kremlin during the Polk administration, met, fell in love with, and married Harriett Beall Williams of Georgetown; hostesses' tongues wagged and wagged, because Miss Williams was a beautiful lass of 16 while the Baron, according to Anne Hollingsworth Wharton's *Social Life in the Early Republic* (1904), was 60 years old, "short and stout, with a broad Kalmuck face, much wrinkled, surmounted by a shining brown wig." Henry Clay gave the bride away and, writes Wharton, the reception, held "at the Baron's house on O Street," was attended by "the President and his Cabinet [and] members of the Diplomatic Corps in full regalia." The union proved a pleasant one ("the monotony of Georgetown relieved by several trips to Russia") until the baron died some years later. But the old boy kept his widow smiling and the neighbors talking even from the grave: before he passed on he "expressed an amiable desire that his wife might marry again," and "Madame Bodisco . . . soon after" managed to find a strapping young "English officer named Scott," whom she took a shine to and married. The stalwart Scott then kept her "as happy as she had made" the Baron.

9 St. John's Episcopal Church

Potomac and O Streets, N.W.

1804 William Thornton
1870 Starkweather and Plowman

Thornton, a trained physician who dabbled in writing, horse-breeding, and political pamphleteering—as well as architecture—worked on the Capitol and designed Tudor Place and the Octagon. He also provided some of the architectural inspiration for this church, if not the actual drawings (the congregation chose not to follow his ideas overly closely). The building has been much modified over the years, but the foundations, bell tower, and most of the walls seem original. The congregation, founded in 1796 by the Rev. Walter Dulany Addison, with the help of Benjamin Stoddert (who lived nearby at 3400 Prospect Avenue), Francis Scott Key, and Thomas Jefferson, is Georgetown's oldest Episcopal parish.

10 Smith Row

3255–3263 N Street, N.W.

1815 Walter and Clement Smith, owner-builders

These five brick federal houses show how minor variations can add to the success of a simple, consistent theme. Comparison with Cox's Row in the adjoining block reveals that the builders of Smith Row favored raised parlor floors, slightly more elaborate door treatments (note 3259), and, in some of the houses, larger and more attenuated windows. In all, it seems clear that the Smiths, who were brothers, kept themselves a bit more *au courant* in matters of design than his honor the mayor, Colonel Cox, did.

11 Cox's Row

3327–3339 N Street, N.W.
1815–1818 John Cox, owner-builder

While some of these five fine houses
show traces of Victorian remodeling—
and of late-20th-century restoration—
enough remains of them all to give a sense
of how they must have looked when new.
With their sunken panels, leaden swags, and arched doorways, they rank
among the finest and purest examples of federal-era architecture in a city
known for its federal-era buildings.

Colonel Cox, builder of the row, was a flourishing Georgetown merchant who had the good sense to marry an heiress. She brought to the
union as dowry the land now filled by Georgetown University. Cox then
gerrymandered the city boundaries so he could run for mayor; he proved
popular and stayed in office a record 22 years. When Lafayette made his
memorable visit to town in 1824, Cox put 3337 N Street at the great
Frenchman's disposal; Lafayette accepted the offer and lived there during
his entire stay. In his honor, it is said, local school girls sketched welcoming
decorative flowers on the floor of the house with their colored chalks. Cox
and his wife lived next door at 3339.

12 Holy Trinity Parish

3513 N Street, N.W.

1794 original church (now Convent of
Mercy): architect unknown
1846–1849 present church: architect
unknown
1869 rectory: Francis Staunton

Three different eras in religious history
have produced three very different structures. The original brick church was the
District's first building erected for public
Catholic worship, and its small scale and simple lines stand as the outward
and visible sign of the tenuous state of Catholicism in 18th-century America. (Before the First Amendment guaranteed freedom of religion to all,
the area's Catholic families, such as the Carrolls, had been forced to celebrate Mass secretively in private chapels.) That tiny structure soon proved
inadequate for the growing congregation; the handsome, Greco-Roman

revival structure replaced it, and the new building's larger size and attention to architectural style suggest American Catholicism's improved condition. Finally, the mansard-roofed rectory, a splendid product of post–Civil War design, accurately manifests the financial stability that was at last ensured when millions of industrial-era immigrants came from Ireland, Italy, and elsewhere, swelling the ranks of the Roman Catholic Church in America.

13 Quality Hill

3425 Prospect Street, N.W.

1798 John Thomson Mason, owner-builder

Washington as the seat of government has always held a mighty attraction to the successful or ambitious: it drew flamboyant merchant princes here in the booming years after the Civil War, and they left scores of Massachusetts Avenue mansions in their wake; a century earlier, power's call had been no less strong and had lured the former colonies' landed gentry to the Potomac. Among the federal-era elite who built houses in and around the capital city were Martha Washington's grandchildren (see Arlington and Tudor Place), John Tayloe of Virginia (the Octagon), and attorney John Thomson Mason, who put up this fine house. (Mason's uncle, George Mason, gained immortality by drafting the Virginia bill of rights and by bringing architect William Buckland to America from England.)

The name Quality Hill is of uncertain origin: for years historians assumed that it generally described the immediate neighborhood and its wealth of fine houses; recent research, however, suggests that a later owner of this house, Dr. Charles Worthington, thought it up specifically for his residence. If so, Dr. Worthington may have been guilty of immodesty but not inaccuracy, for the 2 1/2-story, center hall–plan house, with its justifiably famous interior woodwork, deserves all the praise it gets.

14 Halcyon House (Benjamin Stoddert House)

3400 Prospect Avenue, N.W.

1786 Benjamin Stoddert, owner-builder

c. 1900 A. A. Clemons, owner-builder

In the late 18th century, Philadelphia still reigned as the "Athens of America," the center of the new nation's wealth, learning, and sophistication. Accordingly, Benjamin Stoddert, merchant, landowner, and America's first secretary of the navy, built Halcyon House, he declared, "after the manner of some of the elegant houses I have seen in Philadelphia."

The south façade, which in truth resembles those of several local houses, such as the Bowie-Sevier House, as much as it does anything along the Schuylkill, remains largely intact. The north is another matter. Albert Adsit Clemons acquired the house around 1900 and spent the next 40 years hiding Stoddert's chaste creation in a labyrinth of rooms, hallways, and stairs, most of which no one ever used. According to the *Washington Times-Herald*, Adsit subsisted on money "provided by his wife on condition that he stay away from her"; that condition didn't bother Adsit, who, according to legend, was particularly fond of one of his carpenters and the two happily lived together in the basement, Adsit seldom if ever venturing into the elaborate architectural shell he created to encase himself and his favorite workman. The house's current owners are removing the additions and in so doing will reveal the original structure, which is good; but they will also deprive the District of one of its few eccentric constructions, which, in a regimented place like Washington, is sad.

15 Prospect House

3508 Prospect Street, N.W.

1788 James Maccubbin Lingan,
owner-builder

The view down the Potomac provides the
name for this quintessential freestanding
federal town house. It is currently
thought that Lingan (1751–1812), a
wealthy tobacco merchant, designed the
residence himself, perhaps using one of
the architectural pattern books then so
popular among America's educated builders. But books alone cannot teach
the superlative craftsmanship seen in the brickwork and doorways. Lingan, one of nineteen landowners who agreed to sell their holdings to establish the District of Columbia, decided that the future lay in the new "Capital City" rather than in backwater Georgetown, so he moved there and sold
Prospect House in the 1790s. An outspoken opponent of the War of 1812,
Lingan met his end in Baltimore, when a mob who favored the war stoned
him to death.

John Templeton, who bought Prospect House from Lingan, made a fortune in banking. In this century, James Forrestal, secretary of defense
under Truman, lived here. When the Trumans retreated to Blair House to
avoid construction work at 1600 Pennsylvania Avenue, Forrestal let his
boss entertain foreign VIPs at Prospect House; all went well until the
Washington Times-Herald published an exposé about the "scores of Congressmen" who sullied this dignified Georgetown dwelling with "stag
entertainments . . . featuring liquor and feminine companionship."

16 Washington Canoe Club

K Street, N.W., above Key
Bridge

c. 1890 architect unknown

Heavy-roofed, turreted, and shingley, this structure exemplifies the principles of turn-of-the-century summerhouse architecture. It is easy to imagine the club perched high on a cliff overlooking the rocks of Northeast Harbor or Buzzard's Bay. In actuality, it overlooks the muddy Potomac. Never mind; the view of the club from across the river has been a favorite of generations of Washingtonians, for the club's rambling wooden roofline forms a romantic counterpoint on the shoreline to the lofty, baronial towers of Georgetown University's Healy Building.

17 Forrest-Marbury House

3350 M Street, N.W.

c. 1785 Uriah Forrest, owner-builder; several remodelings
1988 Geier Brown Renfrow Architects; restoration: MMP International

Here in March 1791 Georgetown mayor Uriah Forrest gave a dinner party that produced the District of Columbia. At the urging of George Washington, Forrest gathered together the area's leading land-owners and convinced them to view the proposed capital city as an idea whose time had come. It had been no easy task, and that night Washington wearily wrote in his diary that "the business" was "happily finished." Shortly thereafter, Forrest sold the impressive brick house, whose bulk is made even more impressive by notable splayed and keystoned lintels, and moved away from Georgetown, to lead a more laid-back existence at Rosedale, his farm in what is now Cleveland Park.

Baltimore attorney William Marbury bought the house in 1800. (Three years later the landmark Supreme Court case *Marbury vs. Madison* established the principle of judicial review.) Forrest's old house proved too small for the Marbury clan, who built a two-story addition to the east around 1840 and added a third story to the main block about a decade later. After years of neglect, the house has been adapted to office and condominium use.

18 Dean & Deluca (Georgetown Market)

3276 M Street, N.W.

1866 architect unknown
1992 renovation: Jack
Ceglic, designer; Core
Group, PC, associated
architects

Documents prove that public markets have been held on this site since the
1750s. In 1795 the ground was deeded to the town "for the use of the market aforesaid, and for no other use, interest or purpose whatsoever." This
brick structure dates to the Civil War era. Generations of hucksters
enjoyed a brisk business in the market until chain stores rendered the inde-
pendent vendors obsolete. After a period of neglect, the old building, with
its round-arched windows, bracketed cornices, and central parapet, has
been splendidly restored and again serves as a focus for Georgetown's
gourmets and gourmands.

19 Georgetown Park

3222 M Street, N.W.

1982 Alan J. Lockman &
Associates; Chloethiel
Woodard Smith & Associates,
architectural consultants;
Clark Tribble Harris & Li,
interior design; retail mall:
Yah Yee and Associates

Even though the arched bays of the exterior suggest stylistic links to the
rest of Georgetown, this "park" is probably best viewed as a glitzy escapist
village, an entity unto itself. The complex fills the site that was once the
hub of Georgetown's streetcar lines.

20 City Tavern

3206 M Street, N.W.

1796 architect unknown
1961 reconstruction: Macomber &
Peter

During the 18th century, Georgetown,
located on a much-traveled post road,
boasted several inns and taverns. Some
voyagers used these more or less reputable
establishments as places to refresh themselves with a glass of ale or a spot of din-
ner; others sought rest in the—literally—lousy upstairs sleeping quarters.
While most of the inns went out of business and were destroyed as the
importance of the post road declined in the 19th century, this one managed
to endure. Or, rather, parts of it have endured: the upper-floor rooms are
original, but the lower floor and brick façade are new and date to the building's painstaking restoration. The tavern, now functioning as a private
club, is one of the city's happier preservation success stories.

21 Canal Square

1054 31st Street, N.W.

c. 1850 architect unknown
1971 Arthur Cotton
Moore/Associates P.C.

Moore's new construction
incorporates an old warehouse
into a lively contemporary
center for specialty shops,
restaurants, and offices. This project may be seminal: in it Moore created
what many feel was the nation's first exposed-brick-hanging-fern restaurant. Actually, the older building is no stranger to epochal events, for the
computer age was born here in the 1880s when Herman Hollerith per-
fected his pioneering punch-card tabulating machines under this roof. In
1890 Hollerith won the right to use his new gadget to tabulate that year's
census figures, and he accomplished the job in a few weeks, a vast improvement over the many months it had taken clerks to do the work in 1880.
Hollerith secured several other such commissions, but in 1911 he decided
to sell his Tabulating Machine Company to a vigorous new firm, now
known as IBM.

22 Grace Church

1041 Wisconsin Avenue, N.W.

1866 architect unknown

Set back on a raised and tree-shaded courtyard, this humble granite Gothic revival church, built as a mission for boatmen on the nearby Chesapeake & Ohio Canal, seems unaffected by the passage of time. Indeed, in the right light, the church and its unchanged interior take on the character of a 19th-century stage set.

23 Chesapeake & Ohio Canal Warehouses

Between Potomac Street and Jefferson Place

c. 1828 and after architects unknown

Despite having George Washington and Thomas Jefferson among its backers, the C & O Canal, which ran roughly 185 miles from Cumberland, Maryland, to Alexandria, Virginia, never enjoyed the commercial success its illustrious sponsors had envisioned. The canal, obsolete even when new, could not compete with its arch-rival, the Baltimore & Ohio Railroad, which easily garnered most of the lucrative Ohio Valley trade. This in part explains why Baltimore became a major world port and Washington didn't.

Still, the canal did attract some shippers and merchants, many of whom erected warehouses, mills, and other industrial plants along the route. For example, in the 1820s, '30s, and '40s, the Dodge warehouses at 1000 Wisconsin Avenue and K Street, where the canal slips quietly into Georgetown, formed an integral part of the commercial empire of Massachusetts native Francis Dodge, a merchant who moved to Georgetown and built the impressive house at 1517 30th Street. Closed to commerce since 1923, the canal now attracts hikers, bicyclists, canoeists, and fishermen, and the National Park Service operates a passenger barge, *The Canal Clipper*, as a reminder of other days.

24 The Flour Mill

1000 Potomac Street, N.W.

1845 George Bomford, owner-builder;
much altered
1980 Peter Vercilli

When entrepreneurs laid out the C & O
Canal through Georgetown, many optimistic souls eagerly lined its banks with
industrial buildings in hopes of quick
profits. Mills for cotton and flour proved
especially popular, yet of the many such
buildings erected hereabouts, this is the sole survivor. Col. George Bomford started a cotton mill on this site in the 1840s; later owners converted
that structure into a flour mill in 1866; still later owners built some additions in 1883 and some more in 1932. All this truly shows the triumph of
hope over experience, since the canal never made much money for anyone.
Vercilli used Bomford's extant and much-added-to structure as the base
for this vast condominium complex.

25 Washington Harbour

3000–3020 K Street, N.W.

1986 Arthur Cotton Moore/Associates P.C.

Easily *the* project of the 1980s—at least in terms of press coverage—
Washington Harbour, a large-scale complex of shops, offices, and
condominiums, was designed to extend Georgetown's north-south

streets to the Potomac's edge. The site faces both Georgetown and downtown D.C., and Moore tried to maintain ties to both (very different) sets of older buildings. He said he wanted his work "to reflect . . . the exuberant three-dimensional vocabulary of Victorian Georgetown in an abstract way" while simultaneously acknowledging "the monuments" through "a more classic, rhythmic, columnar quality" and "the use of domes to reflect both classical references to Jeffersonian domes . . . and the Georgetown use of domed buildings to punctuate street corners." The result is a staggering assortment of façades and planes, but Moore defends this diversity by noting that any similar-sized urban neighborhood would contain "anywhere from 40 to 60 different architectural schemes."

26 Jefferson Court

1025 Thomas Jefferson Street, N.W.

1984 Skidmore, Owings & Merrill

In its materials, massing, and roofline, Jefferson Court is one of many new buildings south of M Street that were designed to evoke the architecture of their industrial neighbors.

27 The Foundry

1055 Thomas Jefferson Street, N.W.

1977 Arthur Cotton Moore/Associates P.C.

When he was called in to design a large office and commercial complex for this site, Moore looked at what was already here. He was pleased by William Duvall's 1856 machine shop at 1050 30th Street and based his new work on that utilitarian structure. The terraced plaza, for instance, suggests the old building's raked profile. Moore's work here has in turn provided the aesthetic basis for the many neofoundries built on the sloping sites south of M Street; the sheer number of these projects is visible from the promenade at the Kennedy Center.

28 Georgetown Mews

1111 30th Street, N.W.

1980 Arthur Cotton Moore/Associates P.C.

Moore designed this apartment complex as a transition between the 60-foot-tall renovated warehouses to one side and the more modestly scaled town houses of 29th Street on the other.

29 Four Seasons Hotel

2800 Pennsylvania Avenue, N.W.

1979 Skidmore, Owings & Merrill

This hotel, which offers up luxury à la "Dynasty," is another powerful player in the row of neo-industrial buildings that cling to the steep slopes between M Street and the Potomac. Their intended and much-ballyhooed relationship with the 19th-century warehouses and factories has, however, been obscured by their more powerful and more obvious relationship with each other. Now, intentionally or not, they pack an enormous cumulative visual punch, somewhat akin to that generated by the Federal Triangle, although the Triangle's impact is intentional, not accidental.

30 Corcoran School Development

28th and M Streets, N.W.

1985 Arthur Cotton Moore/Associates P.C.

With its site hard by Rock Creek Park, this mixed-use complex has become M Street's de facto gateway to Georgetown. Moore seems to have planned the project with that very role in mind, and he loaded the new construction with allusions to local landmarks.

31 Embassy of Mongolia

2833 M Street, N.W.

1981 Martin & Jones, Architects

To create this mélange of popular local motifs, Martin and Jones used differently scaled columns to mark the many-sectioned building's varied uses: a single column of a giant order denotes the entrance to the public areas while a pair of smaller columns guard the entrance to what were originally five duplex apartments.

32 3001–3009 M Street, N.W.

1794 Thomas Sim Lee, owner-builder

c. 1805 alterations: architect unknown

c. 1810 Andrew Ross and Robert Getty, owner-builders

c. 1955 restoration: Howe, Foster and Snyder

Lee, a friend of George Washington and an ardent supporter of the patriot cause, served as a delegate to the Continental Congress. He also found time to put in two terms as governor of Maryland. Like many prominent area politicians of the day, Lee dabbled in District real estate. One of his ventures involved building 3001 M Street, originally a six-bay town house. Around 1805, however, Lee decided that he had no use for such a large building, and he divided it in two, selling one part and keeping the other. Lee's original lot extended far to the west and north; in 1810 he sold the unused land to Ross and Getty. Those gentlemen then built 3005–3009 M Street and 1206 and 1210 28th Street.

In the 1950s, after decades of neglect, developers, encouraged by Dorothea de Schweinitz and the nascent Historic Georgetown, Inc., restored the Lee-Ross-Getty houses. The developers' work—and its financial success—spurred others to similar actions and may have been the single most important factor in bringing Georgetown's commercial district back to life.

33 3039–3041 M Street, N.W.

1801–1806 architect unknown

1963 restoration: Macomber & Peter

M Street, where federal and Victorian buildings continuously confront each other, often seems unsure which end of the 19th century it belongs to. The resulting tension, however, generally works to the buildings' advantage, since it gives them an interest their often prosaic façades might lack. These structures, carefully and authentically restored by the Junior League of Washington, harbor no doubts about their allegiance. They clearly place their buckled shoes in the earlier camp.

34 Old Stone House

3051 M Street, N.W.

c. 1766 Christopher Layman, builder

9:30 A.M. TO 5:00 P.M.
WEDNESDAY THROUGH SUNDAY

Some District romantics claim that George Washington head-quartered here in his surveying days; others stoutly maintain that it was in this building that L'Enfant drew up plans for the new capital city. These and other traditional stories have been debunked, and most historians now believe that a Pennsyl-vania-born cabinetmaker built the simple structure to live in and to use as a shop.

Splitting Hairs Dept.: Fans of the Old Stone House claim that the building is the oldest structure built in the District. This is correct, techni-cally: The Lindens, in Kalorama, is a decade older, but it was moved to Washington from Massachusetts.

35 Washington Post Office, Georgetown Branch (Custom House)

1215 31st Street, N.W.

1857 Ammi B. Young

Construction of a custom house here in 1857 indicates that Georgetown remained a viable port of entry well into the 19th century. Young, a native of New Hampshire, had already designed the Vermont State Capitol (1832) and the Boston Custom House (1837) when the federal government called him to Washington in 1852 and made him supervising architect of the Treasury, in charge of revenue-produc-ing buildings such as customs houses. In that capacity Young designed this restrained Italianate building in granite ashlar. During his District stint Young erected several other Tuscany-evoking piles, but Talbot Hamlin, in *Greek Revival Architecture in America* (1944), declared this rather simply massed structure "the best" of Young's Washington buildings.

36 Riggs-Riley House

3038 N Street, N.W.

1816 Romulus Riggs, owner-builder

This is a fine example of a small Georgetown federal house with a side hall plan. It seems a simple enough architectural concept, yet few of today's "neofederal" builders grasp the requisite subtleties, and almost invariably—and disastrously —get little right but the plan. Riggs was a local businessman; a later owner, physician Joseph Riley, added the adjacent office wing to the east.

37 Wheatley Houses

3041–3043 N Street, N.W.

1859 Francis Wheatley, builder

Here is a mirror-image pair of Victorian variations on the flat-façade town house theme. The variations occur in the sinuous and organic cast iron window heads, the strong rhythm of the cornices, and the tall and narrow parlor windows. Wheatley displayed a bit of common sense in placing the windows well above street level, so he could drop them to the floor and still preserve privacy for the rooms inside.

38 Laird-Dunlop House

3014 N Street, N.W.

1799 William Lovering, architect-builder

Lovering, though a self-trained amateur designer, was a prodigiously talented one. He certainly showed what he could do here, picking up the rounded vault of the entrance porch in the brick arches of the flanking windows. These arches, worthy of Sir John Soane and antedating Thornton's work at Tudor Place by more than a decade, form a sort of Lovering leitmotif and appear on most of the District buildings attributed to him (e.g., the Law House). John Laird, a wealthy tobacco merchant, built the house. It later passed to his daughter, Barbara, whose husband, James Dunlop, was a law partner of Francis Scott Key.

39 Foxall House

2908 N Street, N.W.

c. 1820 Henry Foxall, owner-builder

Dwarfed by its three-story neighbors, 2906 and 2912, this small, wall-enclosed three-bay dwelling has been much expanded. Foxall, who owned a thriving munitions foundry on the western outskirts of Georgetown and briefly served as mayor of that city, has gained immortality (and an *h*) thanks to the 20th-century suburban neighborhood that sprawls over the family farm just west of Georgetown University.

40 2812 N Street, N.W.
1813 John S. Williams

The well-articulated doorway of this fine house is similar to the doorway of 3019 P Street, while its window treatment closely resembles that seen at 3038 N Street. These relationships suggest that the houses may have had the same designers and workmen. According to legend, Stephen Decatur's widow, Susan, moved here from Lafayette Square after he was killed on the dueling field in 1820.

41 2806 N Street, N.W.
1817 architect unknown

This building's slightly vertical emphasis and elaborate splayed stone lintels with keystones distinguish it from its many federal-era neighbors, but like most of them it is built on a side hall plan.

42 Trentman House
1350 27th Street, N.W.
1968 Hugh Newell Jacobsen

With a personality secured through quality of design, this house, while thoroughly modern, manages to fit in quietly with its more traditional neighbors. Jacobsen accomplished that desirable result through careful attention to form, scale, proportion, and materials. One wishes he and the house had more emulators.

43 Mount Zion United Methodist Church

1334 29th Street, N.W.
1876–1884 architect unknown

Mount Zion is thought to be the first organized black congregation in the District of Columbia. The original church, built around 1814, stood on 27th Street above P and served as a station on the Underground Railroad. This larger brick building, built after the old church was destroyed by fire, contains a particularly elaborate pressed tin ceiling. Other sites associated with the congregation include the community house at 2906 O Street (built c. 1810, purchased by the church in 1920, and the site of the first public library for blacks in the District) and the cemetery in the center of the 2500 block of Q Street.

44 Christ Church

31st and O Streets, N.W.
1885 Henry Laws

This dark-walled church, with its sharp gables and seemingly precarious tower, looks like a miniature Gothic cathedral; but its imposing, sepia-toned interior and exposed scissor-trussed ceiling move the building well beyond the level of cute eclecticism. The neighboring houses, which date from the same general period, form an appropriate background for the red pressed-brick structure.

45 Linthicum House

3019 P Street, N.W.

1829 Edward Linthicum, owner-builder

The richly detailed, noticeably wide doorway links Linthicum's house stylistically with, among others in Georgetown, the Decatur and Bodisco houses and suggests that some unknown master craftsman enjoyed a wide Georgetown patronage. Linthicum built himself a prosperous career as a merchant, and his wealth eventually enabled him to move into the greater splendors of Dumbarton Oaks.

46 Miller House

1524 28th Street, N.W.

1840 Benjamin Miller, owner-builder

A *wooden* federal format—rather than the usual brick—makes this center hall house a local novelty. Miller, one of Georgetown's master carpenters, obviously kept himself abreast of the latest swings in taste, for the house's dominant front porch, with its fluted Doric columns, distinctly suggests the Greek revival. Miller may have built the place to show prospective clients what he could do. He certainly impressed somebody, because the government hired him to supervise construction of the Potomac Aqueduct.

47 National Society of the Colonial Dames of America (Dumbarton House)

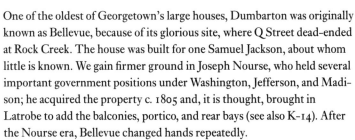

2715 Q Street, N.W.

c. 1798 Samuel Jackson, owner-builder
1805 Benjamin Henry Latrobe
1915 moved to present site
1931 restoration: Horace W. Peaslee and Fiske Kimball

10:00 A.M. TO 1:00 P.M. TUESDAY THROUGH SATURDAY
(CLOSED DURING AUGUST) PHONE: 337-2288

One of the oldest of Georgetown's large houses, Dumbarton was originally known as Bellevue, because of its glorious site, where Q Street dead-ended at Rock Creek. The house was built for one Samuel Jackson, about whom little is known. We gain firmer ground in Joseph Nourse, who held several important government positions under Washington, Jefferson, and Madison; he acquired the property c. 1805 and, it is thought, brought in Latrobe to add the balconies, portico, and rear bays (see also K-14). After the Nourse era, Bellevue changed hands repeatedly.

Demolition seemed imminent in the early 20th century when the District government unveiled plans to extend Q Street—through the house—in hopes of infusing life into sleepy Georgetown by connecting it to the rapidly developing Kalorama neighborhood. Preservationists managed to save the building and move it 100 yards to its present location. The Colonial Dames bought the house in 1928 and made it their national headquarters. Because the house's ownership had changed so often, the Dames sensibly decided to treat the building as a generic five-bay brick federal mansion and not to restore it to reflect a specific date or owner.

---

48 R. E. Lee House

2813 Q Street, N.W.

c. 1890 architect unknown
1959 addition: Hugh Newell Jacobsen

The original late-19th-century structure, the western half of the much-expanded house, proved too small for Lee, its mid-20th-century owner, and Jacobsen was brought in to make enlargements. The results deserve to be better known than they are. Georgetown's large and vocal aesthetic rear guard was up in arms when the addition was announced, yet Jacobsen has proved to all but the most hidebound that the 20th century need not be incompatible with the 19th. He surely and knowingly used new window sashes and other contemporary exterior details in a way that harmonizes with the house's older neighbors but simultaneously declares his creation very much a product of its own modernist times.

49 1633 29th Street, N.W.

1820 Benjamin Mackall, owner-builder

With its five-bay front and center hall plan, this brick house shows how Washington's federal-era design grew increasingly simplified and foursquare. Compare it, for example, to Tudor Place and the Octagon, both earlier and far more complex in massing and plan.

50 Francis Dodge House

1517 30th Street, N.W.

1852 Andrew Jackson Downing and Calvert Vaux

One of a pair of houses designed and built for the Dodge brothers, Francis and Robert, this building, although much added-to, still stands as a textbook example of Victorian Italianate design. (Robert's house occupies the corner of Q and 28th.) Vaux described both dwellings at length in his *Villas and Cottages* (1857). He lumped them together as "Design No. 17, 'Suburban Villa,'" but noted, "although these two houses have their principal features in common, neither is a servile imitation of the other." Vaux also quoted an 1854 letter from Francis Dodge in which client complained to architect that the cost, $15,000, was "much beyond what Mr. Downing led us to expect." Dodge admitted, however, that the over-runs might have been all to the good, since they had produced "fine houses . . . very comfortable and satisfactory in every respect."

---

51 Cooke's Row

3007–3029 Q Street, N.W.

1868 Starkweather and Plowman

Anyone who assumes that Georgetown owes all its character and charm to its crisp federal row houses needs to examine this magnificent run of four detached Victorian villas. The row's two end units are exuberantly Second Empire, and the middle pair are equally elaborately Italianate. While all four sport what may be the best brackets in the city, the ones at 3007 and 3009 deserve particular note.

---

52 Episcopal Home (Bowie-Sevier House)

3124 Q Street, N.W.

1805 Washington Bowie, owner-builder
c. 1890 architect unknown
1957 Horace W. Peaslee

Washington Bowie, a merchant and shipper whose estate once embraced this entire block, built the original five-bay center portion of this now much-expanded house. Bowie's work is a fine, if somewhat conservative, example of federal-era design and suggests the five-part houses so favored by the Chesapeake's colonial elite—think of George Washington's Mount Vernon. Curiously, it was at the close of the 19th century, when John Sevier acquired the property, that Bowie's single-block creation received a century-late five-part massing, to bring it *au courant* with the newly popular colonial revival. Peaslee has adapted the building to serve as the Episcopal Church Home, a residential facility for senior citizens, although looming court battles now make that use uncertain.

53 Tudor Place

1644 31st Street, N.W.

1816 William Thornton

TOURS AT 10:00 A.M., 1:00 P.M., AND 2:30 P.M., TUESDAY THROUGH
SUNDAY, BY APPOINTMENT ONLY   PHONE: 965-0400

Tudor Place—perhaps Thornton's masterpiece—marks a significant and
daring break with the Georgian architecture of the preceding generation
as represented by the Bowie-Sevier House, directly across Q Street.
Thornton gave Tudor Place buff-colored stucco, attenuated proportions,
arched and recessed ground floor windows, and a superb "temple" porch
leading into the shaped saloon, all of which innovations would have been
unthinkable just a few years earlier.

Thornton clearly did his best work when guided by educated clients: at
the Octagon he had John Tayloe to keep him in line; here he had Thomas
and Martha Custis Peter. Using $8,000 left to Mrs. Peter by her grand-
mother, Martha Washington, the couple purchased the sloping, eight-acre
site in 1805. A previous owner had begun to improve the property by
building what are now the house's wings. These didn't suit the Peters, so
they had Thornton remodel them and add the main central block. The
gardens are as fascinating as the house and have evolved with it. Martha
Peter planted some of the Old Blush roses and the boxwood parterre, and
her direct descendants, who continuously owned the property until 1983,
added specimen trees and other features. Both house and garden provide
irreplaceable insights into design dicta of the federal era, while showing
how five later generations embellished and remodeled their inheritance to
reflect the thinking of their own times.

54 3224 R Street, N.W.

1948 Theodore Dominick

Although built onto a federal-era house, this rather European-looking, vine-covered dwelling might be perfectly at home perched on a Provençal hilltop. The rusticated entrance—certainly well defined—and quoins add a rhythm of their own to the rambling structure.

55 Scott-Grant House

3238 R Street, N.W.

1858 A. V. Scott, owner-builder

Almost bombastically Victorian, this pile nevertheless respects the District's classical bent enough to have a well-defined central axis on all three floors. Alabaman A. V. Scott, who built the place, had no use for the house during the Civil War and leased it to a variety of tenants. General Grant himself rented it one summer, hence the second half of the structure's name, but the most memorable lessee may have been Gen. Henry Walker Halleck. General Halleck earned the enmity of his neighbors by quartering enlisted men in the house, turning R Street into a drill field, and having the company bugler sound taps and reveille at dusk and dawn each day.

56 3259 R Street, N.W.

1854 Adams and Haskins

A veritable catalog of mid-19th-century motifs lurks behind the hedges and undergrowth surrounding this house. While the mansard roof and arched windows may be merely typical of the period, the gingerbready cottage-style front porch is good enough to have come directly from Vaux or Downing.

57 Dumbarton Oaks

3101 R Street, N.W.

1801 William Hammond
Dorsey, owner-builder
1822 alterations: Frederick
Brooke
c. 1860 alterations: Edward
Linthicum
1929 music room: Lawrence
White
1922–1959 Beatrix Farrand, landscape architect
c. 1960 garden library: Frederick Rhinelander King
1989 Byzantine gallery: Hartman-Cox Architects

2:00 TO 5:00 TUESDAY THROUGH SUNDAY; GARDENS: 2:00 TO 6:00 DAILY
PHONE: 342-3200

Although the house at Dumbarton Oaks has been so altered and extended that little of the original architecture is visible, it remains a building of great character. One could even argue that its interest has increased with each remodeling. Mr. and Mrs. Robert Woods Bliss (he was heir to a patent medicine fortune) acquired the house and 53 acres in 1920 and proceeded to change the already much-altered dwelling to meet their 20th-century needs. They also set to work on the gardens. The Blisses decided to keep as wilderness 27 acres to the north of the house, the present Dumbarton Oaks Park, but wanted more formal gardens around the house. Beatrix Farrand's 10 acres of terraced gardens and "garden rooms" are both an undisputed masterpiece of American landscape architecture and the summation of her own distinguished career. Her Dumbarton work certainly captures her spirit of romance: she once wrote to the Blisses about a patch of woods near the music room, urging them "to keep it as poetic as possible . . . the sort of place in which thrushes sing and . . . dreams are dreamt."

The Blisses moved to Montecito, California, in 1940 and gave the bulk of Dumbarton Oaks to Harvard University. They sold the balance of the estate to the Danish government, which needed the land for a new embassy. Before heading west, Mrs. Bliss asked Ferrand to draw up some maintenance guidelines for the grounds. Ferrand complied and urged the university always to respect the dual nature of the property: on one hand it offers "a pleasant sense of withdrawal from the nearby streets"; on the other it allows "an intimate connection with all that a great city can offer." So far, so good.

57a Pre-Columbian Museum

Dumbarton Oaks

enter through 1703 32nd Street, N.W.

1963 Philip Johnson

This exquisite gem of a museum—a showcase of teak, marble, bronze, and glass—obviously comes from Johnson's classical period, when he was famous for such statements as "[I] cannot but be classically inspired; symmetry, order, clarity above all. I cannot throw around cardboard boxes or make a pseudo-functional arrangement of air-conditioning ducts into a trouvé-d type of design." Johnson devised a plan that was composed of nine interlocking circles of columns; he domed eight of them but left the ninth, in the center, open to a pool.

58 Montrose Park and Lovers Lane

3001 R Street, N.W.

Montrose Park, equally as popular with dogs and toddlers as with lovers, occupies land that in the early 19th century was owned by ropemaking magnate Richard Parrott, who sportingly let Georgetown's citizens use the tract for picnics and meetings. By the early 20th century Parrott's Woods, as it had come to be called, had fallen into disrepair; so a group of public-spirited women, headed by Sarah Louisa Rittenhouse, goaded Congress to buy the acreage and establish Montrose Park "for the recreation and pleasure of the people." Lovers Lane forms something of a cultural dividing line between the relaxed informality of Montrose Park to the east and the serious intellectualism of Dumbarton Oaks to the west.

59 Oak Hill Cemetery Gatehouse

30th and R Streets, N.W.

1850 George de la Roche

Laid out over four natural terraces in a fashionably romantic manner, Oak Hill Cemetery was chartered by Congress in 1849 on land given by banker and philanthropist William Corcoran. Wonderfully "period" as the landscaping is, the cemetery's buildings also merit attention, especially James Renwick's Gothic revival chapel, George Hadfield's mausoleum, and de la Roche's Italianate gatehouse, with its irregular massing and contrasting brick and sandstone. Local luminaries interred beneath the magnificent trees and alongside the winding paths include architect Adolph Cluss, politico James G. Blaine, diplomat Alexander de Bodisco, and Mr. Corcoran himself. In the segregated Georgetown of the 19th century, black citizens were buried apart from their white neighbors, at Mount Zion Cemetery off Q Street.

60 Oak Hill Chapel

Oak Hill Cemetery

1850 James Renwick

A paperweight in local Potomac gneiss with red sandstone trim, this Gothic revival chapel keeps watch near the entrance of Oak Hill Cemetery. A great success in and of itself, the simple, restrained chapel, when compared with some of Renwick's more ambitious structures, such as the Smithsonian "Castle" and St. Patrick's Cathedral in New York, points up the architect's enormous range and versatility.

61 Van Ness Mausoleum

Oak Hill Cemetery

30th and R Streets, N.W.

1833 George Hadfield

Hadfield, better known for his work at the Capitol and Arlington House, based this monument to the Van Ness family on the Temple of Vesta in Rome. Although it certainly seems at home among the trees and ferns of the cemetery's eastern hill, the mausoleum first graced the family's private burying grounds on 10th and M.

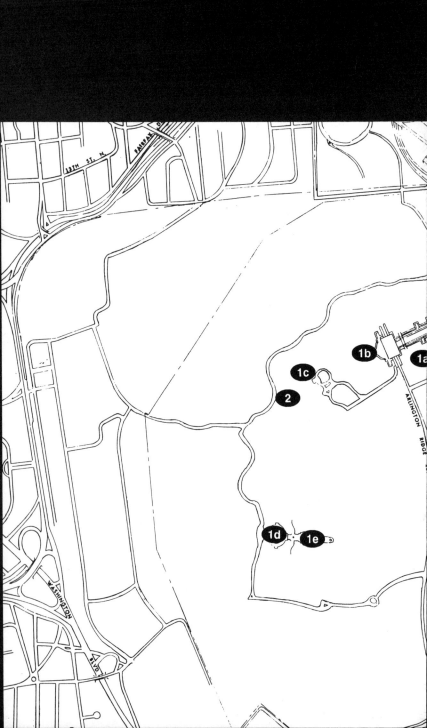

Arlington National Cemetery

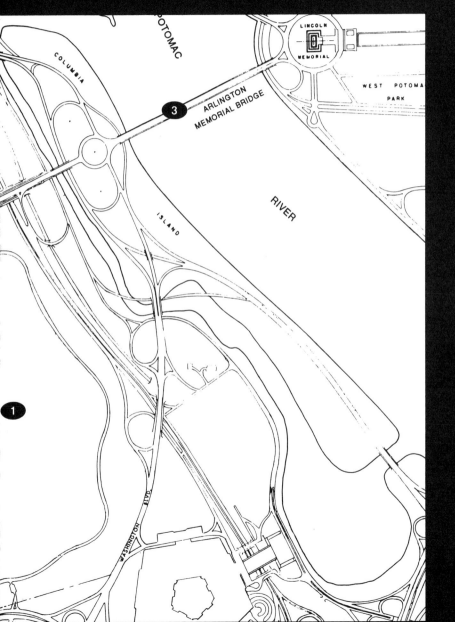

This shaded oasis holds a deep and multilayered significance for nearly all Americans. Art historians value Arlington House, with its massive Doric portico, as one of this country's finest examples of a neoclassical, federal-era villa, one of hundreds of hilltop creations built by the new nation's elite in emulation of Horatian Rome and Medicean Florence. Also, the site, along with the Arlington Memorial Bridge, shows clearly and distinctly what the City Beautiful movement was all about. And, after the federal government established Arlington National Cemetery here during the Civil War, the property assumed its greatest importance; the 200,000 men and women buried here in the past 130 years have imbued the grounds with a near-religious significance.

The Arlington Memorial Bridge was well under way when a photographer snapped this shot in 1927. Note Arlington House, proud and columned, sitting serenely on its hilltop, oblivious to the approaching bridge and the traffic it would bring.

1 Arlington National Cemetery

Arlington, Virginia

Established 1864

APRIL THROUGH SEPTEMBER,
8:00 A.M. TO 7:00 P.M.;
OCTOBER THROUGH MARCH,
8:00 A.M. TO 5:00 P.M.
PHONE: 703-697-2131

A place sacred to nearly all Americans, Arlington Cemetery covers 420 acres, part of the land the federal government acquired from the Robert E. Lee family during the Civil War. A Confederate soldier was the first person interred here. Since then, the shaded hillsides have received more than 200,000 war dead, medal-of-honor recipients, and high-ranking government officials.

This is also one place where the wisdom of Washington's and Jefferson's insistence on neoclassical design for the District becomes clear, for the cemetery, Custis-Lee Mansion, and Lincoln Memorial, all linked together by the Memorial Bridge, form one of the nation's great Beaux-Arts achievements. Subsequent building in and around the cemetery has sensibly adhered to that Greco-Roman theme, and the amphitheater, Memorial Gate, and Visitors' Center are all appropriately monumental. Similar but different, the Tomb of the Unknown Soldier takes the form of a sarcophagus; its effective and restrained decoration is limited to three chaste figures representing valor, victory, and peace, while the rear bears the succinct inscription, "Here rests in honored glory an American soldier known but to God." Flat stones marking unknowns from World War II, Korea, and Vietnam are placed alongside.

President Kennedy is buried on a beautiful hillside beneath a slab of fieldstone from his beloved Cape Cod. As most people know, he admired the site only days before he was murdered in Dallas. Warnecke, who had worked with the First Family to save Lafayette Square, discussed the treatment of the grave at length with Mrs. Kennedy; they eventually settled on a low-key, essentially landscapist approach that emphasizes the eternal flame. As Warnecke says, "the flame is the primary symbol at the grave, stronger than any sculpture or any structure that might be added to it." Mrs. Paul Mellon donated flowering trees, evergreens, and perennials that had been favorites of the slain president. Senator Robert Kennedy was buried near his brother in 1968, in a grave marked by a movingly simply white cross.

1a Visitors' Center

1989 Francis D. Lethbridge & Associates, architects and planners; David Volkert Associates, engineers; Patricia Schifflebeing, associate architect; Coffin and Coffin, landscape architects

1b Memorial Gate

1926–1932 McKim, Mead & White

1c John F. Kennedy's Grave

1966 John Carl Warnecke & Associates

1d Memorial Amphitheater

1920 Carrère & Hastings

1e Tomb of the Unknown Soldier

1921 Lorimer Rich; Thomas Hudson Jones, sculptor

2 Arlington House (Custis-Lee Mansion)

1803 George Washington Parke Custis, owner-builder
1818 George Hadfield
1925 L. M. Leisenring

9:30 A.M. TO 4:30 P.M. DAILY

One of the earliest American examples of Greek revival design, Arlington House remains, according to the father of American architectural history, Fiske Kimball, among "the most notable" of these temples. Custis (1781–1857) was a grandson of Martha Washington (Martha had two children with her first husband, Daniel Parke Custis, who died in 1757; she and George had no children). He began the hilltop house as the seat of his 1,100-acre plantation, building first the elegant wings, with their slightly recessed arched windows; but then he hesitated before beginning work on the center block, perhaps because he knew how important his house would be. Arlington's hillock overlooks the national capital; conversely, the site is visible from virtually any spot in town, and whatever stood here was going to be seen—really seen—by the world's dignitaries. So it had to be good. Custis hired George Hadfield, lately of the Capitol, to come up with something appropriately eye-catching. And Hadfield did just that, placing a 60-foot-long, 25-foot-deep Doric portico across the mansion's Potomac façade. Robert E. Lee, who later owned Arlington, once remarked that the porch made the place "a house any one might see with half an eye."

Lee moved to Arlington when he married Custis's only surviving child, Mary Ann Randolph Custis, in 1831. According to the *Dictionary of American Biography,* Lee once wrote, "My affections and attachments are more strongly placed [at Arlington] than at any other place in the world." The couple and their eventual seven children lived in the house until the Civil War broke out. In 1864 the federal government confiscated Arlington from the Lees for nonpayment of (illegally levied) taxes; Union troops camped in the house and the government turned 200 of the surrounding acres into a cemetery. After General Lee's death, the family brought suit to reclaim the place; the Supreme Court decided in their favor in 1874, but the Lees, pressed for cash, sold it back to the government in the 1880s for $150,000. Since 1933 Arlington House has been maintained by the National Park Service as a memorial to that gentlemanly Confederate.

---

3 Arlington Memorial Bridge

1926–1932 McKim, Mead & White; Leo Friedlander, James Earle Fraser, and C. Paul Jennewein, sculptors

Although this elegantly arched, granite-faced span may seem inevitable, it took a Washington traffic jam to bring it into being. Proposals for a bridge at this point had been bandied about as early as Andrew Jackson's presidency, but it wasn't until Armistice Day, 1921, that anything actually happened. On that day a motorcade attempting to make its way to the Tomb of the Unknown Soldier got snarled in a hopeless traffic gridlock: this caused great embarrassment to many VIPs, and *that* triggered plans for a bridge between the Lincoln Memorial and Arlington. The entirely satisfactory result completely transformed the adjacent areas on both sides of the river into the coherent visual experience that had been envisioned by Charles Moore, secretary to the McMillan Commission, who recalled that, "on the steps of the little temple at the Villa Borghese, the determination was reached that the Memorial Bridge be a low structure on a line from the site of the Lincoln Memorial to the Arlington Mansion—a monumental rather than a traffic bridge, but a significant element in an extensive park scheme." Col. Ulysses S. Grant, grandson and namesake of the great general, supervised construction.

With 16th Street forming its glittering spine, this neighborhood once rivaled Dupont Circle and Kalorama as *the* place to live for the city's rich-rich. It all happened because of Mary Foote, a noted *Belle Époque* hostess and the wife of Missouri senator John Brooks Henderson. In the late 1880s the Hendersons built a gruff stone mansion in what was semirural suburbia. Then, using her immense influence as a power hostess, lobbyist, and philanthropist, Mrs. Henderson worked to have Congress declare the area Washington's official Embassy Row. Unsuccessful, although a few brave—or intimidated—governments did establish outposts here, she then decided 16th Street ought to be rechristened the "Avenue of the Presidents." Unsuccessful again, she decided she wanted to have a new White House built here (no go), after which she tried to acquire the proposed Lincoln Memorial for "her" hill (forget it, lady). Finally, in frustration, she turned her attentions to acquiring socially desirable neighbors. In this she succeeded hugely, and the Pope-Laughlin Meridian House, perhaps the most elegant *hôtel* in town, bears witness to her labors. Mrs. Henderson died in 1931, possibly after learning that Sinclair Lewis wrote most of *Main Street* while living near her at 1814 16th Street.

Upon reflection, Mrs. Henderson's failures seem the city's good luck. She managed to bring some truly superb buildings to this part of town,

Senator and Mrs. John Brooks Henderson's gruff, craggy, and crenelated "Castle" (now the site of the Beekman Place condominiums) doesn't at all suggest the neoclassical palazzi that the couple constructed all along 16th Street.

and if she hadn't been able to coax a few embassies to build here, Massachusetts Avenue would be even more chock-a-block with châteaux than it is. "Henderson Castle" was demolished in 1949, and the site is now occupied by the Beekman Place condominiums.

---

1 Temple of the Scottish Rite

16th and S Streets, N.W.

1911 John Russell Pope; Elliott Woods, consulting architect

8:00 A.M. TO 4:00 P.M. WEEKDAYS
PHONE: 232-3579

Goodness! This fantasy, arguably Pope's most successful project in Washington, is one of the great surprises in the city. In 1909 the Washington Masons commissioned the architect to design a new temple for them. It was the height of the colonial revival era, but Pope (1874–1937) decided to ignore the recent past and looked *waaaay* back, drawing inspiration from King Mausolus, whose Queen Artemisia built the magnificent Temple at Halicarnassus as a memorial to him in 350 B.C. (The original temple, regarded as one of the Seven Wonders of the Ancient World, produced the word *mausoleum*; Pope evidently felt at ease with mausolea, for he also used the form at his second-best Washington job, the National Archives building in the Federal Triangle.) Amidst much masonic pomp, the cornerstone was laid on October 18, 1911, after someone found and dusted off the silver trowel Mason George Washington had used to lay the cornerstone of the Capitol. The temple was dedicated in 1915.

Pope laced the new temple with symbolism. While much of it is obvious, much requires close attention (or esoteric knowledge) on the part of the viewer: The front steps rise in flights of 3, 5, 7, and 9 to reflect the numbers sacred to Pythagoras, and the steps themselves end in a pair of monumental sphinxes, which guard the temple doors. Wisdom, to the right (south), has half-closed eyes and serene features, while the open-eyed Power, to the left, is grimly determined. When the great bronze doors are flung open, one enters the atrium, resplendent in Greek and Egyptian decoration and rich in Masonic associations. The chairs, for example, are modeled after the throne at the Temple of Dionysus, and a pair of statues in Egyptian style, three-dimensional representations of the hieroglyph that precedes the name of a god or a sacred place, flank the grand staircase. It's all a rip-roaring, juicy success that, fortunately, stops just short of theatricality.

---

2 Meridian Hill Park

16th Street between Euclid and Florida Avenues

1912–1935 Horace W. Peaslee; Mrs. John B. Henderson, sponsor

Mary Foote Henderson, teetotaling wife of Missouri senator John Brooks Henderson, did her best to convince Congress that 16th Street was the place to be. Although most of her schemes came to naught, she did succeed in having the lawmakers declare this site "a general congregating point" to attract "visitors from all over the city." That was not quite what she had in mind, but she had lived in Washington long enough to learn to take what she could get.

Construction of the park spanned two decades, time enough to allow for a surprising variety of architectural moods, motifs, and styles. Peaslee (1884–1959) wrote that he based the park's lower level, with its axial plan, 13 graduated pools, and cascading falls, on "the Pincian Hill in Rome." But, since he at various other times said he relied on the Villa d'Este and on Rome's Villa Medici for *ispirazione,* it might be best to call section one simply "generic Italian." The upper terrace is French: dead flat for some 900 feet despite the hill, it is centered on a broad grass mall with promenades and hemlock hedges all terminating in a bronze statue of Joan of Arc.

The park shows how landscape architecture and structural architecture, how the vegetable and the mineral, can be fused into a smooth whole, for Peaslee's luxuriant plantings continuously contrast with and benefit from the aggregate concrete of the massive retaining walls, walks, and basins. In all, as the city's chief engineer observed in 1926, "Meridian Hill Park is neither wholly architecture nor yet is it landscape design. There is nothing like it in this country."

Miraculously, this unique creation has survived more or less as Mrs. Henderson and Peaslee envisioned it: it has survived plots to build a replica of Old Faithful geyser in it, and it has survived—so far—the drug dealers and hooligans who have recently made it a favorite point of rendezvous.

3 Meridian House (Washington International Center)

1630 Crescent Place, N.W.

1920 John Russell Pope

Just breathing the air here summons up visions of vanished Society. Meridian House's richness of space and decor—qualities sometimes lacking in Pope's other Washington work—make it easy to conjure up the monied intellectuals who peopled the pages of Edith Wharton and Henry James.

Pope designed the house for Irwin Boyle Laughlin, heir to one of the country's more sizeable steel fortunes. Laughlin, a career diplomat, purchased the land for his château in 1912 (and what a superb hilltop site he chose), but postings abroad kept him from doing anything about construction until 1920. A recognized scholar of 18th-century French art, Laughlin worked closely with Pope on the project. A 1929 article on the building in *Architectural Record* commented, "Because of his [Laughlin's, not Pope's] detailed knowledge of the art and architecture of that period and because of his indefatigable interest in every detail, Meridian was immediately recognized as one of the finest examples of architecture in the French style in America." Laughlin continued the French themes out into the terraced garden, and nowhere else in town will one find the polled plane trees and raked gravel that so evoke an elegant *place* or a quiet *bois*.

Laughlin maintained his interest in art and architecture throughout his life. He helped his friend Andrew Mellon organize and plan the new National Gallery and, according to David Finley, the gallery's first director, the steel heir influenced everything about the new building—down to details such as choosing the fountains for the garden courtyards and the paint colors for the galleries. This distinguished man died in 1941, just missing the National Gallery's opening. His beloved Meridian House, however, makes a fine memorial to him, a splendid, civilized gentleman, a superb example of a nearly vanished and forgotten breed.

4 Ecuadorian Embassy

2535 15th Street, N.W.

1922 George Oakley Totten, Jr.

Architect Totten, egged on and paid by Mary Foote Henderson, built a dozen or so residences in the Meridian Hill area, all part of his sponsor's grand plan to make the neighborhood a center of international society. This is one of the group; others, all designed in sympathetic eclectic architectural styles, include 2401 and 2437 15th Street, 2640 and 2600 16th Street, and the Spanish Embassy, on the corner of 16th and Fuller Streets.

5 Inter-American Defense Board ("Pink Palace")

2600 16th Street, N.W.

1906 George Oakley Totten, Jr.

The writer James Morris advanced one dispassionate way to analyze the seductive charms of Venetian architecture; he argued that the Italian city is greater than the sum of its parts, that the palaces which line the canals are not in themselves particularly "good," and that if one imagined Ca' This or Palazzo That in another location, far away from the lambent Venetian light, the building simply wouldn't work. Readers may test that theory here.

Built for secretary of the treasury, Franklin MacVeagh, and his wife, Nellie, this Venetian Gothic mansion was one of Mary Foote Henderson's efforts to have Meridian Hill dazzle with Washington social life. The MacVeaghs certainly did their bit for the cause; after living here for a few years, they built 2829 16th Street, which now houses the Mexican embassy.

6 Lutheran Church Center (Warder-Totten House)

2633 16th Street, N.W.

1885 H. H. Richardson
1902 reconstruction: George Oakley
Totten, Jr.

The Richardson attribution seems a bit
shaky: while the design did come from his office, the house's pale, smooth
sandstone and its reliance on 16th-century France—as opposed to the
Master's usual insistence on pure Americana rendered in rough granite—
make it likelier that it represents the thinking of his underlings, Shepley
and Coolidge—or of Totten, himself a pupil of Richardson. When Totten
learned that the house, originally built on K Street between 15th and 16th,
was being demolished, he bought the remains from the wrecker, hauled
them across town, and reconstructed them on this site.

7 All Souls Unitarian Church

16th Street and Harvard Square, N.W.

1924 Coolidge & Shattuck

St. Martin-in-the-Fields, London, by
James Gibbs provided the architectural
inspiration for this building as it did for so
many other churches throughout America, Britain, and Canada.

8 Church of Jesus Christ of Latter-day Saints

16th and Harvard Streets, N.W.

1933 Young & Hansen

Designed to suggest the Mormon Taber-
nacle in Salt Lake City and capped by the
Angel Moroni, the building, with its delicate, linear detailing, stratified stone skin,
and consistent verticality, creates one of
the most elegant small churches in town.
Or perhaps the sense of success is relative and results from comparing it to
its distinctly unsubtle neighbors across the street.

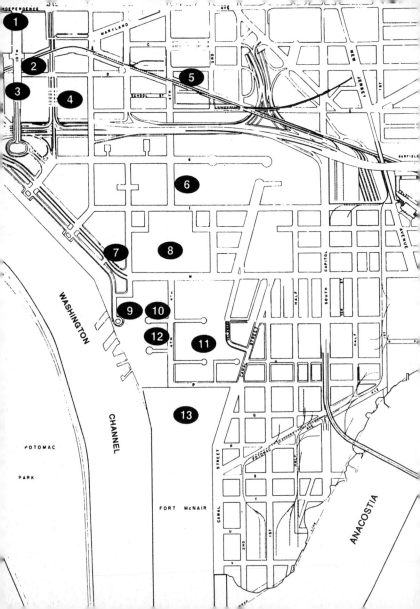

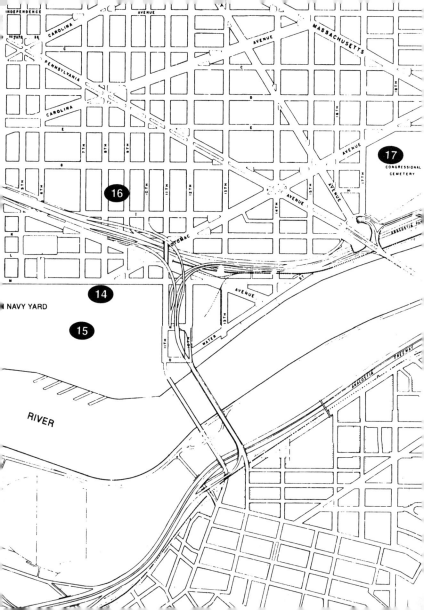

This strategic site, at the confluence of the Potomac and Anacostia Rivers, has prevailed through a roller-coaster history that might have left less resilient neighborhoods breathless. Land speculators swarmed along the Anacostia in the 1790s, hoping to cash-in on anticipated growth in the newly established capital city. John Greenleaf, who gave his name to the point of land at the rivers' convergence, struck a particularly memorable deal with Congress: he was allowed to purchase 3,000 city lots cheap, but he was expected to lend the municipal government funds to be used for public improvements. Wheat Row resulted from this cozy arrangement, but little else did, because Greenleaf went bust in 1797. Greenleaf's peers and rivals included William Duncanson, whose mansion has been incorporated into Harbour Square, and Thomas Law, whose house still stands at 6th and N Streets.

For several years all went beautifully here. Thomas Jefferson chose Greenleaf Point as the site of the new Washington Navy Yard; the Dis-

L'Enfant, Jefferson, and Washington all believed that the city would grow along the then-navigable Anacostia River (not into the distant hills to the northwest). So, evidently, did Louis Clover; when he published this view of the city in 1837 he made the White House (left distance) and Bulfinch's newly domed Capitol subservient to the bustling Navy Yard, which dominates the foreground. Note also the Marine compound (with the huge flag) just beyond the Yard.

trict's first newspaper, the *Impartial Observer and Washington Advertiser,* was headquartered nearby; and Washington's first mayor, Robert Brent, lived in the neighborhood, at Maryland Avenue and 12th Street. The English writer and observer Frances Trollope, sailing into town in 1832, recorded that "the Potomac, on arriving in Washington, makes a beautiful sweep, which forms a sort of bay, round which the city is built. . . . The navy-yard and arsenal . . . make a handsome appearance on the edge of the river, following the sweep above-mentioned."

Conditions in the area began to deteriorate early in this century, and by World War II the neighborhood had degenerated into perhaps the city's most notorious slum. Photographers such as Gordon Parks documented the shameful state of things—half the dwellings lacked plumbing, 70 percent lacked central heating—and eventually the city and federal governments were goaded into action.

And did they act! Beginning in the 1950s they created a 550-acre "renewal zone"; they then demolished some 6,000 dwellings (displacing over 15,000 people) and filled some of the newly vacant land with parks, some with town houses, some with apartments, some with office towers, all built along sternly efficient modernist lines. Thus, with the exception of the few historical town houses specifically selected for preservation and a smattering of old commercial buildings along the waterfront, virtually all the architecture hereabouts dates to the Cold War era. When these buildings were new, they were not without their detractors; but with the passage of time, historians have come to value much of this work as a huge outdoor museum of period design.

---

1   Forrestal Building

Independence Avenue and
10th Street, S.W.

1970   Curtis & Davis; Fordyce
& Hamby Associates; Frank
Grad and Sons

Three structures of heroic scale
make up the Forrestal "building." Historians might view the trio as one element in the continuum of Washington formalism—the Vietnam generation's version of their parents' Federal Triangle and their children's Market Square.

2 National Aeronautics and Space Administration, Aerospace Building

370 L'Enfant Plaza, S.W.

1987 Cooper, Robertson + Partners; Jaquelin T. Robertson, architect in charge

This firm's internationally known prowess at dealing with thorny city planning issues becomes self-evident at the NASA building. Its design elements were dictated by the dilemma of how to fit a new building into an existing cityscape, and Robertson's work for NASA provides one exemplary answer: he gave the upper parts of the massive structure three distinct elements joined by a spine that runs parallel to D Street; a plaza then links the building to 10th Street and the almost ceremonial entrance establishes a well-defined relationship to the entire L'Enfant Plaza complex.

3 L'Enfant Plaza

10th and D Streets, S.W.

1965 I. M. Pei & Partners
1968 Dan Kiley, landscape architect
1970–1973 hotel and west office building: Vlastimil Koubek

Now a generation old, the first two office buildings here, fronting the north and south sides of the plaza, are generally regarded not only as sophisticated examples of design in concrete but also as technological innovations, for Pei integrated the mechanical and electrical systems into the exposed coffered ceilings, a practice by no means common in the 1960s. The complex, an outgrowth of the Zeckendorf-Pei plan for southwest Washington, maintains an air of quiet dignity, despite being located at an exit ramp of I-395.

4 Department of Housing and Urban Development

451 7th Street, S.W.

1968 Marcel Breuer & Associates; Nolen, Swinburne & Associates

The curved form and deeply molded window panels seen here are all well-known characteristics of Breuer's work. It is high-octane stuff, and, in the hands of lesser talents, these and other favorite Breuer devices all too easily become dangerous, dehumanizing clichés. In Breuer's hands, of course, they become buildings that double as superlative abstract sculpture. Breuer guaranteed an extra bit of panache for HUD by contrasting its light precast-concrete main façades with dark stone facing on the projecting end walls.

5 Washington Design Center

300 D Street, S.W.

1983 Keyes Condon Florance Architects

Originally a 1920s refrigerated warehouse, this building has been adapted to contain the Washington Design Center, the first expansion of Chicago's Merchandise Mart outside that city. Keyes Condon Florance managed to retain a high percentage of the warehouse's old brick walls, but the new wholesale showrooms—the first major marketplace for interior furnishings and household *objets* in the District—required a good deal more space, which the architects created in a sleek, mirror-sheathed addition.

6 Capitol Park Apartments (South)

800 4th Street, S.W.

1958 Satterlee & Smith

The first of a group of similar structures in the area, this landmark still meets its architects' hopes of providing scale, intimacy, and variety in a large apartment building.

7 Arena Stage

6th and M Streets, S.W.

1961 Harry Weese & Associates
1970 Harry Weese & Associates

One of the District's most significant modern cultural institutions, the Arena Stage deserved—and got—the best architectural treatment possible when it abandoned its earlier somewhat vagabond existence in favor of a permanent home here. Weese piled strength upon strength to create Arena's admirable new quarters, and the building works on many levels: in the clear division and appropriate expression of usage, in the imaginative structure and details, and in the sequence of space one encounters moving from entrance to performance hall.

Arena Stage's landmark-filled history contains two especially notable moments: the first came in 1951 when, violating every local practice, the repertory group performed before an integrated audience; the second came in 1967 when Arena gave the world premier of Howard Sackler's *The Great White Hope,* a play that won a Pulitzer Prize for Sackler and that launched James Earl Jones on his highly successful career.

8   Town Center Plaza

1100 block of 3rd Street, S.W.
and 1100 block of 6th Street,
S.W.

1961–1962   I. M. Pei &
Partners
1972   Chloethiel Woodard
Smith & Associates

Pei's original apartment complex, unlike most others in the area, had neither town houses nor balconies—nothing could detract from the building's lean, tight-skinned, modern silhouette. Smith, who with Charles Goodman and Waldron Faulkner boldly kept the modernist banner flying in a sometimes hostile and conservative Washington, respected and underscored Pei's aesthetic when she added the larger commercial center ten years later to fill out the block.

9   Law House

6th and N Streets, S.W.

1796   attributed to William Lovering

When Congress authorized the new federal city in 1790, the event set off a spate of speculative building. Thomas Law, an influential businessman who made a fortune in India, was among those speculators. He put up this elegant, center hall, *piano nobile* structure for himself and his bride, née Eliza Parke Custis, one of Martha Washington's granddaughters. (It is unclear whether Lovering or Law—or, indeed, Eliza Custis—should be given credit for the dwelling's refined touches.) In 1797 Law optimistically built a sugar refinery nearby, the District's first heavy industry; but he overextended himself and, notwithstanding his rich wife, promptly went bankrupt. The Laws' house has survived these and other vicissitudes and now serves as the Tiber Island Center for Cultural and Community Activities.

10 Tiber Island

429 N Street, S.W.

1965 Keyes, Lethbridge &
Condon, Architects
1993 concrete restoration:
architrave p.c., architects

Judges awarded this (and the
adjoining Carrollsburg Square
development east of 4th Street) prizes in two successive Redevelopment
Land Agency architectural competitions. The awards seem thoroughly
justified, for Tiber Island boasts many laudable features, including
closely juxtaposed apartment towers and town houses, a covered central
plaza, and a carefully limited—and thereby unifying—range of materials
and colors.

11 River Park Apartments

4th Street and Delaware
Avenue, S.W.

1962 Charles M. Goodman
Associates

This apartment building, distinctive in its vaulted roofs and
aluminum screens, serves as a
boundary to separate the adjoining town houses from public housing
beyond. Goodman grouped his apartments around residential courts, a
pleasantly humane treatment sadly rare for that time.

Born in 1906, Charles Goodman helped pioneer Bauhaus modernism in
Washington. Francis Lethbridge has called Goodman the District's "most
innovative modern architect." Although he displayed this innovativeness
in individual structures such as this building, he probably achieved his
greatest triumphs in large-scale works such as the Hollin Hills development in Arlington and the new town of Reston.

12 Wheat Row–Harbour Square

1313–1321 4th Street, S.W.

1794 attributed to William Lovering
1966 Chloethiel Woodard Smith &
Associates

Wheat Row typifies the speculative housing ventures that characterized early
building in Washington. Actually this
row, named for John Wheat (who lived at
1315) and erected by wheeler-dealer John
Greenleaf, typifies the *best* of such ven-
tures, for Lovering clearly took pains with the four side-hall units. Saved
and renovated when most of the neighborhood was destroyed in a 1950s fit
of urban renewal, this group of federal houses (with the Duncanson-
Cranch House and the Washington-Lewis House around the corner of N
Street) has been incorporated into the construction of the Harbour Square
complex. The row houses' fanlights and stone keystones provide soothing
grace notes amongst the modernist sensibility that otherwise dominates
the area.

13 Fort Leslie J. McNair and Army War College

4th and P Streets, S.W.

1903–1907 McKim, Mead &
White

TOURS BY APPOINTMENT
PHONE: 475-1822

What a checkered career for one of the most beautiful sites in the city!
Greenleaf Point, named for famed land speculator John Greenleaf, has
been the site of the District's federal penitentiary (the convicted Lincoln
assassins were hanged here), and since 1804 has also been the site of Fort
McNair, which was burned by the British in 1814 and rebuilt shortly
thereafter. Upon assuming the presidency on the death of William
McKinley, Theodore Roosevelt established the war college here, at the
point's apex. He hoped that the institution might modernize the U.S.
Army and correct the deficiencies he had seen during his stint with the
Rough Riders. The college building itself—a burly three-story product of

the Beaux-Arts, solidly executed in brick with granite trim—couldn't be more TR if it tried, and its central three-story rotunda—complete with balustraded galleries—forms a particularly memorable space. The idyllic officers' houses, along the backwaters of the Washington Channel, create an enclave unique unto themselves.

14 Navy Yard Entrance Gate

8th and M Streets, S.E.

1804 Benjamin Henry Latrobe

In 1800 Thomas Jefferson established this naval yard, now the oldest surviving in America. Building proceeded in a some-
what hit-or-miss manner, which displeased the architecturally-minded Jefferson, so in 1803 he brought in Benjamin Henry Latrobe to regularize matters. Latrobe kept himself busy at the yard. Working with Jefferson and Commodore John Rodgers, he developed an innovative dry-dock system, which Jefferson liked because it saved money in ship repair. (Rodgers liked it because it saved ships; Latrobe because it was novel.) In 1807 Latrobe, promoted to the post of official engineer to the Navy Department, convinced Congress to build one of America's first steam engines here; completed in 1810, the engine powered a saw mill, block mill, and forge before the British destroyed it when they captured Washington in 1814.

Sadly, of all Latrobe's ventures at the Navy Yard, only the Doric, stuccoed-brick entrance gate remains—and *it* has been heavily altered. Still, what's left of the gate deserves respect as one of the earliest examples of Greek revival building on this side of the Atlantic. But it isn't all Greek revival here, and the yard's magnificent Victorian-era officers' houses also merit visitors' attention.

15 Commandant's House (Tingey House)

The Navy Yard

c. 1804 attributed to William Lovering

Very "regular" without and within, with a center hall plan and Aquia Creek stone trim, this brick house is the sole substantial survivor of the original naval complex, the British having torched most of the rest when they stormed into town in 1814. Much of the house's interior—mantels, staircase, etc.—dates from a mid-19th-century renovation, but the federal era's clean lines remain discernible on the exterior. The government built the house for Capt. Thomas Tingey, first commandant of the yard. Tingey, a Jefferson favorite, helped the president get Congress to approve a naval revolution whereby bulky sailing ships were replaced with small, easily maneuvered "gun boats." Tingey told Congress that the importance of the gun boats was "obvious to every person capable of reflection" (no polite weasel-words in that era!) and both Senate and House overwhelmingly supported the plan. But then, when Madison became president, he—evidently incapable of reflection—dropped the project.

16 Marine Barracks and Commandant's House

801 G Street, S.E.

1805 George Hadfield
1891 additions: Hornblower & Marshall

Framed by the simple arcaded brick barracks and with the drill field stretching out as a mall, the Commandant's House forms the focal point of this cloistered block. The residence of every Marine Corps Commandant since 1806, its many remodelings bear witness to the shifting tastes of several generations.

17 Congressional Cemetery

18th and E Streets, S.E.

Established in 1807

TOURS AVAILABLE   PHONE: 543-0539

Although this was once the official congressional burial ground, architects
Thornton, Hadfield, and Mills managed
to squeeze their way in among the politicians. Many of the latter chose to be
buried in their home districts, but they are commemorated here in the
more than 80 official cenotaphs. Use of the cenotaphs, designed by Benjamin Henry Latrobe and paid for by Congress, began in 1816 but abruptly
ended in 1877, when Senator George Hoar of Massachusetts remarked on
the floor of the Senate that the structures added a new terror to death.

Among the great (and near-great) actually interred here are John Philip
Sousa, Commodore John Rodgers, Push-Ma-Ta-Ha (a Chocktaw chief
who died while in Washington negotiating a treaty), Marion Kahlert
(killed at age 10 in 1904, the city's first automobile victim), J. Edgar
Hoover, photographer Mathew Brady, and George Watterson (first
Librarian of Congress). Elbridge Gerry is also buried here: although a
signer of the Declaration of Independence, governor of Massachusetts,
and vice president under Madison, he is undoubtedly best known for giving rise to the term *gerrymander*.

Other Places of Interest

Washington began as a square, ten miles on each side, with the Capitol in the center. Since 1846 it has been a square with one large corner removed, because in that year the government ceded back to Virginia the portion of the District south of the Potomac, leaving the Capitol no longer at the geographical center of the city. For that matter, because of the willy-nilly nature of urban growth, it doesn't form the District's fashionable center either, since generations of the city's trendsetters have marched inexorably to the northwest. As a result, a number of significant structures, formerly enjoying prime locations, have been left high and dry.

The impression of this c. 1910 engraving of Howard University and the McMillan Reservoir (right) *is positively rural.*

1   Le Droit Park

Florida and Rhode Island Avenues between 2nd and 7th Streets, N.W.

1873–1877 James McGill; Amzi L. Barber and Andrew Langdon, developers

Since its founding, Le Droit Park has played a key role in the cultural and social life of nearby Howard University. Poet Paul Lawrence Dunbar lived here, as did

Anna J. Cooper, who founded Frelinghuysen University in her home at 201 T Street.

McGill elected to design most of the neighborhood's houses in the highly popular romantic styles of the period: Gothic cottage, Italian villa, and Second Empire mini-château. Built on speculation a century ago, they remain a significant contribution to the architectural interest and variety of the city. Le Droit remains largely intact, too, for 50 of the original 64 dwellings still stand.

---

2   Howard Hall

Howard University

607 Howard Place, N.W.

1867 architect unknown

8:00 A.M. TO 5:00 P.M. WEEKDAYS
PHONE: 806-6100

A fine, early example of the French Renaissance style in America, this yellow brick structure was the home of Gen. Oliver Howard, founder of Howard University and a commissioner of the Freed-men's Bureau. The university purchased the house in 1909 and, despite the building's present state of neglect, it still dominates the neighborhood like a shabby but genteel dowager.

Howard University has distinguished itself in many areas, but nowhere has it played a more dramatic and vital role than in supplying the legal talent that powered the civil rights movement. As Haynes Johnson wrote in his 1963 book, *Dusk at the Mountain,* Howard Law School produced "the men who have carried the burden of legal argument in segregation cases throughout the nation." To cite but one alumnus, Thurgood Marshall, counsel to the NAACP, solicitor general of the United States, and associate justice of the Supreme Court, earned his LL.B. here, after being denied admission to the whites-only University of Maryland Law School.

3 National Shrine of the Immaculate Conception

4th Street and Michigan Avenue, N.E.

1920 Maginnis & Walsh; Frederick Vernon Murphy

NOVEMBER 1 TO APRIL 1, 7:00 A.M. TO
6:00 P.M. DAILY; APRIL 2 TO OCTOBER 31,
7:00 A.M. TO 7:00 P.M. DAILY
PHONE: 526-8300

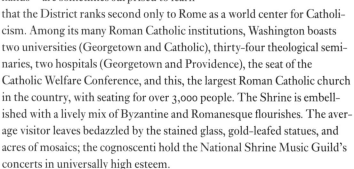

Visitors—and even old Washington hands—are sometimes surprised to learn that the District ranks second only to Rome as a world center for Catholicism. Among its many Roman Catholic institutions, Washington boasts two universities (Georgetown and Catholic), thirty-four theological seminaries, two hospitals (Georgetown and Providence), the seat of the Catholic Welfare Conference, and this, the largest Roman Catholic church in the country, with seating for over 3,000 people. The Shrine is embellished with a lively mix of Byzantine and Romanesque flourishes. The average visitor leaves bedazzled by the stained glass, gold-leafed statues, and acres of mosaics; the cognoscenti hold the National Shrine Music Guild's concerts in universally high esteem.

4 Franciscan Monastery

1400 Quincy Street, N.E.

1899 Aristides Leonori

8:00 A.M. TO 5:00 P.M.
MONDAY THROUGH SATURDAY,
1:00 P.M. TO 4:00 P.M. SUNDAY

This highly romantic creation—the official "Commissariat of the Holy Land for the United States"—contains copies of shrines to evoke Jerusalem and Bethlehem, copies of catacombs to evoke Rome, and the Portincula Chapel to evoke Assisi. The monastery's 44 acres of buildings, woodlands, and gardens are bordered by some equally romantic neighbors, such as the Shrine of the Immaculate Conception; the Chapel of Notre Dame (at the north side of the Trinity College grounds, Michigan Avenue and Harewood Road) also merits visitors' attention.

5 U.S. Soldiers' and Airmen's Home

Rock Creek Church Road at Upshur Street, N.W.

1851 (and earlier) architect unknown; several additions

In 1851 Gen. Winfield Scott, hero of the war with Mexico, used the indemnity paid him by that defeated nation to establish this, the oldest veterans' home in the United States. A single sentence sums up the institution's purpose: "Here comfortable quarters are provided for men who have served for 20 years in the United States Army or who have been disabled by wounds or disease." Anderson Cottage, which predates the Soldiers' Home, is probably the oldest of the many structures nestled into the site's 300 acres. Built about 1843 by banker G. W. Riggs, the cottage remained a popular retreat throughout the 19th century. (Lincoln, for instance, stayed here in 1862 while working on the Emancipation Proclamation.) Other notable structures on the vast property include the Sherman Building (c. 1852), all marble beneath a hipped roof and turrets, and the 1897 Gothic revival Stanley Hall.

6 St. Paul's Church

Rock Creek Cemetery

Webster and 3rd Streets, N.W.

c. 1775 architect unknown
1921 restoration: Delos H. Smith

This old brick chapel, the first church built in what would become the District of Columbia, has had as tumultuous a history as the federal city itself. Begun in 1719 it was replaced in 1775; the replacement was remodeled in 1868, and all went smoothly until it burned to the ground in 1921. The present one-story brick church, with its central entrance tower and projecting chancel, is a reconstruction of the 1775 building.

7 Adams Memorial, "Grief"

Rock Creek Cemetery

Rock Creek Church Road, N.W.

1890 statue: Augustus Saint Gaudens; base: Stanford White

Henry Adams commissioned this heavily shrouded bronze as a memorial to his wife, Marian, after her suicide, and it almost immediately became one of the most revered works of art in Washington. Lorado Taft, who sculpted the Columbus Fountain near Union Station, said that to look on the figure's face was like "confronting eternity"; Saint Gaudens himself felt the sculpture "beyond pain and beyond joy. It is the human soul face to face with the greatest of all mysteries." Adams wrote that the degree of effect depended on the observer. "Like all great artists, Saint Gaudens held up the mirror and no more. The American layman had lost sight of ideals; the American priest had lost sight of faith. . . . The old, half-witted soldiers . . . denounced the wasting, on a mere grave, of money which should have been given for drink."

Once cloaked by a grove of holly and other evergreens (recently removed for fear their roots might disturb nearby gravesites), the figure sits on a rough stone with a simple bench in front. Novelist John Galsworthy had Soames Forsyte sit on the bench and reflect on the statue: "It was the best thing he had come across in America: the one that gave him the most pleasure, in spite of all the water he had seen at Niagara and those skyscrapers of New York."

Henry Adams died in 1918 and was buried here beside his wife.

8 Gallaudet University

7th Street and Florida Avenue, N.E.

1866 Frederick Law Olmsted, Sr., and Calvert Vaux
1874–1877 Frederick C. Withers and Daniel Chester French

Founded as the first institution of higher learning for the deaf in America and named for Thomas Hopkins Gallaudet, a pioneering educator of the hearing impaired, the university's buildings and grounds are nestled in a park-like setting far from the bustle of downtown. School officials hired no less than Frederick Law Olmsted, Sr., and Calvert Vaux to lay out the campus. The pair produced a masterpiece of informality, and that quality has remained the dominant aesthetic at Gallaudet to this day. But while all the buildings harmonize with their landscape, many possess great individual character as well: both Chapel Hall (Calvert Vaux, 1867), built of contrasting-colored stone and possibly the earliest Ruskinian Gothic college structure in America, and College Hall (Frederick C. Withers, 1877), a delight in brownstone and brick, merit special attention.

Two asides, one to please the sports-minded, one for the artistically inclined: It is not generally known, but in the 1890s Gallaudet students invented the football huddle, a device born out of necessity so the opposition couldn't read the team's signed plans for the next play. In addition, mention must be made of French's bronze of Professor Gallaudet signing the letter *a* to a child, for the sculpture holds a revered place in the District's collection of commemorative art.

9   National Arboretum

24th and R Streets, N.E.

1963 administration building: Deigert & Yerkes & Associates
1976, 1978, 1980 revisions: Sasaki Associates Inc.
1990 Corinthian column garden: Russell Page, with EDAW Inc.
1993 bird garden and grove of state trees: HOH Associates

8:00 A.M. TO 5:00 P.M.
PHONE: 475-4857

Four hundred and forty-four hilly acres of trees and flowering shrubs, pools and gazebos and fountains do much to soften this somewhat unappealing stretch of New York Avenue. Lobbying for an arboretum began at least as far back as 1901, and in 1927 Congress approved legislation to "establish and maintain a national arboretum for purposes of research and education concerning tree and plant life." Since then the institution has grown into one of the largest, most advanced arboreta in America. The fern and woodland garden, the Bonsai and Penjing Museum, and the metasequoia grove have achieved national importance. In addition, the arboretum maintains diverse educational programs; and, thanks to the staff's interest in plant propagation, many local gardens now sparkle with new, hardy species of camellia, crape myrtle, and azalea hybridized by arboretum scientists.

One of the arboretum's most recent gardens focuses on the 34-foot sandstone Corinthian columns, 22 of them, removed from the Capitol when that building experienced expansions in the 1950s. The columns, designed by Benjamin Henry Latrobe and erected under the supervision of Charles Bulfinch, seemed, despite that pedigree, to be destined for some Anacostia landfill until Mrs. George Garrett intervened and rescued them. After years of negotiations and hassles, the columns finally were taken out of storage and placed in the arboretum, and the brilliant English landscape architect Russell Page designed a setting for them on a knoll near the main entrance. Page died in 1985, but EDAW faithfully carried out his low-key plans: a small fountain adds the elements of gentle noise and soft movement to the composition and spills over to form a reflecting pool below. Planting has been kept simple, with red tulips in the spring growing out of a carpet of native groundcovers.

---

10 Woodson High School

55th and Eads Streets, N.E.

1972 McLeod, Ferrara & Ensign

Woodson broke from the past when it became Washington's first high-rise high school. The building might also be viewed as an intelligent response to the twin pressures of ever-increasing needs and an ever-diminishing number of usable sites.

---

11 Fairfax Village Recreation Center

41st Street and Alabama Avenue, S.E.

1969 Hartman-Cox Architects

12:30 P.M. TO 9:00 P.M. WEEKDAYS

This neighborhood recreation building was sited at the bottom of a hill and designed so that the best parts of the lot were kept clear for playing fields. While maintaining a playful scale appropriate to its use, the well-articulated structure creates a surprisingly grand space within.

12 Frederick Douglass National Historic Site (Cedar Hill)

1411 W Street, S.E.

c. 1855 architect unknown

APRIL THROUGH OCTOBER, 9:00 A.M. TO 5:00 P.M.; NOVEMBER THROUGH MARCH, 9:00 A.M. TO 4:00 P.M.   PHONE: 426-5961

Frederick Douglass, author, abolitionist, and editor, moved to this house in 1877 when he became U.S. marshal of the District of Columbia; he named the place to honor the cedar trees that shaded the house (most are now gone) and lived here the rest of his eventful life. In buying property in what had been a segregated neighborhood, Douglass launched the first serious attack on the District's racist housing laws.

That was all business as usual for Douglass, a man who devoted his life to ridding the nation of all forms of injustice. Born into bondage in Talbot County, Maryland, in 1817, Douglass was taken by his owner to Baltimore, but in 1839 he managed to escape. He fled to New England, where he purchased his freedom and started the antislavery newspaper *North Star,* whose masthead bore his credo, "Right is of no sex—Truth is of no color—God is the Father of us all and we are all Brethren." After the Civil War, Douglass became the first black American to achieve ambassadorial rank, representing this country in Haiti. He died in this house in 1895 from a heart attack suffered during a women's rights meeting. His widow, Helen, opened Cedar Hill for tours in 1903; and in 1962 the property was acquired by the National Park Service, which maintains it as a memorial to this fascinating and important person.

13 St. Elizabeth's Hospital

2700 Martin Luther King, Jr., Avenue, S.E.

1852 Thomas U. Walter

In the 1850s, outraged by the shameful condition of her generation's homeless and mentally ill, Dorothea Dix led the federal government to do *something* to improve the condition of the "many persons from various parts of the Union, whose minds are more or less erratic," and who "find their way to the metropolis of the country [and] ramble about . . . poorly clad and suffering for want of food and shelter." Congress listened, approved funds, and hired Walter. Working closely with the hospital's first chief of staff, Dr. C. H. Nichol, the architect created a dignified structure whose brick façades receive interest from a stone belt course and splayed stone window arches and whose rooms are shaded by rambling arcades and two-tier porches.

The hospital still performs its original task and, over the years, thousands have received treatment beneath its tiled roofs. Of these men and women, the poet Ezra Pound was probably St. E's most noted resident; released from here in 1958, the pro-Mussolini Pound returned to his beloved Italy stating, "All America is an insane asylum."

In 1854, partly to provide housing for hospital workers, land developers laid out Anacostia, known as Uniontown until 1886. So, although residents of Baltimore's Roland Park and Philadelphia's Chestnut Hill might protest, Anacostia wins the title of America's first planned suburb.

Index

U.S. News and World Report Complex (H-29), 163
U.S. Soldiers' and Airmen's Home (Q-5), 289
U.S. Tax Court Building (C-10), 80

Valmarana, Mario di, viii, 156
Van Ness Center (K-12), 209
Van Ness Mansion, 153
Van Ness Mausoleum (M-61), 255
Vaughn, Henry, 201–202
Vaux, Calvert, 9, 10, 64, 249–250, 290–291
Venturi, Rauch & Scott Brown, 21, 102–103
Vercilli, Peter, 237
Veterans Administration Building, 133
Vietnam Veterans Memorial (B-12), viii, 63
Volta Bureau (M-6), 226

Wadsworth, Herbert, 177
Waiting Station (at U.S. Capitol) (A-3), 36
Walsh, Thomas, 108–109, 179–180
Walsh-McLean House, 179–180
Walter, Thomas U., 8, 28, 33, 76, 79, 294
Wardman-Park Hotel (K-7), 205–206
Warnecke, John Carl, 20, 134, 140–141, 169, 224, 259, 261
Warner Theater Project, 102–103, 160
War of 1812, 7, 131, 150
Warren, Herbert Langford, 172
Warren and Wetmore, 123
Washington, George, 3, 18, 28, 65–67
Washington, Martha Dandridge Custis, 251, 261, 279
Washington Canoe Club (M-16), 232–233
Washington Chapter/AIA (I-15), 175
Washington Club (I-20), 166, 167
Washington Convention Center (E-41), 15, 115
Washington Design Center, 277
Washington, D.C.: building height limitation in, 14, 172; establishment of, 1–2
Washington Harbour (M-25), viii, 20, 237–238
Washington Hotel (E-22), 105

Washington Metropolitan Transit Authority (Metro), 16, 73; Operations Control Building (C-4), 75–76
Washington Monument (B-16), 22, 47, 65–67
Washington National Cathedral (K-1), 201–202
Washington Square (F-14), 125
Watergate, The (H-16), 146, 156
Weeks, John C., 174
Weeks House (I-14), 174
Weese, Harry, and Associates, 16, 48–50, 73, 278
Weinstein, Amy, 22, 48
Weinstein Associates, 48
Welles, Sumner, 182
Wharton, Anne Hollingsworth, 210, 227
Wharton, Edith (*Decoration of Houses*), 191
Wheatley, Francis, 243
Wheatley Houses (M-37), 243
Wheat Row–Harbour Square (P-12), 224, 274, 281
Wheeler, Perry, 207–208
White, Frank Russell, 160–161
White, George M., 28
White, Lawrence, 253
White House, The (G-1), 6, 9, 22, 128–132
Whitney, Gertrude Vanderbilt, 152–153
Wilkes and Faulkner, 161
Wilkins House (I-6), 170
Willard Hotel (E-21), 104–105, 159
Wilson, Woodrow. *See* Woodrow Wilson House
Winder Building (H-1), 147
Windrim, James, 111
Winslow, Lorenzo, 129–131
Withers, Frederick C., 290–291
Women's National Democratic Club (I-14), 174
Wood, Donn & Deming, 110, 113–114
Wood, Waddy Butler, 110, 113–114, 142, 153, 190–191
Woodley House (K-2), 202–203
Woodrow Wilson House (J-7), 190–191
Woods, Ellicott, 28, 267

Photo Credits